The Global Debt Trap

How to Escape the Danger and Build a Fortune

Claus Vogt
Roland Leuschel

WILEY

John Wiley & Sons, Inc.

Published by John Wiley & Sons, Inc., Hoboken, New Jersey.
Published simultaneously in Canada.

A German edition *Die Inflationsfalle: Retten Sie Ihr Vermogen!* was published by
John Wiley & Sons in 2010.

For general information on our other products and services or for technical support, please
contact our Customer Care Department within the United States at (800) 762-2974, outside
the United States at (317) 572-3993 or fax (317) 572-4002.

Wiley also publishes its books in a variety of electronic formats. Some content that appears in
print may not be available in electronic books. For more information about Wiley products,
visit our web site at www.wiley.com.

Library of Congress Cataloging-in-Publication Data:

Vogt, Claus.
    The global debt trap : how to escape the danger and build a fortune / Claus Vogt,
Roland Leuschel, Martin D. Weiss.
      p. cm.
    Includes index.
    ISBN 978-0-470-76723-8
      1. Finance, Personal.   2. Global Financial Crisis, 2008–2010.   I. Leuschel, Roland.
II. Weiss, Martin D.   III. Title.
HG179.V65   2010
332.024'01—dc22

                                                                    2010042166

Printed in the United States of America
10 9 8 7 6 5 4 3 2 1

*To Our Children
and Grandchildren*

Contents

Foreword

In the days after the real estate bust of 2007, scores of pundits came out of the woodwork declaring that they had predicted the crisis. Still others made similar claims after the debt collapse of 2008, and again, following the sovereign debt crisis of 2010.

But how many analysts truly foresaw each of these three crises, wrote about them extensively ahead of time, carefully explained the causes, and clearly spelled out the consequences?

I don't have a precise answer. But I do know that Claus Vogt and Roland Leuschel, the authors of this book, are definitely among them.

In their 2004 German bestseller, *Das Greenspan Dossier,* they exposed, in great detail, how the monetary policies pursued by the former Fed chairman were creating an unprecedented real estate bubble. They showed how the bubble would inevitably collapse. And they predicted how that collapse would lead to a series of financial disasters of unthinkable dimensions.

"When the U.S. real estate bubble bursts," they wrote in *Das Greenspan Dossier,* "it will not only trigger a recession and a stock market crash, but it will endanger the entire financial system, especially Fannie Mae and Freddie Mac."

That one sentence alone—plus their constant reminders throughout the book about the enormous magnitude of the expected crisis—gave readers an unambiguous forewarning of the precise sequence of events that followed:

- First, the bursting of the housing bubble.
- Then, the worst recession and stock market crash since the Great Depression.
- Next, a near meltdown in the entire financial system.
- And finally, the near demise of Fannie Mae and Freddie Mac.

Indeed, not only were these two government-sponsored mortgage giants the primary victims *during* the debt crisis of 2008, they are also the two largest institutions whose troubles have most obviously endured *after* that crisis. Clearly, Vogt and Leuschel singled them out in their book for the right reasons.

The irony of this story, however is that *Das Greenspan Dossier,* although a bestseller in Germany, was never translated into English. So unless you happen to be an avid reader of German language treatises on international finance, you missed it.

I didn't miss it—but mostly by coincidence: I happen to work closely with Claus Vogt because we were co-editing *Sicheres Geld,* the German edition of our U.S. investment newsletter, *The Safe Money Report.* So when Claus first brought *Das Greenspan Dossier* to my attention, my first question was the natural one "This book is about America and should be of intense interest to all American investors. So why wasn't it translated and published in the United States?"

The answer: Although American books about Germany, Japan, or other countries are almost automatically translated into their languages, the reverse is not true: Foreign books about the United States are *rarely* translated into English.

It seems few in the United States seek out the opinions of overseas authors—let alone about the United States itself. Indeed, to find a time when American readers were measurably intrigued by the analysis of a foreign observer, you might have to go back to Alexis de Tocqueville and his *Democracy in America,* first published 175 years ago.

That's a shame.

Foreign authors can shed fresh light on America's dilemmas and suggest novel solutions that U.S.-based analysts might miss. Foreign authors do not suffer from the same biases; they rarely have the same academic or political turfs to defend.

Moreover, as I explain in a moment, these two authors, in particular, have talents and insights that help them rise head and shoulders above their peers abroad.

"Clearly," I said to the authors, "we must not let this happen again! When you write your next book, revealing your forecasts for what's likely to happen in the *next* phase of this crisis, we must find a way to get it promptly translated and made available to everyone in the English-speaking world."

Fortunately, John Wiley & Sons, which has published three of my books, agreed; and the product of that effort is in your hands right now—the fully translated and updated edition of the authors' original German bestseller published in 2009—*Die Inflationsfalle*.

I was asked to review the translated manuscript, and I was pleased to find that the authors' track record for prescient forecasts was reconfirmed. Indeed, in the relatively short time it took to find a U.S. publisher and translate the original, some of the authors' key new forecasts were already beginning to unfold.

For example, in their 2009 German edition of this book, they wrote that the "cure" for the 2008 debt crisis that many sovereign governments were pursuing—massive bailouts—were worse than the disease. They explained that it would merely lead to a *new* crisis, this time in the debts of the sovereign governments themselves. In other words, the authors clearly predicted the *sovereign debt crisis*.

Sure enough, even as I was reading the manuscript, this is precisely what the world was experiencing or fearing—not only in financially vulnerable countries like Greece, Spain, or Portugal, but also in supposedly stronger economies like the United Kingdom, Japan, and even the United States.

The 2009 German edition of this book also predicted that the U.S. Federal Reserve under Chairman Ben Bernanke would embark on an increasingly more aggressive program of "quantitative easing"—outright *money printing*. This is precisely what the Fed has done. And right now, how much further the Fed travels down this dangerous path has become *the* defining policy issue of our time.

But the authors' proven forecasting abilities are not the only unique strengths they bring to this work.

They are former banking industry insiders who never accepted the established economic theories that prevail in their world. Instead, they are eclectic, independent thinkers, drawing heavily from one of the few schools of thought that can logically explain the true causes and consequences of the busts we are now experiencing.

They fully understand—and explain—what *money* really is, what our governments have done to abuse it, and what the ultimate cost could be to society.

They are also ardent students of one particularly extreme boom-and-bust cycle that most government officials would prefer to forget: the rampant abuse of money printing presses in 1920s Germany, the destruction of the German currency and all of its terrifying consequences. More so than most other German authors, they are vividly aware of how that singular episode unfolded and the lessons it can teach us today.

Most important, the authors are major advocates for everything that has made the United States the envy of the world. Mr. Vogt writes weekly to 500,000 American readers to convey his views. And Mr. Leuschel was the co-author—along with Congressman Jack Kemp—of the German bestseller, *Die Amerikanische Idee [The American Idea]*. This book was translated into French and Dutch and became a bestseller in Belgium. An important chapter of this book was dedicated to the idea of sound money. In following Ludwig von Mises's ideas, the authors tried to convince European readers that a return to growth and full employment was only achievable with sound money and tax cuts (Kemp-Roth Bill in 1981). Both are ardent critics of today's U.S. policy, particularly under Fed chiefs Greenspan and Bernanke. But both have always been passionate supporters of America.

Looking ahead, no one can predict the future with precision. But Claus Vogt and Roland Leuschel provide a clear vision of what's possible. If you want to protect and grow your wealth even in the worst of times, heed their warnings and seriously consider their recommendations.

MARTIN D. WEISS, PhD

INTRODUCTION

The Global Debt Trap

N early every advanced industrial nation on the planet is ensnared in the greatest debt trap of all time.

The debt trap is not a far-off danger that we can worry about some other day. Nor is it merely a concern for armchair theorists.

Quite the contrary, the debts are so large, so widespread, and so deeply entrenched around the world that virtually every policy decision by our leaders, every strategic move by investors, and every financial choice by billions of citizens is influenced, constrained, or driven by the need to compensate for—or the desire to escape from—the great trap that these debts have created.

The most recent 15-year sequence of events provides the best historical evidence.

First came the tech boom and bust.

In the mid-1990s, mostly thanks to aggressive money easing by U.S. Fed chairman Alan Greenspan, U.S. technology stocks enjoyed a massive bubble that culminated in an equally massive bust in the year 2000.

In the wake of the bust, the Fed chairman, vividly aware of the debt trap, feared the market decline would set off a deflationary debt collapse.

So he eased money even further, engineering America's lowest interest rates since World War II.

Second, we saw the housing boom and bust.

By overreacting to the tech stock bust, Greenspan helped create another, even larger bubble—this time in U.S. real estate.

And when that bubble also burst, his successor at the Fed, Ben Bernanke, confronted an even greater problem. This time, not only did U.S. authorities harbor the *fear* of a debt collapse, they faced an actual, real-time collapse that threatened the entire global financial system.

Third was the Great Recession.

The world stumbled into the most severe economic downturn since the Great Depression of the 1930s. The banking system did not only come to the brink of a total collapse, but actually fell over the brink.

In a concerted effort to prevent a global collapse, the United States, Western Europe, and others embarked on the most expensive program of financial bailouts, economic stimulus, and money printing in the history of mankind.

In the United States, the Special Inspector General for the Troubled Asset Relief Program (SIGTARP)—the government agency responsible for tracking the $700 billion bank rescue package of 2008, reported to Congress that, by mid-year 2010, the U.S. government had spent $3.7 trillion in financial bailouts and bond-buying operations. If you add other measures taken to stem the debt crisis—such as U.S. government guarantees of bank deposits, credit markets, and other institutions—the total bill and liability is over $14 trillion. And if you consider parallel rescue efforts in Europe, it easily exceeds $20 trillion.

But none of these great rescues came without a cost. Quite the contrary, to save the banking system and financial markets from the global debt trap, the sovereign governments of the United States and Europe have gutted their own finances, instantly creating the largest peacetime deficits of all time.

Fourth, the sovereign debt crisis struck.

Given this sequence of events, it should have come as no surprise. Global investors rebelled, dumping the bonds of sovereign governments, targeting first the weakest among them.

Suddenly, Greek government bonds plunged in price as their interest rates soared from as low as 2 percent to 18 percent. Suddenly the Greek state was at the brink of default, and other European countries like Spain,

Ireland, Portugal, and Italy were also in jeopardy. Suddenly, the acronym PIIGS—Portugal, Italy, Ireland, Greece, and Spain—largely unknown to the public, became a household word, denoting countries buried in the muddy world of the sovereign debt crisis.

The European Union was initially very reluctant to intervene with yet another major financial rescue. But ultimately, the threat was deemed so great that European leaders were forced to do what many swore never to do—join with the International Monetary Fund (IMF) to bail out their weaker members with a massive $1 trillion rescue package.

The Global Debt Trap Is Clearly Driving Policy

Thus, it should be clear that monetary and fiscal policy are no longer driven by reason—let alone by any semblance of sounder principles established in earlier decades. Clearly, it is driven almost entirely by the global debt trap and the fear of its inevitable consequences—a global depression.

The global debt trap has driven monetary and fiscal policy makers to take ever more desperate measures to escape its fangs. But alas, the only solutions they have been able to come with so far have merely added *more* debts, created *bigger* speculative bubbles and ensnared them into a *deeper* trap, raising the specter of even *harsher* long-term consequences for billions of their citizens.

The Bank of International Settlements (BIS), the world's "central bank of central banks," helps gives us a clear vision regarding what some of those consequences might be. In its most recent annual report, it first gives us a snapshot of the massive, global deterioration in government finances, summarized in Table I.1.

This table itself is devastating in its implications. It shows that:

- We have witnessed an increase in government debt that is both dramatic and ubiquitous. Not one country listed by the BIS escaped the trend. Not one took effective measures to stop it.
- The government debts of two pivotal countries in the global financial system—the United States and the United Kingdom—are no less threatening than those of two countries that have already been victims of the sovereign debt crisis—Portugal and Spain. Indeed, for 2011, the BIS estimated that the government debts of Portugal and Spain to be

Table I.1 Conclusive Evidence of the Global Debt Trap

	Government Debt			Fiscal Balance		
	As a Percentage of GDP					
	2007	2010	2011	2007	2010	2011
Austria	62	74	77	−0.5	−4.7	−4.6
France	70	94	99	−2.7	−7.8	−6.9
Germany	65	81	84	0.2	−5.4	−4.5
Greece	104	129	139	−5.4	−8.1	−7.1
Ireland	28	83	92	0.1	−11.7	−10.8
Italy	112	132	135	−1.5	−5.2	−5.0
Japan	167	199	205	−2.4	−7.6	−8.3
Netherlands	52	75	79	0.2	−6.4	−5.4
Portugal	71	95	99	−2.7	−7.4	−5.6
Spain	42	73	78	1.9	−9.4	−7
United Kingdom	47	82	91	−2.7	−11.5	−10.3
United States	62	90	95	−2.8	−10.7	−8.9

SOURCE: Bank for International Settlements.

99 and 78 percent of GDP, respectively. For the same year, the BIS estimated that the government debts of the United States and the United Kingdom to be 91 and 95 percent of GDP, respectively. The debt burdens of these two larger countries are similar—or larger—than those of the two PIIGS countries.

- Japan has the biggest government debt problem of all. So some apologists for large U.S. government debts use Japan as an argument for how much debt is possible without risking a bigger disaster. But Japan, unlike the United States, has been able to finance its debts almost exclusively with the savings of its own citizens, while the United States relies on foreign lenders for most of its financing. Moreover, any implication that Japan's economy has *not* been severely hurt by its debt burden ignores Japan's two lost decades of chronic, on-again–off-again recession and deflation.
- The changes in the fiscal balance of every one of these countries is shown in the second group of columns. And they show that the fiscal

balance has clearly deteriorated sharply, especially in the past two to three years.

- Moreover, the BIS numbers show that the pace of deterioration in fiscal balance has actually been much faster in the United States and the United Kingdom than in four of the PIIGS countries—Italy, Portugal, Spain, and even Greece. This directly refutes anyone who might deny the possibility that the United Kingdom and the United States could be the next victims of the sovereign debt crisis.

But if you think this snapshot of the *current* global debt trap is shocking, wait till you see what the BIS projects for the future, as illustrated in Figure I.1.

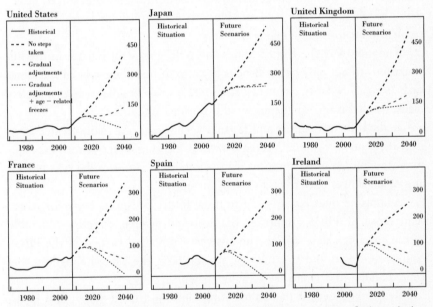

The debts in these charts refer to general government debt, with the future scenarios reflecting projections by the OECD (2010–2011) and BIS (2012–2040). The vertical line corresponds to 2008, the first full year of the debt crisis. For the "no steps taken" scenario (thick broken line) the BIS assumes (1) constant growth of potential real GDP at the rate estimated by the OECD for 2012–2025; (2) constant real effective interest rate at the 10-year precrisis average; (3) 2011 revenue and non-age-related spending (both as a percentage of GDP) held constant. The "gradual adjustments scenario" (thin broken line) assumes improvement from the 2011 level by one percentage point per year for the first 10 years of the projection and remains at that level for the remaining period. The least adverse scenario (dotted line) makes the additional assumption that age-related expenditures as a percentage of GDP remain constant at the 2011 level.

Figure I.1 Gross Public Debt Projections (as a Percentage of GDP)
SOURCES: OECD; BIS calculations.

Here you can see that for each country, the BIS estimates three scenarios:

In the first scenario, deficits continue to grow at the current pace with little or no efforts to change course. In this case, the resulting global debt trap would be *many* times worse than we have today. Not only would it be entirely intolerable, creating a burden so massive it would sink every economy . . . it is also entirely unthinkable, threatening an end to governments as we know them and a twenty-first Century of Dark Ages.

Therefore, the BIS assumes that governments must and *will* take steps to change course. The only questions are: how, how much, and when?

The big dilemma: even if the United States, Japan, and the United Kingdom can cut deficits by 1 percent of GDP per year for the next 10 years, the BIS projects that their accumulated debt burden will *still* increase. They will still be incurring new debts and those will still be larger than the old ones they pay off. Plus, to accomplish that unsatisfactory result will be, in itself, a major challenge.

The only way the United States can reduce its debt burden in the BIS scenario is to not only cut its deficits but also to freeze age-related spending, such as Social Security payments, at current levels—in other words, austerity measures that most Americans would consider draconian.

In the United Kingdom and Japan, the challenge is actually greater. Even *with* the 1 percent annual decrease *and* the freezing of age-related expenditures, the burden of government debt continues to rise over the years, albeit at a much slower pace than it's rising currently.

Again, the question arises: Are these future prospects better or worse than those of PIIGS countries that were considered directly vulnerable to the sovereign debt crisis? The answer: Compared to two of the PIIGS countries—Spain and Ireland—the prospects of the United Kingdom, the United States, and Japan are actually far worse.

Remember: even if the United Kingdom, the United States, and Japan can impose austerity in the years ahead, their government debt burdens could still increase. But Spain and Ireland (plus France) are better off in this scenario. If they do pursue austerity measures, their government debt burdens will ease markedly, according to the BIS.

Another big dilemma: all three of the BIS scenarios assume healthy growth in the global economy. If the expected economic growth fails to materialize, or worse, if the global economy suffers another contraction, the explosion in growth in government deficits will be greater. At the same time, any tangible results from austerity programs will, at best, be delayed for many years.

Certainly the "healthy growth scenario" is far from guaranteed. Quite to the contrary, as we put the finishing touches on this English-language edition of our book, our forecasting model, which correctly warned of the 2001–2003 and of 2007–2009 declines, is again showing a very high risk of another recession. Hence, if anything, the BIS scenarios may be too optimistic.

So again we ask: when global bond investors pick their next sovereign governments for dumping sovereign bonds, which ones will they pick? Will they target the ones that have taken—or have the ability to take—measures to counter these trends? Or will they target those that have neither the political will nor the financial flexibility to do so?

And again, we say emphatically: anyone who thinks the United States and the United Kingdom—or Japan—are invulnerable to a sovereign debt crisis such as the one that has struck Greece must awaken from their slumber and look carefully at these hard facts.

This is why the United Kingdom has already embarked on a shock-and-awe austerity program that far exceeds what most observers might have expected. And it is why political pressure is likely to build for the United States and Japan to do the same. Whether it will be possible to pursue austerity, however, seems doubtful. And how monetary authorities will react to the resulting economic shocks is equally uncertain.

No matter what the outcome, the only conclusion that can be drawn from the BIS study is a future of turmoil and economic pain.

What Will Actually Happen?

In theory, there are six ways to resolve the global debt trap—six escape hatches. So as a preview of the arguments we make in this book, let's briefly review each one:

Escape hatch 1: An economic growth miracle. It's highly unlikely that the developed world will stage a growth miracle during the coming years. Even the most optimistic economists don't dare forecast such an event. The debt burdens themselves are massive obstacles to growth. Nor have any of the highly indebted countries made the investments in infrastructure or technology that would be needed to generate rapid growth. It would indeed be a miracle, and it's so unlikely that it merits no further discussion.

Escape hatch 2: Major interest rate cuts. Also not possible. Interest rates have already been falling dramatically since 1981, with short-term official rates near zero. They cannot fall below zero. And there is virtually no more room for additional substantial declines in long-term rates. In short, all developed countries have already played this card. They can't play it again.

Escape hatch 3: Bailouts by other governments. This was apparently possible—at least temporarily—for PIIGS countries, all of which are a part of the euro zone. But it would be far more difficult to justify for countries outside the euro zone. Moreover, what country or entity is large enough to bail out the United Kingdom or Japan. And who could possibly bail out the United States itself? Certainly not smaller countries. Even if it were willing, China is not big enough, either. And a bailout from the IMF, whose funding comes mostly from the United States, would also not be possible.

Obviously these first three escape hatches from the global debt trap are not available—especially for the United States, the United Kingdom, and Japan. They must choose from one of the other three escapes, none of which is painless. . . .

Escape hatch 4: Outright default. This may be possible for smaller nations that can subsist under dictatorships that isolate them from the global economy. But it is not possible for the United States, which depends on its credit with foreign lenders, to survive. Even if the United States is willing to give up its status as the world's economic leader, an outright default on its government debts would be a disaster and blunder of such obvious and great magnitude that it is highly unlikely it would ever be seriously considered—let alone pursued as an escape hatch.

Escape hatch 5: Austerity. Austerity policies include tax hikes and massive spending cuts—both with dramatic political consequences and painful economic impacts.

So far, virtually the whole world has responded to the Great Recession with the largest government stimulus program in peacetime, and still the results have been very disappointing. Thus, it doesn't take a PhD in economics to imagine what might happen if those same governments did precisely the opposite—instead of pouring money into the economy, pulling money back out. The result would be a vicious cycle of government cutbacks, falling income, shortfalls in income taxes, even larger deficits, and still more cutbacks needed. In sum—a depression.

This scenario is possible. But we don't see it as the most probable, at least not until the final alternative is pushed to the limit.

Escape hatch 6: Money printing. Governments can and do default on their debts in a more subtle and sly manner—through inflation. Central banks can monetize government debt and seek to inflate the debt away. And it is this escape hatch that is typically the most appealing to most politicians.

In their minds, the major byproduct—inflation—is distributed through the society. And more importantly, the inevitability of that byproduct is not fully understood by large segments of the public, giving politicians the opportunity to inflate their country's currency and let their successors or other scapegoats take the blame.

It is this escape hatch from the global debt that we deem to be the most probable. But it comes with a high risk. It may soon career out of control and usher in a period of hyperinflation. Unfortunately, financial history holds many examples of this very sad outcome.

In the balance of this book, we explain why. We show you how we arrived at this unfortunate predicament, how our leaders have failed us and how they are likely to continue to do so.

No matter what, the coming years promise to be both frightening and exciting. Both as an investor and as a citizen, you need to be as flexible as ever before to circumvent the many pitfalls. But always remember: the bigger the crisis, the greater the opportunity for those who can prudently prepare ahead of time. In the chapters that follow, we will show you how.

CHAPTER 1

Why the Debt Crisis
Was Predictable

How was it that we, of all people, were able to successfully predict the major financial and economic crisis that continues even as we write these words today? What differentiates us from the army of economists, professors, analysts, bankers, fund managers, central bankers, politicians, and journalists who only recognized the impending calamity after it was well under way?

We are not whiz kids or members of Mensa. Nor do we have any secret access to knowledge.

Rather, our only strategic advantage is the willingness to swim against the tide, and to remain immune to the siren songs. Most human beings are gregarious animals who can believe—and sometimes, *must* believe—almost anything, as long as they are part of a group that subscribes to the same viewpoint. It seems no theory or thought is too absurd to be accepted by vast numbers of otherwise thoughtful people. Fictions that few could ever believe individually are trusted implicitly within the shelter of the group. Individuals who otherwise might be totally rational are swept up into irrational groups that suppress and inhibit even the most basic of common sense.

The second factor that has helped us distance ourselves from the crowd is the absence of any conflicts of interest. We view market analysis—which necessarily includes political analysis, social analysis, and even mass psychology—as one of the most worthy pure intellectual challenges that the world has to offer. We have no professional ties, contracts, or commitments that interfere with or bias that endeavor.

From a technical point of view, the key is our intensive focus on the phenomenon of the speculative bubble. A comprehension of its causes, its dynamics, its bursting—and the consequences thereof—has enabled us to see the period since the mid-1990s, when the largest stock market bubble of all time began, through different eyes from the majority of our colleagues. Furthermore, the internal logic of the speculative bubble forced us to ask further critical questions and to connect the dots to what others may have seen as unthinkable conclusions.

Finally, and most important, our understanding would be woefully incomplete if we were not familiar with the Austrian School of economics. The brilliance and consistency of its approach, dedicated to the cause of freedom, is both inspiring and persuasive. Its logic will propel you toward insights that cannot be reconciled with ready-made views of the world. But therein lies one of its great strengths. Moreover, it does not stop at the gates of institutions that continue to be regarded as sacrosanct. Quite the contrary, the Austrian School debunks the wisdom of the state's monetary monopoly, reveals the danger of its resulting system of central banks and fractional reserve banking, and exposes this monetary complex for precisely what it is. As we will document here, this monetary complex is the underlying root of the crisis now unfolding. Worse, the global official response to the crisis—unprecedented interventionism—threatens the continued existence of our free market system and, with it, individual freedom itself.

Keynes versus Mises and Hayek

Let us start this chapter about the huge differences between classical liberal thinking and Keynesianism with a central quote about money from F.A. von Hayek.

The past instability of the market economy is the consequence of the exclusion of the most important regulator of the market mechanism, money, from itself being regulated by the market process.[1]

We refer again and again in our analyses to the insights of the Austrian School of economics, whose preeminent thinkers were Carl Menger, Eugen von Böhm-Bawerk, Ludwig von Mises, Friedrich August von Hayek, Walter Eucken, and Murray N. Rothbard.

At the heart of this school of thought, which extends far beyond the realm of economics, is freedom of the individual. And inextricably tied to freedom is, of course, property—specifically including ownership of the means of production. Freedom of contract and self-responsibility are the most important additions to these key concepts, which underpin classical liberalism and from which the political program of a free society emerges.

It goes without saying that the boundaries of the freedom of one individual lie where the freedom of another begins. It is easy to derive the rules governing cooperation from this basic principle.

At the same time, there are also thieves, liars, and fraudsters, seeking to acquire other people's property for themselves. It follows that certain measures must exist to protect property rights. Furthermore, freedom of contract would have little meaning were there no mechanism in place for the enforcement of contractual agreements.

At discussion of the precise form of such mechanisms—and what concrete proposals classical liberalism offers for their regulation—is beyond the scope of this book. Suffice it to point out that individual freedom continually faces a series of specific threats and that the greater threat to individual freedom comes not from other individuals but rather from powerful organizations.

Organized crime, like the Mafia, is a common example that springs to mind, but it is not the one that affects the most people most of the time. Rather, the single greatest threat to individual freedom comes not from common criminals, but from the mightiest organization of all—the state.

The Road to Serfdom

History is littered with examples of horrendous crimes. But the biggest, the worst, and the most devastating have, almost without exception, been perpetrated in the name of the state. This unmistakable conclusion has led the philosophers of freedom to adopt a healthy mistrust of government and its representatives.

Based on the most thorough analytical and empirical arguments, they see the government as the greatest threat to freedom, against which a society must protect itself at all costs, lest it degenerate into dictatorship. The separation of powers is one such protective mechanism. But equally important is strict adherence to a currency that *cannot* be multiplied at will, thus forcing the government to treat the nation's finances in a responsible manner, while protecting the people from the greed of the politicians.

In principle, there are two ways freedom can be abolished and slavery introduced: through revolution or evolution. The reader will certainly be familiar with revolutions that have led to the rise of dictatorships. The communist revolutions, causing untold suffering and poverty across great swaths of the globe have, after all, only recently been consigned to history. A repeat of this ghastly period in history hardly appears to be an imminent threat today, while the threat of Islamist revolutions seem more current, threatening the introduction of new tyrannies in several parts of the world.

In Europe, most of the Americas, and other regions, freedom is not currently threatened by domestic groups demanding revolution. Instead, the greater threat stems from an evolutionary process initiated long ago—a not-so-subtle, insidious progression in which the government spreads gradually like a cancerous tumor, increasingly limiting or abolishing individual freedoms.

To describe this process, Hayek coined the phrase "the road to serfdom."[2]

In this book we refer primarily to *Keynesianism*—to embody not only John Maynard Keynes's economic program, but also, to some degree, all schools of economic thought that seek to accord the government a sphere of influence extending far beyond the essential sovereign tasks of ensuring security at home and abroad.

For the sake of simplicity, we draw no distinction among multiple schools of economic thought, all of which have one major commonality: namely that they all demand an overly robust role for the government in the economy and society.

In this broader sense, we also characterize *monetarists* as Keynesians inasmuch as they advocate the government monopoly over money and the system of central banks, which that monopoly necessarily entails. Granted, in other realms, monetarists espouse thoroughly non-Keynesian positions that may seem to favor freedom. But for the purposes of this book, they continue to fall under the broader rubric of Keynesians.

The administration of former president George W. Bush and the neoconservatives, despite all their rhetoric to the contrary, were, in fact, out-and-out Keynesians. This is so obvious it should not even be worth mentioning. However, in the wake of the debt crisis, since the blame game and search for scapegoats is so ubiquitous, and since neoliberalism is first in the firing line, this observation is nonetheless necessary. It's ironic that liberalism and free market philosophies are getting lynched, when the real culprit that deserves to stand trial is Keynesianism.

The key point here is not whether government intervention in the economy—including massive economic stimulus programs—are financed by deficits or not. We know that Keynes proposed that the government should accumulate reserves in good times so that it could afford to finance stimulus programs in bad times. But because Keynes himself was, in large measure, a politician, it is inconceivable that even he considered the implementation of this proposal to be possible—let alone probable. The interests of politicians who depend on votes are diametrically opposed to Keynes's proposition of accumulating reserves in times of plenty. Voters almost invariably demand that surpluses be spent *today*—not in some elusive future.

To reveal a government's hidden agenda—even behind its smokescreen of public relations and propaganda—all that is typically required is to consider a few key variables: you can look at the trend in the government's share of total economic activity, the amount of legislation passed or, more commonly, the level of national debt. If each of these is expanding, you can be almost certain that the government is *not* pursuing a liberal agenda. It is immaterial what kind of rhetoric or propaganda the government is deploying. Do not let them fool you. And don't be hoodwinked by false critics, either. Judge both sides not by their words, but by their deeds.

Classical liberalism and the Austrian School of economics stand, as we do, for freedom of the individual—with no ifs or buts. Classical liberalism and the Austrian School are the offspring of unwavering philosophers of freedom. And these are philosophers who think ideas through to their logical conclusion with inexorable consistency, even in circumstances in which others would prefer to take a more relaxed view—to further their career or to avoid established taboos. It should therefore come as no surprise that thinkers of this provenance have no powerful friends. They are a thorn in the side of the powerful.

In *The Denationalisation of Money*, F.A. von Hayek sums it up as follows: "I fear that since 'Keynesian' propaganda has filtered through to the masses, has made inflation respectable and provided agitators with arguments which professional politicians are unable to refute, the only way to avoid being driven by continuing inflation into a controlled and directed economy, and [the only way to] ultimately save civilization, will be to deprive governments of their power over the supply of money."[3]

We agree. But some of the most powerful men—controlling trillions of a nation's money supply—do not.

Dr. Greenspan's Great Experiment

"Dr Greenspan's great experiment" was the title of an important chapter in our book *Das Greenspan Dossier*. We coined this term, with good reason, to refer to the policy of unrestricted use of the printing press to create money—a policy pursued aggressively at that time to counteract the consequences of the technology stock bust (the *Tech Wreck*) between 2000 and 2002.

The United States had witnessed the bursting of a giant stock market bubble once before, in 1929. And the Crash of 1929 proved to be the prelude to a serious banking crisis and a global recession that would later go down in history as the Great Depression. The causes of this historic crisis are the subject of extremely heated debate even today. Nonetheless, in recent years, the Keynesian view has increasingly prevailed—a view we regard as mistaken.

Believers in Government Omnipotence

On one side of this dispute are John Maynard Keynes and the school of thought that is now followed by the vast majority of economists. Above all, this school places its faith in the government. It maintains that the massive monetary and fiscal measures taken in the 1930s were fundamentally correct; it was simply the extent of government intervention that was believed to be insufficient to prevent the catastrophe. "Too little, too late" is the shorthand version of the analysis that predominates today.

Strangely, in their theory and worldview, the preceding boom, made possible by the lax monetary policy of the 1920s, plays no role. To be precise, it does not even appear in this theory at all.

Nevertheless, virtually every central banker and policy advisor, together with almost every economist in government, subscribes to this school. Naturally, he who pays the piper calls the tune. Unfortunately, it's ultimately the average citizen that gets stuck with the bill.

Free Market Economists and Skeptics of the State

On the other side of the debate are Friedrich August von Hayek and a beleaguered minority that's been consistently skeptical of government. They see the true cause of the 1930s bust not in the inadequacy of the government's response, but rather, in the monetary excesses that created the speculative boom that preceded it.

It was lax monetary policy that drove the credit-financed boom and stock market bubble of the 1920s. And it was the unprecedented monetary and fiscal government responses in the 1930s that prevented or postponed a long-overdue correction process, serving merely to prolong and deepen the depression.

As we said at the outset, we subscribe, without reservation, to the second point of view, based largely on the insights of the Austrian School of economics.

This school is the primary foundation of our analyses and forecasts. And it's the Austrian School's far-reaching perspective that enabled us to give our readers advance warning of the dangers of the 1990s stock market bubble and, later, of the real estate bubble. It is also this approach that enabled us to recognize the extent of bad investments and economic imbalances associated with the real estate bubble early on, together with the enormous attendant risks.

To drive home the importance of this approach, don't be surprised if we sometimes repeat ourselves. The repetition is deliberate, as many of our observations and conclusions will be new to most readers, and perhaps a little disconcerting.

Dr. Greenspan's Great Experiment

When the stock market bubble burst in the year 2000, Alan Greenspan's Fed reacted with drastic cuts in interest rates and massive borrowing to finance ever-larger government intervention. America's monetary policy makers, virtually all of whom subscribe to the Keynesian worldview, wanted to avoid what they believed to be the great blunders of the 1930s. So they opted for no half measures.

Around the world, central bankers, all believers in government by virtue of their office, followed Greenspan's lead and pursued some of the most lax monetary policies of all time in each of their respective countries.

At first, the extraordinarily low interest rates had the desired impact. A correction process, which had begun when the stock market bubble burst, was indeed halted. The recession of 2001 was short and shallow, and a new economic upturn began. But by almost any established measure, it was one of the weakest recoveries since the end of World War II.

Nevertheless, despite the weak results, a very high price was paid: the largest real estate bubble of all time. And this real estate bubble emerged as the central axis around which the bulk of the economic upturn revolved. In a nutshell, the true consequence of Dr. Greenspan's great monetary experiment—to combat the stock market bust—was simply the creation of a far *larger* bubble, this time in the global market for homes.

In *Das Greenspan Dossier,* we gave our appraisal of Greenspan's high-risk experiment, warning that he was creating a bubble; that the bubble was likely to burst; and that it risked crashing the stock market, triggering a severe recession, toppling America's mortgage giants, even threatening the entire financial system.

How did we know? Because anyone with some knowledge of the Austrian School—and a modicum of common sense—could see that the consequence of an asset bubble is an asset bust. There is no other likely outcome.

The Long Road to the Worst Central Banker of All Time

Fast forward to 2010 and we now have, strewn before us, the undeniable results of Greenspan's irresponsible series of experiments in monetary policy. As we commented in *Das Greenspan Dossier:*

> Because we are ourselves primarily and irresistibly propelled through life by Faustian curiosity, we can fully appreciate the significance and beauty of this experiment and also the pleasure that

the maestro may derive from its execution. However, we would feel considerably more at ease if it were only the poor soul of the experimenter which were at stake, and not the economic well-being of us all.[4]

Thus, we stand by our earlier prediction that Alan Greenspan will finally take his well-earned place in history as one of the worst central bankers of all time, a fate that his self-righteous autobiography cannot prevent. Whether we're right or wrong, however, it will be cold comfort to the millions of innocent people who have had to suffer the consequences of his blunders.

Today, Greenspan's successor, Ben Bernanke, is sparing no effort to upstage him. But, at their core, his policies are merely a continuation of the Greenspan doctrine. Yes, they break new ground in regard to tactics (as we explain further on), but not by virtue of their rationale or goals. Alas, despite Bernanke's best efforts to destroy your prosperity, it remains to be seen if he will someday inherit the title of worst central banker of all time.

Whiskey for the Alcoholic

The central engine of lax Greenspan-Bernanke monetary policy is the concept of fighting fire with kerosene, flushing whiskey down the throat of an alcoholic, using Beelzebub to drive out the devil. Worse, the economic distortions and disasters that inevitably flow from their misguided monetary excesses are met with a repetition—or even massive escalation—of precisely the same excesses.

Again and again, we have compared this course of action to the treatment of a drug addict suffering from the initial stages of withdrawal. Repeatedly, we have warned against the disastrous long-term consequences of this myopic approach. And never have we left any doubt as to what the result would be: more bubbles, more busts, and ultimately, a far deeper economic crisis than the one they're seeking so desperately to avoid.

Failure without Insight

From an analytical point of view, recognizing the bubble, understanding its consequences, and forecasting its bust was relatively straightforward. But we were not particularly surprised when Keynesians, with their blind faith

in government, stuck their heads in the sand. What is very surprising—
even shocking—is that they have persisted in their failed theory even in the
wake of its self-destruction during the 2008–2009 debt crisis. Even though
the Keynesian experiment failed miserably, they stood stubbornly by their
government-based theories, prescribing even larger doses of the very same
policies that caused the disaster in the first place.

Meanwhile, free market solutions—corrections that have historically
been instrumental in restoring balance in line with market forces—are not
permitted. Instead, politicians and their central bankers experiment with
ever more expansionary manipulations of the market. Only by this means,
they tell us, can they prevent an even darker scenario—a "systemic collapse"
that they refuse to define or describe beyond vague references.

What's most unfortunate is that, with their interventions, governments
punish all those who would save or invest prudently, help build a nation's
capital base, and promote stability. Simultaneously, they reward those who
spend lavishly, speculate wildly and, in the long run, undermine the nation's
future growth. Worst of all, this ultimate moral hazard, which we discussed
at length in *Das Greenspan Dossier*, has now been taken to such an extreme
that it threatens the very foundation of capitalism and Western society.

Nationalization as a Response to Burst Bubbles and the Shattered Dreams of Central Bankers

The forecast we published back in 2004—that a future housing bust would
bring the entire financial system to its knees, with Fannie Mae and Freddie
Mac among the prime casualties—has since been borne out in dramatic style.

The two mortgage giants, which underwrote almost 80 percent of the
entire U.S. mortgage credit market in 2007, are *de facto* bankrupt. Yes,
the U.S. government prevented a potentially ugly free market resolution
of the bankruptcies—a deeper housing depression. But in the long run,
the path it chose instead—outright nationalization—could be the greater
of the evils.

From the outset, Fannie Mae and Freddie Mac owed their existence to
the U.S. government and enjoyed a close relationship with its policy makers. Fannie Mae was formed by the government in 1938 to breathe new
life into the mortgage market, and Freddie Mac followed 32 years later.

Armed with a government mandate and an implicit government guarantee, they were able to gain an enormous market share—mostly based on a business model that was, at best superfluous, and, at worst, a major force that greatly distorted the marketplace.

In the final analysis, Fannie and Freddie crowded out the less privileged private sectors, took on huge risks, and helped foster the greatest debt bubble of all time—all centered around home mortgages. They also stood at the very crest of a huge wave of bankruptcies that swept through the banking sector.

Fannie and Freddie have already cost the taxpayer dearly, and there is no end in sight. In the third quarter of 2008, Freddie Mac alone, the smaller of the two, posted a loss of $25 billion. And subsequent losses were even worse. And looking ahead, we confidently anticipate that considerable *additional* losses will be laid at the taxpayer's feet in the coming quarters, if not years. For shareholders, too, the institutions nationalized at the start of September 2008 proved to be massive destroyers of money.

As you can see in Figure 1.1, the shortsighted risk taking of Fannie Mae's management has totally destroyed the value the stock. Stockholders have suffered huge losses. But unfortunately, that's not the end of the story. Now you, the U.S. taxpayer, are on the hook for further losses, very much

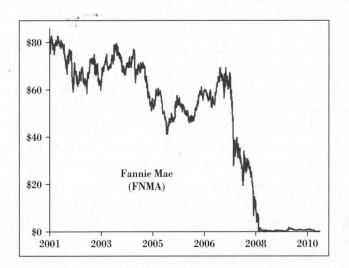

Figure 1.1   Riches to Rags: Fannie Mae (Stock Price of Fannie Mae)

to the delight of the holders of Fannie Mae's bonds who have been bailed out by the government's rescue package, as have the bondholders of many other de facto bankrupt financial institutions rescued by the government.

Fannie and Freddie have now become wards of the state. Nor are they alone. All over the world, major segments of the credit markets and banking system are passing from private to government hands in the wake of massive losses.

The nationalization of the banking system, a traditional demand of socialists and communists, is rapidly being implemented by the very same leaders who, in any other circumstances, would be steadfastly opposed to such demands.

And ironically, Great Britain, the cradle of free market economics, has been leading the movement to nationalize big banks, and we expect this process to resume as soon as the next phase of the current crisis gets under way. Indeed, by the end of the Great Recession, which may ultimately be recognized as a depression, much of the financial sector could be nationalized— not just in the United Kingdom, but throughout most of Europe and the United States as well.

East Germany as a Model?

Surprisingly, few are taking the needed time out to engage in a higher-level political discussion about the true, unintended consequences of these measures. Free market principles are being thrown overboard. Giant steps are being taken along the path toward socialism and serfdom. But voices of protests are muted or deliberately drowned out.

Nevertheless, current and historical evidence of the longer-term economic consequences of this policy is everywhere: the obvious failures of every economy locked behind the Cold War Iron Curtain, the declining ability of socialist-leaning nations to compete in the global economy, and, now, the existential threats to the euro and the entire European Union.

The big picture that emerges is a protracted decline in prosperity with ever-greater curtailments and encroachments of freedom. If you want a better grasp of where this road may take us, then recall the decay and rot that permeated former communist East Germany. Slowly and stealthily, the country degenerated into a mere caricature of its former self, riddled by political capriciousness, nepotism, bureaucracy, and worse.

Looking ahead, as we put the finishing touches on the English-language edition of this book in the summer of 2010, we proceed from the assumption that the shocking and spectacular bankruptcies witnessed in recent months are not over. More are to come in the United States, Europe, and indeed, throughout the world. And more countries—especially the large ones in the epicenter of the global debt trap—are bound to fall victim to the contagion now commonly called "the sovereign debt crisis."

Some analysts worry that governments will, at some point, simply let corporations, banks, and even entire nations fail, much as the United States did with Lehman Brothers in September 2009. But what would, in our view, be even more worrisome is the opposite outcome: a commitment to save them all, ultimately driving virtually the entire financial sector into government hands. The redemptive hand of powerful friends, who can only afford to exercise that friendship through the use of taxpayers' money, will seek to make this a certainty.

The Financial Arsonists Remain Vigilant

Reuters News amused us on September 10, 2008, with the headline "The financial crisis continues—ECB chief warns against complacency."[5]

They were referring to European Central Bank president Jean-Claude Trichet. But to whom Trichet was addressing this landmark warning remains an open question.

Reason: most banks affected by the crisis have found out the hard way that the crisis is far from over. On the executive floors of Citibank, Goldman Sachs, and other financial giants, the erstwhile dancers on the rim of the volcano were certainly greedy, shortsighted, and deficient in their judgment. But they never struck us as particularly complacent.

Rather, complacency was far more evident among the world's central bankers—Greenspan, Bernanke, and Trichet himself. Each failed to recognize the dramatic consequences of the real estate bubbles, which had been made possible only by their own monetary policies. On Sunday talk shows, each sought to exonerate himself by pontificating (correctly) about the moral hazard of rewarding risk . . . only to trample their own insights in their Monday-to-Friday policy making.

Bernanke warns Congress about federal deficits. Trichet and others declare, "*We must remain vigilant.*"[6]

Agreed. But does that now mean we can all relax, safe in the knowledge that they will keep the vigil to prevent double-digit monetary growth and the next speculative bubble? We think not. They are the true financial arsonists. They are the foxes guarding the chicken coops.

We cannot underscore this point more forcefully: it was the misguided policies of these arsonists in the guise of central bankers that started the fires now still raging throughout the financial system. It was their misguided response to these fires that has brought us the sovereign debt crisis. And it is thanks to them that the largest and supposedly most powerful economies of the world are now caught so deeply in the global debt trap.

The outcome of their policies was—and is—easy to predict. And now these same arsonists are telling each other to remain vigilant? If the likely consequences were not so serious, such performances would be comical.

Are Falling Asset Values Good or Bad?

In 2008, values fell globally and across many asset classes—not only in the United States, but also in Europe and Asia; not only in the real estate sector and in stocks, but also in corporate bonds, commodities, and even a variety of other supposedly safe investments.

Until early 2009, those declines continued. And despite a temporary, government-engineered recovery through early 2010, similar or greater declines are bound to return.

Here's the key: most people—including consumers, investors, analysts, and policy makers—automatically assume that falling values are bad, while rising values are good.

But, in reality, that depends on whether you own them or you're seeking an opportunity to buy them; whether you were caught flat-footed by the declines or were prepared for them.

If you were seeking to buy a home in the United States in the early 2000s, surging prices were bad. Likewise, the subsequent housing price declines were good, giving middle class families new opportunities to own a home.

If you were looking for a chance to invest in the stock market, before the recent declines, the pricy valuations of most worthy stocks represented a major obstacle to your investment success. Conversely, price declines that created low valuations created attractive opportunities.

And if you have good tools to help you anticipate the declines, the profit opportunities—both during the declines and after—are even greater.

Many analysts and commentators described 2008 as a very bad and difficult year—in relation to both economic trends and the equity markets. But we do not subscribe to this assessment. It only applies to the vast majority—those experts for whom the property slump, the recession, the banking crisis and, of course, the bear market in stocks were a surprise.

But for the objective minority—those with eyes to see, an open mind, and a willingness to understand the lessons of history—it was actually an opportunity.

How the Objective Minority
Saw the 2008 Recession

The 2008 recession was clearly and unmistakably signaled in advance by a series of relatively reliable alarm bells—not only the stock market itself, but also an inverted yield curve and sharp declines in the U.S. index of leading indicators.

These are not rare, unknown indicators that only a few people can see. They are classic early signals of recession that were largely ignored or explained away by some of the nation's leading economists and politicians.

In the prior economic cycle, these economists conjured up the image of the grand Internet superhighway to justify bad business models and bad investment decisions. This time, the spin doctors used what was called the *decoupling theory* to ignore the handwriting on the wall.

The grand boom in Asia, went the theory, had completely altered the global economy. It more than compensated, they said, for any signs of weakness in the United States. Thus, they concluded, the global boom would continue unabated.

These were the same pundits who, in the earlier bust, had blustered— even back then—about the abolition of the economic cycle, enabling them to believe in their theory of a boom without end. In both cycles, they urged their followers to hold their stocks and even buy more. Then, as now, they caused untold financial misery.

The bursting of the stock market bubble in the year 2000 marked a watershed event. World stock markets have been in a secular downtrend

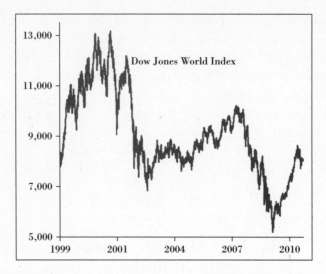

Figure 1.2   Decade-Long Global Bear Market Began in 2000 (Dow Jones World Stock Index in Euros)

since then, as you can see in Figure 1.2. The buy-and-hold mantra has delivered nothing but huge losses. Unfortunately, the end of this secular bear market has not yet come.

Yet, even as they touted more stocks, equity markets had long since risen to historic levels of overvaluation. And even as they continued to chant their "buy-buy-buy" mantra, the world's leading stock market indices were already breaking down from well-developed topping formations. It's not just in retrospect that those signals were clear. Even then, it was hard to imagine a clearer advance warning of a bear market and a recession.

Now, in the summer of 2010, the picture looks similarly bleak. But most pundits are looking the other way again, still predicting prosperity and rising stock prices.

The reason highly remunerated experts saw no recession or financial crisis coming cannot be explained by the complexity of our times. Instead, it lies in these two factors:

1. Career risk and the herd instinct.
2. Questionable models, questionable theories.

Career Risk and the Herd Instinct

In the first instance, the all-too human self-interest of the principal actors creates a tendency toward bullish forecasts, come what may. Far less effort— or none at all—is made to predict economic downturns and recessions.

The primary reason: No analyst was ever fired and no wise man of economics ever thrown onto the street for failing to predict a stock market slump or recession. But anyone who stands out as one of the few who fails to foresee—or make money in—boom times is at risk of losing one's job and damaging one's career. In the United States, this rather distasteful tendency is known by the term *career risk*.

Result: both Wall Street pros and Washington policy makers have a clearly discernible inclination to provide bullish or optimistic forecasts, while it is well known that a terrible fate has historically awaited the proverbial messenger of bad news.

There is also an important psychological reason underlying the systematic bias of financial and economic forecasts toward optimistic outlooks that cannot be supported by objective facts: in his memoirs, Henry Kaufman, once among the most influential analysts in America and well known for his ability to swim against the tide, explained it this way:

> Most predictions fall within a rather narrow range that does not deviate from consensus views in the financial community. In large measure, this reflects an all-too-human propensity to minimize risk and avoid isolation. There is, after all, comfort in running with the crowd. Doing so makes it impossible to be singled out for being wrong, and allows one to avoid envy or resentment that often afflicts those who are right more often than not.[7]

Questionable Models, Questionable Theories

Secondly, the models and theories used by the overwhelming majority of modern economists almost invariably lead to an incorrect assessment of the actual situation.

"We are all Keynesians now," wrote Nobel Prize-winning economist Milton Friedman in the 1965 year-end issue of *Time* magazine; and "I am now a Keynesian in economics" echoed President Richard Nixon as he took the United States off the gold standard in 1971. More so than ever before, this same statement applies to the vast majority of economists.[8]

Keynesian theory, which we never found convincing, dominates economics curricula at universities, research departments at major Wall Street firms, and think tanks in Washington. Entire generations of economists, financial advisors, and management experts were brought up with Keynesian theory.

Keynesian theory drives politics itself, serving to justify and promote the increasing expansion of bureaucracy and boundless government intervention. Indeed, Keynesian theory supports a self-fulfilling cycle of success for politicians. The theory is used to rationalize almost any form of intervention, which, in turn, imbues them with ever more power over the economy and society.

Ultimately, Keynes's theories have now come to dominate not only the United States, but also the central banks of most major nations—not to mention their oversized bureaucracies. Around the world, central bankers, who administer the government's monopoly over money, were supposed to protect the value of their currencies. Instead, they are now among the most zealous Keynesians promoting inflation. If one believes what they say, one must conclude that they seriously believe in their ability to solve economic problems and provide for the general welfare—strictly with the aid of the money printing press.

The Austrian School and Common Sense

We repeat: in place of Keynesian macroeconomic models, the sound common-sense insights and theories of the liberal Austrian School of economics stand at the heart of our analyses. This school provides substantially more convincing explanations of economic realities and relationships than do the models of modern economists.

In essence, modern economists are playing Hermann Hesse's glass bead game,[9] in which the rules of the game are forever shrouded in mystery. Their attempt to apply mathematical approaches—which work successfully in the natural sciences—to economics, which reflects politics, social interaction, and mass psychology, seems to us extraordinarily naïve and distant from reality.

This is especially true regarding the economic cycles since the late 1990s, each characterized by huge speculative booms and busts. The insights of the Austrian School enabled us to detect early on the treacherous trends that were emerging—and the threats to the economy, the financial system, and the stock market that they entailed. Armed with the insights and foresights of the Austrian School, the widespread asset destruction of 2008 came as no surprise.

The events of 2009, however, were not so predictable. As we wrote in the German original from which this book is derived, "The massive government interventions termed variously *rescue packages* and *economic stimulus programs* will inevitably have effects and side effects that render free market processes more or less inoperative, thus making the work of an analyst much more difficult."

But governments can alter the natural economic tides only temporarily. And in 2010, those same governments suddenly suffered Mother Nature's revenge, as market forces unleashed the sovereign debt crisis, first pounding the weakest countries like Greece and then spreading to Spain, Portugal, the United Kingdom, and ultimately, even the United States.

The Brilliant Failure of the Keynesian Model

Science teaches us that models should achieve three things: they must describe that part of the world to which they refer; they must explain its processes; and they must help make forecasts that are, more often than not, borne out in fact.

Measured against these established requirements, recent years have demonstrated, in the most convincing manner, that the Keynesian stimulus programs—implemented as a response to the bursting of the stock market bubble between 2000 and 2003—failed monumentally. They did not overcome the undesirable trends and imbalances that were obvious even then; they merely delayed their negative consequences, creating an additional layer of even greater dangers.

In the wake of the bear market of the early 2000s, they merely created a new bubble in real estate, which was echoed in the equity markets. These bubbles, in turn, tricked the financial world and participants in the real economy into thinking that everything was in perfect order once again, that central bankers had things under control, and that the groundwork for "a new, sustainable recovery" had been laid. The consumer regained confidence. An orgy of debt gathered greater momentum, particularly in the United States and United Kingdom. Finally, share prices in many countries reached record heights once more, as the Dow Jones World Stock Index exceeded its high water mark for the year 2000 by about 25 percent. And in contrast to the bull market of the 1990s, many commodity prices also climbed to spectacular new highs.

Money printing has unwelcome side effects. Sooner or later it leads to rising prices, somewhere, somehow. During the mid-2000s, not only housing prices surged, but commodity prices were also driven to extreme highs as Figure 1.3 demonstrates.

In reality, however, these new bubbles of the mid-2000s only served to drive the devil out with Beelzebub. The alcoholic suffering the initial stages of withdrawal was again treated with a large dose of whiskey. The result of this policy was soon evident: the near-collapse of the entire financial system, prevented only by massive government intervention and huge

Figure 1.3   Money Printing in Early 2000s Leads to Commodity Surge in Mid-2000s
SOURCE: Reuters/Jefferies.

government guarantees. It was the greatest crisis since the 1930s, which, in many respects, had—and still has—the potential to dwarf even the Great Depression.

One would think that this disastrous outcome would cause any rational supporters of the Keynesian model to rethink their theories and reverse course. At the same time, one would expect that it would prompt established economists to acknowledge the obvious—that the few analysts who predicted the debt crisis did so thanks largely to their understanding of the Austrian School. This is no coincidence; indeed it is almost a precondition, since it is only the Austrian School that provides an insight into the root cause of this extreme boom-and-bust cycle: central bank manipulation of interest rates.

Despite Everything, Keynes Is *Still* on the Rise!

Ironically, however instead of discarding the discredited Keynesian models, adopting the theory that has now proven itself to be scientifically correct, and following the path of common sense, establishment economists have, so far, sought to do precisely the opposite. Indeed, the insights of the Austrian School and their clear success in forecasting the events of recent years remain, as before, almost completely ignored.

Virtually everywhere in the world, another, even larger wave of Keynesian stimulus measures was set into motion. What about the simple, common-sense reality that governments did not have the money? Until the sovereign debt crisis erupted, the question wasn't even asked! Billions, nay, trillions were patronizingly frittered away. Why? And most important . . .

Where did all that stimulus money come from?

From China to Singapore, from the United States to the United Kingdom, and from every financial center to the ends of the earth, governments felt compelled to combat the recession through Keynesian stimulus programs. Trillions of dollars, euros, yen, and yuan were poured into this well-intentioned global project. But as is so often the case, good intentions are not sufficient to achieve good results. The obvious reason: The sources of the money.

In theory, three principal sources of money are available.

1. Domestic savings.
2. Foreign savings.
3. The printing press or, to put it more precisely, money creation within the financial system.

In practice, however, although all played some role in the greatest Keynesian stimulus programs in history, it was the printing presses that were deployed by most Western governments most of the time.

When the government taps domestic savings to finance its expenditures, it competes with the credit needs of private enterprises, which often depend on external capital for their investment plans. There is consequently a crowding-out effect at the expense of the private sector. This is obviously counterproductive. The aim of an economic stimulus program is to support the economy. But if the government depletes the available supply of domestic savings and pushes up interest rates, its stimulus has the opposite effect, dampening growth or even helping to precipitate the next recession.

If, instead of domestic savings, external ones are accessed, then the crowding effect does not impact home-based corporations. But because almost all countries reacted to the global economic crisis with similar economic measures and because of the interconnectedness of the global economy, only a few countries have had the privilege of financing their government debt at the cost of other countries.

The third possible path is printing presses and the resulting inflation. We fear that this source of money will, at the end of the day, be the primary one. In any case, beginning in September 2008, the world's two most powerful central banks—the U.S. Federal Reserve and the European Central Bank (ECB)—set a clear course for inflation. The balance sheet totals of both, a necessary precondition for all further money creation by the banking system, were expanded dramatically.

In fact, just in the first four months following the failure of Lehman Brothers in September of 2008, the consolidated balance sheet total of the ECB and the national central banks in Europe rose from 1.5 trillion euros to 2.0 trillion euros; that is, by a third. And in the United States the explosion was even more drastic. The Fed's balance sheet total rose from $950 billion to $2.2 trillion, or 130 percent.

What's most shocking of all is this: in prior, smaller episodes of money printing—such as in preparation for a feared Y2K crisis in 1999 and in the wake of the terrorist attacks of 2001—as soon as the crisis subsided, the Federal Reserve quickly restored its balance sheet by sopping up the excess funds from the economy. But this time, the Federal Reserve, along with the ECB, have done nothing of the kind. Quite the contrary, they have continued to expand their balance sheets throughout 2009 and into the first half of 2010.

This is the basic stuff inflation is made of. This is why we are convinced that inflation is on the way. The inflation creators are on the warpath. They have been forewarned. But they have failed to change course.

Politicians Want Us to Believe
They Know What They're Doing

Let us now turn our attention to the question of *why* the politicians are doing what they're doing. Why are they, as Friedman wrote 45 years earlier, all Keynesians now? Why do they keep on doing the wrong thing? There is a straightforward answer: politicians always try to give the impression that what they are doing is not only beneficial, but essential. There is of course an abundance of both theoretical and empirical evidence pointing to the futility of political intervention, particularly when it comes to the economy. Everybody understands, in principle, that politicians cannot create prosperity, but can only redistribute the prosperity created by certain segments of the electorate to particular interest groups that support them. Furthermore, following the bankruptcy of the communist bloc in Eastern Europe, everyone should know that a planned economy is an economic system categorically inferior to free markets.

In this context, the burden of proof is on politicians to continually seek a way to justify their actions. When an economic boom occurs, they must be able to point to the economic measures that they have themselves taken, so they can claim credit for the recovery and exploit it for political ends. And when a downturn occurs, they must revert to herculean measures to set the course for the next upturn or somehow convince voters that it was they who prevented an even worse outcome. They can get away with it for the simple reason that, in the final analysis, no one can say, with any certainty, what could or would have happened had the politicians done nothing.

When one considers this nexus, the success of Keynesian theory is immediately comprehensible, for it provides politicians the arguments they need to pursue massive state intervention. It helps them justify their devil-may-care politics that has been their hallmark for decades, leaving future generations to pay the bills. Because nobody knows where the end of the flagpole may be, each politician can live in that hope that the poisoned chalice will pass him by, and that dealing with the inevitable dire consequences of their irresponsible policies will always fall to a future successor. The United States and Western Europe, including Germany, have been governed by this sad scheme for decades. And now the whole world has begun to extend the flagpole once more—even though the dire consequences are now far more visible.

The First Results of Mr. Greenspan's Great Experiment

One of the most important aims of this book is to bear witness to the entire trend of recent years, which is now reaching its sorry climax, as *not* a consequence of the free market. Quite the contrary, the real estate bubble itself would quite simply not have been possible without the fateful decisions made by central bankers like Mr. Alan Greenspan.

Central banks are not part of freely operating markets. Even if their bureaucrats are nominally empowered to make independent decisions, the fact remains they are part and parcel of the government. Central banks are monopolies under government guarantee, which have constructed a banking cartel around themselves. This system has little to do with free markets. Indeed, especially in recent years, central banks in capitalist economies have been, in many respects, akin to central committees in former communist economies, manned by individuals who owe their primary allegiance to the state.

In the United States, unlike their predecessors William McChesney Martin and Paul Volcker, Fed Chairmen Greenspan and Bernanke have rarely defied the policy agenda of the executive branch and have almost invariably been its most aggressive militants. In Germany, the Federal Debt Administration—along with the Labor Office—has already been renamed in true Orwellian newspeak style. It is now called the Finance Agency. We can't wait to learn when the central bank will get its new name, one that obscures its true character even further. And everywhere, the fox is minding the chicken coop, as the very people who have done the most to create inflation are dubbed *monetary guardians*—another so-far successful experiment in obscuring the truth.

The big picture: the events we've witnessed since the dawn of the new millennium and continue to experience today—the late 1990s stock market bubble and the ensuing bust, followed by the housing bubble and collapse, and now the sovereign debt crisis—have nothing whatsoever to do with capitalism. Neither can it be termed socialism. Capitalism is steeped in the fundamental principle that both profits and *losses* are a private concern. And even under socialism, both profits (although rarer) and losses are kept in the same realm—under the umbrella of the state.

What we've seen in the Western nations of the early third millennium, however, is neither an example of capitalism nor socialism. Instead, thanks to the policies aggressively pursued by America's two central bankers of our era—Alan Greenspan and Ben Bernanke—what we have is an entirely unholy and unsustainable mix whereby *profits may be private but losses are socialized.*

It is the ultimate moral hazard.

This corrupted economic system is nothing more and nothing less than an extreme form of crony capitalism—a very unique kind of nepotism—that, if pursued, can ultimately only lead to a fate similar to that of Iron Curtain countries themselves.

The banking crisis of 2008 and the sovereign debt crisis of 2010 are not failures of the market, but rather the consequences of monumental failures in monetary policy. This central truth is rarely recognized in the media or policy circles. Wall Street and Washington portray the inflationists as monetary defenders, and the arsonists as the fire chiefs. Don't let them fool you. And never forget: Politicians do not create prosperity. They merely redistribute it.

CHAPTER 2

Real Estate, Banks, Bubbles, and Debts

A Look at the Extent of the Real Estate Bubble

To better understand the current situation, one needs to grasp the extent and significance of the real estate bubble. We generally make the United States the primary focus of our analysis because it remains, more than ever, the undisputed leading power in the world—politically, militarily, economically, and especially in the realms of monetary policy and influence on global financial markets.

For this reason, we believe it makes no sense for investors to consider European or Asian countries in isolation from developments in the United States. Our analysis is therefore generally grounded in our outlook for the United States, with the results then cautiously extrapolated and properly adapted to the unique circumstances of the rest of the world. Tellingly, we hear again and again from our American friends that they view not only the emerging markets but also the German DAX as leveraged versions of their own stock markets, not as independent entities.

Particularly in 2007, as the crisis emanating from the United States began to unfold, we found ourselves the odd men out in applying these tried and tested methods. Why? Because, at the time, the so-called decoupling thesis was in vogue among traders, analysts, and economists. According to this theory, the world had fundamentally changed, largely due to the economic upturn in the Asian economies, drastically reducing its interdependence with the United States.

As we explained earlier, career optimists used this decoupling thesis as the key argument for explaining away the obvious signs of weakness in the U.S. economy. The positive economic trend in Asia, they said, would serve to offset or reduce any cooling effect in the United States. But it was a classic case of Wall Street wishful thinking, which has probably done more harm than any other. "Everything is different this time around," they argued. "Lessons learned from the past are of no relevance."

That kind of broad-brushed, simplistic—and almost invariably false— argument is what has enabled financial leaders to persist in their bullish outlook far beyond the point at which all indicators point down. And this rampant rationalizing of irrational human behavior—going to extraordinary lengths to justify a cherished belief, a trusted conviction or long-held prejudice—is, unfortunately, especially common at the very pinnacle of global power, that is, in Washington and on Wall Street.

Figure 2.1 shows a fundamental indicator for valuing residential property, namely median home prices as a multiple of household income. You can see how far this indicator drifted away from its normal level. And you may also consider, that despite their awareness of these kinds of indicators, key decision makers like Greenspan and Bernanke were apparently unable to recognize the property bubble until long after it burst.

No less a figure than the serving chairman of the U.S. Federal Reserve, Ben Bernanke, stated, at the height of the real estate bubble, that the price increases merely reflected the strength of the U.S. economy. Looking at the chart, one can hardly believe that a man as intelligent as Bernanke could be capable of such an absurd misjudgment. Does the job of a central banker impair the senses? Or is the possession of impaired senses a prerequisite for a successful career as a central banker? And would you trust a man to solve the problems unleashed by the housing bubble who, in many respects, stood before the Himalayas and failed to see the mountains? We do not.

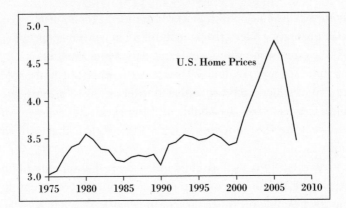

Figure 2.1   Early Warnings of U.S. Housing Bubble and Bust Should Have Been Obvious (Median Home Prices as a Multiple of Household Income)
SOURCES: National Association of Realtors; U.S. Census Bureau.

Neither does the graph of this important indicator hold out much hope of an imminent end to the real estate slump. Even though home prices temporarily stabilized, to be expected when governments intervene in the wake of a major burst, further price declines appear inevitable.

A key basis for our negative outlook: The situation appears little better in the United Kingdom, Ireland, Spain, Portugal, Australia, and population centers of Eastern Europe and Asia. And in some cases, it is far worse. None of this supports hope for a rapid end to the crisis. On the contrary, we fear a significant new round of deterioration in the global economic landscape.

The Macroeconomic Impact of the U.S. Real Estate Crisis

When asset prices rise, it naturally encourages more consumption and speculation while discouraging savings. Those who see their properties and portfolios go up in value understandably tend to save less and enjoy the fruits of their labor more than they would if asset values had remained constant or fallen. Economists call this the *wealth effect*.

However, there is a notable difference between the wealth effect of real estate compared to that of stocks: Rises in real estate prices have more than *doubled* the wealth effect. According to U.S. economists, every $100 increase in property values generates about $9 in consumer spending, while every $100 gain in stock values generates only $4 in spending.

This makes sense. Around 70 percent of American households own the property in which they live, either outright or with a mortgage. Only around 50 percent are stockholders. Moreover, the average value of properties held by U.S. households is far greater than that of their stock portfolios.

So with these two factors combined—more households holding far more property than stocks—you can judge for yourself how great the effect of the housing bubble on American consumer behavior has been in recent years. Trillions of additional dollars found their way into the consumer economy by way of the wealth effect, and it was this key factor that made and broke the economic boom of recent years.

Real Estate Price Rises Were Immediately Converted into Cash

The wealth effect alone would have been big enough. But even more impactful was the way millions of homes were converted into private, perpetual, and powerful ATM machines—a uniquely American invention called "mortgage equity withdrawal" (MEW).

For compatriots of the authors—German citizens who typically rent or buy their homes for cash, and almost never refinance a mortgage—this sounded like science fiction. But in the United States, and some other countries as well, it was not only possible, it was common practice. Home values rose. Millions rushed to refinance. And trillions of dollars in paper profits were converted into trillions to spend on SUVs, summer vacations, Hummers, and Harleys.

Adding even more fuel to the fire, most of the refinancing occurred in an environment of sharply falling interest rates, helping households reduce their monthly payments and drive up consumption even further. This meant that, from 2001 onward, people could benefit greatly from dramatic reductions in interest rates engineered by the central banks. And still more property price inflation was converted into cash, with still larger portions spent on consumer goods.

Trillions of Dollars Flowed into the Consumer Economy

The effect of this process, which appears rather exotic to German eyes and which is certainly very risky, was immense in the early-to-mid-2000s. Ironically, no less a figure than Alan Greenspan, the father of the U.S. housing bubble thanks to his monetary policy, published a study in the final days of his chairmanship that discussed the mortgage equity withdrawal effect in detail.

In the 1990s, an average of approximately $25 billion per quarter, or about 1 percent of disposable income, was freed up, thanks to mortgage equity withdrawals, and at the end of the 1990s, rising real estate prices began to generate an increase in these activities. But it was not until 2002, when interest rates were reduced to a level not seen since the 1960s, that the excesses really began. MEWs jumped to $150 billion per quarter, or 6 percent of disposable income, and in the 2004–2005 period, they reached $200 billion per quarter, or a surprisingly large *10 percent of disposable income*—10 times the 1990s levels. These are highly significant orders of magnitude, especially for the U.S. economy, with its $15 trillion GDP.

The Effect on Economic Growth Was Immense

How great was the effect of this unprecedented cash windfall on the U.S. economy? The American strategist Barry Ritholtz has presented a study that investigates precisely this question. He comes to the conclusion that, without it, the U.S. economy would have actually contracted slightly in 2001 and 2002 and would have been close to stagnation between 2004 and 2006, with growth at 1 percent.

To reach this conclusion, he used Greenspan's own study referred to earlier together with data from the Federal Reserve. Based on that study, Ritholtz assumes that only half of all MEW cash flowed into the consumer economy—a somewhat conservative estimate.

Regardless of underlying assumptions, however, it is undeniable that the effects of the housing bubble on American economic growth were immense. Without it, the U.S. economy would hardly have grown at all in the first decade of the new millennium!

In light of these facts, is the conclusion not inescapable that the U.S. economy has feet of clay? That any economic growth created in this way would come to an abrupt end when the bubble burst? And that, at the end of the day, the price for all this excess would have to be paid—probably over many years?

Presumably, it takes a lot of formal training and discipline—the hallmarks of establishment economists and central bankers—*not* to allow such banal ideas to enter one's head and, instead, to adhere to cherished economic models far removed from reality.

Figure 2.2 shows the huge impact the housing bubble had on GDP growth. If you conservatively adjust U.S. GDP growth by the mortgage equity withdrawal effect, you get significantly smaller growth rates from 2001 to 2008.

Figure 2.3 shows the massive dollar amounts homeowners withdrew from their homes each quarter. This source of money has fallen dry since the bubble burst.

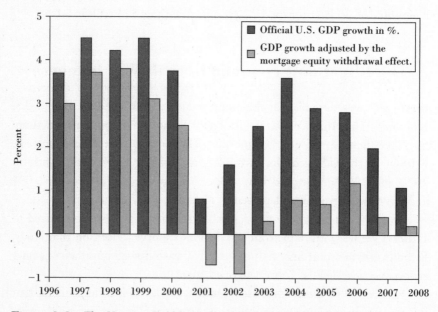

Figure 2.2 The Housing Bubble Had a Huge Impact on GDP Growth
SOURCE: Quirinbank.

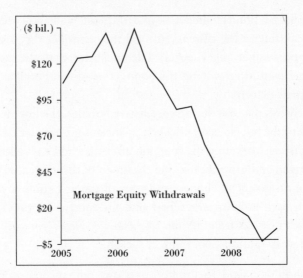

Figure 2.3   Mortgage Equity Withdrawals Plunge to Zero!
SOURCE: Federal Reserve.

Shut the Stable Door! The Horse Has Bolted!

We repeat: A necessary—but insufficient—condition for the emergence of a speculative bubble is excess growth in the supply of the money and credit. U.S. central bankers, together with their money-printing accomplices in the rest of the world, created this necessary condition with their extremely expansionary monetary policy of recent years. At the same time, commercial banks ensured, through their absurdly lax lending policies, that easy money could find its way onto the property market.

This retreat from tried-and-tested rules of creditworthiness was facilitated and encouraged by the rapidly growing market for collateralized debt obligations. In contrast to earlier times, many loans were no longer held by the credit issuer, but were packaged up, securitized, and passed on to institutional investors.

That this mechanism produces very lax credit standards was abundantly clear. Critics of the housing bubble pointed out this connection again and again. However, the Wall Street credit rating agencies tasked with grading these structured bonds failed to—and did not want to—recognize this blatant weak link in the system. Nor did they consider the possibility that property prices might fall. The record demonstrates that, because they were paid by the institutions issuing the bonds, this obvious conflict of interest impaired their objectivity.

As is always the case during speculative bubbles, the hot air must begin to leak out of the bubble before the first politicians begin to tackle the subject. They only discuss covering the fountain after the child has fallen in.

Congressman Barney Frank, the chairman of the influential U.S. House Committee on Financial Services, was one of the first to discover the issue for himself, back in 2007, when he found the courage to state the obvious. Here is a short extract from the *San Jose Mercury News* (passages in brackets are not direct quotations, but indirect speech):

> You shouldn't lend [to home buyers or refinancers] more than they can afford to pay back, and you don't lend them more than their house is worth. You can't just make a loan and then sell it [to investors, forget about it, and expect no legal liability for putting people into a mortgage that never made sense for their situation].[1]

Déjà Vu

Remember the corporate scandals that made the headlines between 2001 and 2004 in the wake of the tech wreck? It's always the same. Folks go round in circles and learn little from the lessons of history—at least not in the financial markets.

Every speculative bubble provides fertile soil for scandalous behavior, and this one was certainly no exception. We witnessed the mass issuance of credit to noncreditworthy borrowers, people with no means of servicing a loan. But only later, when the bubble had burst, did these processes suddenly become well-publicized scandals.

It is against this backdrop, for example, that Bernard Madoff's giant Ponzi scheme must be understood. Although there was abundant, detailed evidence pointing toward his fraudulent activity, the U.S. government's regulatory authorities did nothing. It therefore fits the scope and duration of the speculative bubble perfectly (including the echo bubble in the equity markets) that the Madoff fraud was left uninvestigated for years and now stands as the greatest of all time.

But was it really the largest? No. It is merely *the greatest fraud that was not perpetrated by a government*. The unbridled attacks and wars governments have waged on your retirement and pensions—through the monetary expansion we have described here and the debasing of currencies that inevitably follows—makes the Madoff scandal seem harmless by comparison.

Still an Issue: The Burst Property Bubble in the United States

We have repeatedly referred to how important the real estate bubble was for the current economic cycle. It was the engine behind the boom that followed the recession of 2001—and its bursting was the easily predictable trigger for the crisis that began in 2007, including the ensuing recession and stock market slump.

Property slumps are relatively protracted affairs. Based on fundamental indicators—such as the ratio of average income to average home prices—we anticipate that residential property prices in the United States could fall by at least another 20 percent.

By the time housing prices reached a cyclical low in 2009, their price decline already amounted to at least 25 percent. And that decline alone was already sufficient to trigger a global banking crisis during the course of which nearly all of the United States's largest investment banks and a large number of commercial banks became de facto bankrupt. Looking ahead, after a temporary lull in the crisis, a continuation of the real estate slump could cause a further intensification of the banking crisis. But unfortunately, it is not the only problem that bank managers, their shareholders, and government regulators will have to face in the years ahead.

Remember: the crisis began in 2007 with massive defaults on subprime mortgage loans. This was the riskiest mortgage loan sector in the United States. By the end of 2008, most of this huge mountain of subprime credit issued at the height of the real estate bubble went into default and was written down. A relaxation of stress in the financial system and the financial markets came promptly at the start of 2009 and endured until the onset of the sovereign debt crisis. But that period of calm was deceptive. A key reason: until early 2012, further mountains of mortgage debt problems await lenders.

Yes, a good portion of the bad subprime mortgages have been written off or moved over to government ownership. But in addition to subprime loans, still other dangerous credit variants—option ARMs, for example— were marketed in grand style, especially at the height of the property speculation phase. Most are mortgages that require low or no interest payments at the start of their term. Only after a certain waiting period do higher interest or higher payments kick in. And a veritable flood of these interest and payment resets is now under way, with more waves of the same expected to continue until early 2012. Result: in mid-2010, we could already see a new wave of home sales declines, price declines, and defaults, with untold impacts on the banking and financial system.

As you can see in Figure 2.4, U.S. banks are still holding a high percentage of their portfolios in real estate loans. In spite of the huge losses already suffered during the past years, the total risk position of the banking system is still historically high.

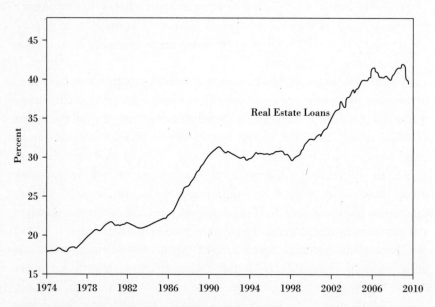

Figure 2.4   U.S. Banks Remain Mired in Real Estate Loans (Real Estate Loans as a Percentage of Total Loans and Leases)
SOURCE: Board of Governors of the Federal Reserve System.

What Next?

Apart from the credit problems resulting from the burst housing bubble, we see other areas that will lead to substantial credit defaults and a potentially heavy burden on the banking system.

First among these is the private equity sector. In recent years, a large number of "fair-weather deals" were financed by private capital, based on the assumption that good times would last forever. Alongside the undesirable trends in the property sector, it was in the hedge funds and the private equity sector that the largest excesses were played out. The former already underwent a correction in 2008, but a correction in the latter is still pending.

Another major sector bound to deliver spectacular corporate failures and headlines is the commercial real estate sector—and not only in the United States. While expenditures on home construction had approximately halved by the start of 2009, expenditures on nonresidential construction continued to rise. That's why we forecast that commercial real estate would be the next sector to collapse and why we continue to see big declines ahead.

In the United States, a rapid deterioration in commercial real estate portfolios of regional banks is among the chief reasons so many failed and were taken over by the FDIC in 2010. In Germany, meanwhile, many real estate funds were simply closed to prevent the distress sales of commercial property. As the law stands—for whatever that is worth these days—these closures may last for up to two years. Only then will investors have the opportunity to demand the return of their money, or whatever is left of it.

In March 2009, the John Hancock Tower in Boston, the largest office skyscraper in New England, changed hands at the price of $661 million. In 2006, it had been sold for $1.3 billion, and even in 2003, before the bubble, it was valued at $935 million. These price drops of 49 percent and 29 percent, respectively, are merely a sneak preview of what lies in store for other commercial real estate—not only in the United States, but around the world.

The other sword of Damocles that we see hanging above the banking sector and the financial system is the precarious financial situation of many emerging markets, particularly in Eastern Europe. Falling local currencies, financial crises, payment difficulties, and even defaults on government bonds are to be expected.

Against this background there is a realistic fear of a second, double-dip global recession—one that could be very severe and last a long time. This forecast should come as no surprise to our readers. It is based upon a simple correlation: the larger the speculative boom, the greater the subsequent speculative bust; and the greater the bust, the more severe the consequences will be for the financial markets and the real economy.

This insight, to which we accorded central importance in *Das Greenspan Dossier,* was subsequently validated by important empirical data contained in a 2009 academic study, "The Aftermath of Financial Crises" by Carmen M. Reinhart (University of Maryland) and Kenneth S. Rogoff (Harvard University).

The authors concern themselves with the consequences of economic crises whose starting points can be found in a banking or financial crisis. They do not delve into the cause of the banking crisis itself—in the present case, the greatest speculative bubble of all time. Nevertheless, their observations do deliver some critical conclusions:

- Financial crises are long, drawn-out affairs, with important characteristics in common.
- The average price drop in real estate prices was 35 percent in real terms, and the real estate slump lasted around six years.
- The average decline in equity markets was 55 percent, lasting three and a half years.
- Within a period of approximately four years, the unemployment rate rose, on average, to a level that was 7 percentage points higher than its low of the preceding boom.
- The economy contracted, on average, by more than 9 percent and for a period of two years.
- Government debt rose dramatically, by an average of 86 percent.

These empirical results match very closely our analysis of speculative bubbles and the consequences of speculative busts. They should make abundantly clear that recent hopes for a quick end to the bad times have almost no basis in fact.

Poverty as a Consequence of Inflation—The Gap between Rich and Poor Is Becoming Ever Greater

With the phenomenon centered in the United States, but also replicated in many other parts of the world, the gap between rich and poor is becoming ever wider. The small number of super-rich today hold a far greater share of total wealth than was the case even a few years ago. This is not always a bad thing in and of itself, as long as the wealth accumulation is generated by entrepreneurial effort. Yet it is precisely this connection—between effort and reward—that is increasingly weakened during speculative booms and inflationary periods. The government bloats the money supply. Rich rewards are lavished on those who contribute little value to society. And the connection between effort and reward becomes so arbitrary as to become meaningless.

In that environment, how can you honestly counsel your child or grandchild to put money aside for savings? In the real world, the government has ensured, through its easy-money policies, that the best advice you can give your offspring is that they'd be foolish to save. After taxes and inflation, the saver will, in fact, lose money. Is it any wonder that the savings rate in the United States fell to its lowest level of all time—below zero? And is it not shocking to see the government itself do everything in its power to discourage the minor recovery in U.S. savings rates that we've witnessed since?

Inflation leads to an impoverishment of great cross-sections of the population. During hyperinflationary phases, such as experienced by Germany in the early twentieth century or by Zimbabwe in the twenty-first, this process occurs extremely rapidly. With relatively moderate inflation rates, it occurs far more slowly. But in either scenario, thrift is replaced by theft—it reduces your wealth.

Why? The newly created money, which is not backed by tangible assets of any description, must always go into circulation at some point within the economy. In other words, someone is always the first to possess the new money and the first to be able to spend it. These first beneficiaries are the inflation winners—they enjoy an incalculable advantage, for they can make purchases on the market at old prices, before the new demand drives prices higher. However, those who are last in line to get the new money are the inflation losers, forced to pay much higher prices.

The effect is very similar if inflation manifests itself in the form of speculative bubbles. The new money causes asset prices—especially in stocks or real estate—to rise sharply. Those who own one or both may see their wealth grow significantly at least in nominal terms while those who own neither are unable to compete or cope—let alone catch up. They lag further and further behind, and the gap between rich and poor widens still further.

Not "Poor through Work" but "Poor through Inflation"

"Poor through work" was the title feature of a 2007 issue of the German magazine *Der Spiegel*.[2]

In it, the journalists completely ignored—or overlooked—the significance of monetary policy for the subject under discussion. The word *inflation* is not even mentioned in their article. This omission is enormously sad, because it renders impossible any analytical investigation of the most significant cause of the growing gulf between rich and poor. Perhaps someday, *Der Spiegel* will produce Part Two of the article, including the much-needed research of these causes—too much easy money.[3]

Stable, reliable money is the foundation of healthy, balanced, and sustainable economic growth. In contrast, the use and abuse of the printing press to create money leads to the impoverishment of broad sections of the population. In hyperinflationary periods, this effect can, to some extent, be viewed as if in a time warp—it happens almost instantly. During periods of relatively moderate inflation, such as the last few decades, it has been a more insidious process—income inequality emerges relatively slowly, but still inexorably.

Applying the classic definition of the term *inflation* as growing quantities of money, recent years have been characterized around the world by high levels of government-induced inflation—in other words, sharp growth in the supply of money and credit. In contrast to the inflationary period of the 1970s, this inflation did not lead to big price rises in the baskets of consumer goods used in official price calculations. And this difference, in turn, has allowed today's politicians and their Keynesian-influenced economists to continually boast about low inflation rates. Conveniently, they were able to ignore the fact that the expansion of money and credit progressed at a faster clip than economic growth.

Sharp rises in other asset prices—such as stocks, real estate, or art and antiques—were simply not captured in the consumer price baskets. And like magic, the inflation effect vanished, or never appeared. Nonetheless, rapid increases in the supply of money and credit are, of course, every bit as real as the asset price increases that they give rise to—even if politicians and Keynesians choose to ignore them. These price increases ensure that the relatively small group of asset holders becomes ever richer, while those depending on fixed incomes or earning low wages become the losers.

The policy of extreme easy money pursued across the globe for many years is also, in many respects, a fundamental assault on society. Not only does it lead to growing income inequality, but it also threatens to disrupt the very social harmony that Keynesian politicians are so keen to pay lip service to.

Guilty! Jeremy Grantham's View of the Debt Overhang

We have already referred to the most central problem for the world financial system and the global economy—the historically unique level of the United States's aggregate debt. Jeremy Grantham, a critical financial analyst highly regarded in the United States and beyond, has provided a description of this problem that is very easy to comprehend.[4]

He points out that when the housing bubble burst what was lost was not true wealth, but only an imaginary wealth. The practical utility value of property—its actual usage—had not actually changed in recent years. It had neither increased during the years of rising prices, nor did it decline during the housing slump. When a family's home price rose, they still lived in it, even if some homes changed owners in the meantime. Thus, in that sense, no real wealth was created when home prices rose—all that was created was the *illusion* of wealth. For resident homeowners, the only means of converting that illusion into actual prosperity was through a sale and moving into a rented apartment. Nevertheless, the illusion did have thoroughly real effects on the behavior of a vast number of people. They felt rich. And as we stressed earlier, people who feel rich tend to save less and consume more. Result: the savings rate in the United States fell to zero and even lower, while consumption and indebtedness grew by leaps and bounds.

Compounding the illusion, rising property prices served as collateral for additional mortgage loans. We have already discussed this mechanism earlier. For this context, suffice it to say that indebtedness rose drastically, both in absolute terms and in relation to GDP, while the level of indebtedness in relation to the inflated home prices initially grew only disproportionately. Then the bubble burst and home prices tumbled. But the debts, of course, remained.

The end result is millions of households upside down in their mortgage— so deep under water that many have decided to abandon their homes, en masse, even if they can afford to make mortgage payments.

There are more than 10 trillion dollars of excess debt in the United States alone.

Grantham presents a rough calculation for the United States that we regard as meaningful and illuminating. It covers not only residential property, but also the equity markets and commercial real estate. At the height of asset price inflation in 2007, these three asset classes were valued at approximately $50 trillion. If one assumes price declines of 50 percent for stocks, 35 percent for residential property and 35 percent for commercial property, the total loss compared with this peak value comes to $20 trillion. Of course, this dramatic collapse not only means that the people affected by it feel significantly poorer; it also leads to a dramatic deterioration of debt in relation to the underlying assets.

The commercially sound basis for issuing credit is the borrower's current income plus collateral. Normally, banks set their lending limits significantly below the market value of the collateral. They also attempt to ensure, through credit checks, that the borrower's income is sufficient to easily cover interest and principal payments. (The fact that these basic principles of proper lending were mostly abandoned during the housing bubble is a major topic, but best saved for another context.)

Grantham calls the $50 trillion valuation of the three asset classes the "national private asset base." This base, in turn, supported private household and corporate debt of around $25 trillion. In other words, an indebtedness ratio of 50 percent. But around half of all U.S. real estate is debt free, as are most equity holdings. So a 50 percent debt ratio means that most Americans who do owe money are actually far deeper in debt, and the ratio is actually dangerously high. So when that private asset base is down dramatically in value—to as low as to $30 trillion—we calculate the ratio could be up to a very worrisome 83 percent.

A return to a 50 percent indebtedness ratio, which cannot be characterized as particularly conservative, would mean that the shrunken national private asset base would justify debts of only around $15 trillion. And assuming a more reasonable 40 percent indebtedness ratio, it would only be $12 trillion. In other words, measured against these more or less normal indebtedness ratios, the U.S. private sector has at least 10 to 13 trillion dollars in *excess* debt.

Bottom line: since the debt crisis erupted in 2007, at least $1 trillion has been written off. *But this represents only about 10 percent of the total correction needed to clean out the estimated $10 trillion of excess debts.*

One more word of warning: this rough calculation is based on recent low values for equities and real estate. If those lows succumb to even steeper declines, a scenario we consider very possible over the course of the coming years, the debt liquidation process may have to be even more severe.

The Risk of Higher Interest Rates

A further risk stems from the possibility of rising interest rates, a far from improbable scenario. Higher interest rates, of course, make new loans and refinancing more expensive. Also, they come with principal losses on existing bonds, which can depress the bond and loan portfolios of insurance companies, pension funds, and banks. Worst of all, when steeper interest costs help trigger higher default rates, they can bring on a whole new wave of writedowns and loan losses.

One thing seems clear: the inflationary monetary and fiscal policies pursued around the world, and particularly in the United States, will sooner or later lead to rising prices and rising official inflation rates. Interest rate rises will then be unavoidable. Furthermore, Asian central banks, which in recent years have become the largest purchasers of U.S. government securities, could alter this policy at some stage, adding further pressure to rising interest rates, and forcing the government to rely more heavily on domestic savings to finance its deficit.

But persuading U.S. households to save more and buy more U.S. debt will be no easy task. Washington will have to bid far higher rates and accept the fact that higher domestic savings rates to finance the deficit, would, in turn, come with other serious consequences as well—a big squeeze on the consumer spending and a negative impact on the broader global economy.

Four Ways to Reduce the Debt Overhang

Revisiting the topic we highlighted in the Introduction, there are only certain ways of returning to a more sustainable indebtedness ratio.

First, the debt overhang could be written down. Most observers believe that this would be short-term radical solution, a very painful break with the past. And up until now, governments and their central bank bureaucrats have left little doubt about their views—they regard this free market solution as invalid.

Second, governments could seek to follow Japan's example of the last two decades—to prolong the agony. Japan's stock market bubble burst in 1990 and its real estate bust followed within two years. The Japanese government did everything it could to cushion the necessary adjustment process with massive monetary and fiscal interventions. As a result, rather than putting it behind them, the adjustment process was stretched out over a long period of time, while consumers were forced to tighten their belts, and high savings rates gradually filled the gap.

This example, characterized by repeated recessions and weak overall growth, is known as the "lost decade"—a euphemism that incorrectly implies that the close of the 1990s somehow ended Japan's lean years. But the stock market's continued weakness throughout much of the 2000s belies that notion: Japan's Nikkei 225, which stood at nearly 40,000 points in December 1989, fell to below 8,000 at the start of 2009, on par with 1982 levels. And despite a feeble recovery, by mid-2010, the Nikkei was still far *below* its lowest level reached during the 1990s. Japan's real estate prices have behaved in a similar fashion.

But even during the worst years of Japan's lost decade, the country had an advantage that nations infected by the sovereign debt contagion may not enjoy in the 2010s—it was buoyed by a global economy that remained largely intact and helped support Japan's export business throughout the 1990s.

Third, the possibility exists, in principle, of creating a new, even bigger speculative bubble than the one that burst in 2008. This path, so strongly criticized by us in *Das Greenspan Dossier,* was the one chosen by the United States and large parts of the world following the bursting of the stock market bubble in the early 2000s. In the short term, it actually seems to work, albeit at an extremely high price. But it soon becomes apparent that it merely postpones the inevitable day of reckoning while magnifying existing problems. Comparatively smaller disasters are papered over while the risk of a future financial catastrophe is greatly magnified. We've already seen this once—in the disastrous bubble-generating policies adopted from 2001 to 2005. Now that we have experienced it—a stock market bubble and a housing bubble in quick succession—a growing minority of individuals have begun to understand the relationships at the heart of *Das Greenspan Dossier*. For this reason, we believe a further bubble to be improbable. Once bitten, twice shy. Apart from this, we cannot imagine what asset class could possibly be big enough to assume that role.

Fourth, governments may seek to solve the problem through consumer price inflation and a de facto devaluation of the currency. Devaluation reduces the real value of debts. It is state-sanctioned deception of creditors. And it allows debtors to pay the piper with cheaper money.

We are convinced that this is the primary path already chosen by the government's inflation mongers—led by Fed Chairman Ben Bernanke. This path, too, is anything but simple. It also brings with it enormous risks. It can and will have dramatic consequences for the economy and society.

Inflation causes the degradation of nearly all assets and leads to the impoverishment of great segments of the population—in particular, the middle classes. Worse, its disastrous effects can pave the way for extremist politics, even dictators, who seem to always claim to have the wellbeing of the people at heart, a convenient cover for the erosion and abolishment of freedoms.

We expressed these same fears in *Das Greenspan Dossier*. At that time, it was the third path—to overcome a bust with a new bubble—that was being pursued. But that was in response to what, in retrospect, was a minor threat compared to the housing bust and sovereign debt crisis. Today, five years later, the global debt trap looms far larger.

Stimulus Programs: Everything Must Go!

No Alternative to State Intervention?

In a rush of knee-jerk reactions to the global debt trap, politicians around the world are showering other people's money on their favorite interest groups and segments of the electorate. The sums have now reached such orders of magnitude that most people have no concept of the number of zeros involved.

The media respond with the cry: "This is the only possible solution." Even the many voices that until recently professed to adhere to free market principles have defected, in droves, to the camp of those who place their faith in the state. "Yes," they admit, "these measures are politically problematic, but there is simply no other alternative."

No alternative? The free market is suddenly no longer an alternative? The long-overdue return to the principles of the free market is now reduced to an impossibility? In other words, the transition to socialism is now inevitable?

We are aghast at this appalling prospect.

No one can deny the fact that, at some point, someone has to pay. Yet, at the same time, nearly everyone seems to be taking for granted that our children or grandchildren are the ones who must pick up the tab for our failures.

We are fathers with children of our own, and we are deeply disturbed by this facile proposal. Why is it that, in their private lives, most parents and grandparents are ready and willing to make every sacrifice for the benefit of their children, while, in their public persona, politicians are so willing to sacrifice their children's future on the altar of instant gratification?

What they may not realize is that the bills for their follies will not fall strictly to future generations. Already, here and now, we can see the consequences. We already see a sovereign debt crisis that takes immediate victims. And we can see abundant collateral damage from the massive spending and intervention of the last two years.

The Biggest Government Stimulus Package of All Time—By a Wide Margin

Thanks to research provided by Jim Grant's Interest Rate Observer, we can summarize the key data from all U.S. recessions since the Great Depression in Table 2.1.

Since the early 1930s, there have been 13 recessions in the United States. Most of them did not last very long—between 6 and 16 months. Most were not catastrophic, with real economic output shrinking by between 0.2 and 3.4 percent.

In each case, the government invariably intervened by means of Keynesian economic stimulus programs, with only one exception—the

Table 2.1 U.S. Recessions and Monetary plus Fiscal Stimulus

Peak	Trough	Length (Months)	Decline in Real GDP	Stimulus as % of GDP		
				Monetary	Fiscal	Combined
Aug 1929	Mar 1933	43	27%	3.4%	4.9%	8.3%
May 1937	Jun 1938	13	3.4	0.0	2.2	2.2
Nov 1948	Oct 1949	11	1.7	−2.2	7.6	5.4
Jul 1953	May 1954	10	2.7	0.0	−3.5	−3.5
Aug 1957	Apr 1958	8	3.2	0.7	3.2	3.9
Apr 1960	Feb 1961	10	1.0	0.7	1.0	1.7
Dec 1969	Nov 1970	11	0.2	0.3	2.4	2.7
Nov 1973	Mar 1975	16	3.1	0.9	3.1	4.0
Jan 1980	Jul 1980	6	2.2	0.4	0.9	1.3
Jul 1981	Nov 1982	16	2.6	0.3	3.2	3.5
Jul 1990	Mar 1991	8	1.3	1.0	1.7	2.7
Mar 2001	Nov 2001	8	0.2	1.3	5.9	7.2
Dec 2007	Jun 2009	18	4.1	10.3	11.8	22.1

SOURCE: Grant's Interest Rate Observer.

recession of 1953–1954. Nevertheless, despite the lack of state intervention, and contrary to what Keynesians might expect, this recession *also* ended after only 10 months.

The total value of the monetary and fiscal stimulus programs was generally very modest, typically ranging between 1.5 and 4.0 percent of GDP. However, the Great Depression was an exception. The U.S. government believed at that time that it needed to rush to the aid of the economy with much greater force. The sum total of its monetary and fiscal stimulus experiments: an unusually large 8.3 percent of GDP.

It is well known that these efforts were not crowned with success. Indeed, a study of Table 2.1 leads to the conclusion that the consequences of government intervention were exactly the opposite of what was intended.

Murray N. Rothbard, a pupil of Ludwig von Mises, came to precisely this conclusion in his book *America's Great Depression*: The massive government interventions merely served to prevent much-needed adjustments in the economy to bring it into better alignment with market forces of supply and demand. And ultimately, the interventions made the situation considerably worse.

It wasn't until the recession of 2001, however, that we began to see the magnitude of government stimulus reach levels equal to those of the Great Depression. With 7.2 percent of GDP, Greenspan's Fed and the Bush administration pulled out all the Keynesian stops.

Result: yes, the recession ended quickly. But in its place, there emerged the largest real estate bubble of all time. And when that bubble burst, the financial system lay in tatters, the global economic crisis began, and the ensuing recession was the worst since the 1930s.

What's most surprising, however, is that neither the politicians—nor the central bankers they appointed—seem to have learned anything from these terrible experiences. Quite the contrary, the very same kinds of policies that gave us the current crisis are now being used to combat it.

The big difference this time around: as you can see in Table 2.1, the sums spent or poured into the economy—which reached 22.9 percent of GDP through mid-2009 and are now closer to a shocking 30 percent of GDP—are at least four times greater, with still more stimulus and money printing in the works. And that's without even including new, wide-ranging government guarantees of bank deposits, commercial paper, and other debts. If you add the guarantees, the total present and contingent value of the government's intervention jumps to 100 percent of GDP.

These numbers leave no doubt: we are witnesses to an unprecedented experiment in government economic intervention. The orders of magnitude depicted here are truly breathtaking. We are in uncharted territory. And these policies will have drastic consequences, just as prior excessive interventions have had.

No one can possibly know the precise nature of these consequences. Nor should you be fooled into thinking that those responsible have an inkling as to where this road is leading us. Our advice, therefore, is threefold: Hope for a return to reason, expect extremely volatile times, and, prepare yourself for the worst.

There is no such thing as a free lunch.

The Invisible Effects of Visible Policies

The title of Milton Friedman's 1975 book, *There's No Such Thing as a Free Lunch*, says it all: alongside the visible consequences of a government rescue package, there are also invisible, unintended consequences—a form of opportunity cost.[5]

The government decides to save a certain bank from bankruptcy using taxpayer money. Needless to say, the most visible consequence is the bank's continuing operations, together with any jobs it may provide.

However, what remains invisible to the casual observer is the profit and growth that competing banks could have achieved absent the intervention. If the moribund bank had been allowed to fail, its customers would have sought a new bank to handle their accounts. Moreover, in the field of asset management and advice in particular, there were certain companies, even in the present cycle, that did a better job than others. Should those asset managers not be rewarded for their superior performance?

The market share of the surviving banks, clearly better managed than failing institutions, would grow, along with their profitability. Assets of the bankrupt bank could then be snapped up by the competition to further their business operations and growth, often at fire sale prices. And at the end of the day, the failed bank's qualified staff would enter the labor market and be prepared to work for former competitors, accepting less exorbitant bonuses.

A classic example of the folly of government rescues is Bank of America, which was allowed to take over the failing investment bank Merrill Lynch with the aid of a $20 billion injection of government capital plus a government guarantee worth *another* $118 billion.

In the process, Merrill Lynch CEO John Thain spared no expense in furnishing his new office, reportedly paying $1.2 million for his snug little workspace. The underlying attitude: What's a million and change next to the magnitude of government aid monies, and compared to the ensuing quarterly loss of $15.3 billion? And why not throw a few crumbs—$230,000 per year—to Thain's chauffer while you're at it? Heck, maybe the chauffer should even get a fat bonus, which would still be a pittance in comparison to the billions lavished on investment bankers, even if their high-risk wagers crashed and burned.

Alongside these invisible consequences, there is also another more latent class of side effects, emerging from this question: What else could have been done with the money diverted to the failed bank?

For example, suppose the money had been returned to the profitable, tax-paying segments of the private sector by means of tax reductions. Precisely what they would have done with this money is, of course, not predictable. However, the unwavering truth, based upon the soundest of theories and confirmed repeatedly by empirical evidence, is this: The private sector is far more efficient than government bureaucracy. Almost invariably, enterprises and individuals like us would have used the money in a more sensible manner, creating greater benefits for all concerned.

A Free-Market Approach to Solving the Banking Crisis?

Around the world, federal governments and central banks have decided to guarantee the survival of ailing banks through almost any means available. Their closing arguments to justify these do-or-die steps, despite incipient corruption and high-powered lobbying, is the catch-all concept of *system risk*. Without the intervention of the state and the squandering of tax revenue, the argument goes, the entire financial system would collapse. However, the sheer impossibility of proving the falsity of this horrific scenario gives the powers that be a free hand to do as they please.

The great fallacy of their argument: if the system collapse scenario is truly as realistic as those in power maintain, then one must also conclude that any government rescue will be inadequate and will presumably fail. The collapse will be merely postponed. And in the interim, with the transfer of gigantic losses from the private to the public sector, the stakes are raised to an even higher plane, the genesis of sovereign debt crises. As we forecast in our original German edition of this book over a year ago, "instead of banks and insurance companies failing, we will be talking about entire countries going bankrupt."

What the pundits and powers that be seem to ignore is that the free market already has clear rules governing banking collapses. On the basis of previous experience, precisely this eventuality is provided for: the banking authorities are entrusted with the task of taking over the failing institution, finding a worthy buyer or winding down its operations. Insured depositors get first priority, uninsured depositors are second in line, and investors in bonds, debentures, or shares are last. In almost all cases, customers' money is not at risk. But in extraordinary financial rescues, à la Citibank or AIG, it is not necessarily the saver's money that get first-priority protection, but rather, the bank's lenders of external capital, that is, the holders of bank bonds and shares.

An Exemplary Liquidation

Hedge fund manager John P. Hussman has demonstrated very clearly how a bank liquidation should unfold, according to the letter and spirit of the law, using the example of Citibank—once the largest in the world. We follow his thought process here.

We start by looking back at the Citibank bailout of 2009 and consider the alternatives that could have been pursued: in the third quarter of 2008, Citibank reported total assets of $2 trillion and a net worth of $132 billion. That was a great deal of leverage—a debt-to-equity ratio of 16 to 1. But it also means that losses of just over 6 percent of the bank's asset value would almost wipe out the bank's entire equity capital.

At this juncture, it is perhaps worth noting that only particularly hard-nosed private investors—nay, only hardened gamblers—would be prepared to enter into risks of this magnitude. Alternatively, can you imagine pursuing an investment strategy whereby a loss of just 6 percent would leave you bankrupt? Hardly. Modern bank managers must be cut from a different cloth than we are cut.

At that time, Citibank had more than $300 billion of long-term external capital on its balance sheet, with bonds and shorter-term external capital to the tune of roughly $200 billion, that is, more than half a trillion dollars in total. This money is not to be confused with deposits. It was expressly risk capital, for which the external investors were able to receive, over the years, a correspondingly higher rate of return than was paid to depositors. More risk, more yield—the standard quid pro quo of the capital markets.

Thus, on Citibank's balance sheet, we found $132 billion plus $300 billion plus $200 billion, for a total of $632 billion in capital, or 35 percent of total assets, which would be actually liable if the bank went bankrupt.

In essence, this was the money specifically available to cover losses in the case of bankruptcy. So before the first saver would lose a penny of deposits, and before the Federal Deposit Insurance Corporation (FDIC) might get involved, 35 percent of all assets held by Citibank would have to be written down to zero.

That was a huge sum. Even Citibank's managers couldn't have been so stupid as to allow a situation in which 35 percent of all of its loans are dead losses. And if Citibank became insolvent, then it should have trod the path laid out for it—it should not have been bailed out but put through the tried-and-tested, traditional process of dismemberment, sale, or liquidation.

To cover the losses, equity capital would have been used in the first instance, followed by external creditors and investors, each in proper queue. If anything remained, then that portion would be distributed among external investors. At the same time, those operations of the bank that are still of value would be sold to solvent competitors. In this way—and in no other—should banking failures be handled in a free market.

An alternative path: banking regulators may choose not to sell off the assets, but instead, seek a new, hopefully more competent management team for the bank, while the losses are handled as described earlier. In this way, a healthy bank is created, for which, presumably, investors can be found. At the end of the day, these investors could now be certain that there are no more skeletons in the closet, with the complete transparency they need to evaluate the investment.

Let the Dinosaurs Die Out!

Bank failures are nothing new. They are as old as maturity transformation and the invention of fractional reserve banking. They have always happened in the past and they will always happen in the future. That they have now become a mass phenomenon is thanks to central banks. But this alone is no reason to discard the tried and tested, sensible principles for dealing with banking failures. Market economics can only function if failed companies disappear from the market and make way for other, more efficient competitors. Even if the failure is grandiose. Even if the failure is the result of heeding the siren songs of central bankers.

There were, after all, not only savvy individuals, but also thousands of prudent, far-sighted bankers who refused to take part in the madness.

These should now be given the opportunity to fill the gaps created by the failures of speculative mania and myopia. Instead of providing life support for dinosaurs, these must now be allowed to grow, and even given the opportunity to emerge as the new leaders of their industry.

If our argument—that this path is based upon decades of experience with prior banking collapses—is insufficient to convince you, we provide an even more compelling one.

By creating zombie banks, the government has already frittered away untold sums, as we have said, quite clearly to protect anonymous risk-savvy investors. But if, as our leaders maintain, the system risk is so large and so dangerous, then it follows that:

- The root cause of the system risk—the global debt trap—is equally large and dangerous.
- The global debts are endemic, not going away on their own, and certainly not going away by adding more government debt to the heap.
- The money being squandered now will probably *not* be there in the future when more institutions—and entire governments themselves—are ensnared by the global debt trap.
- Nor will the money be there when and where it is truly needed—to help the market generate worthy employment for those who have lost their jobs, or to make homes more affordable for those who have lost the roof over their head.

Another "Bad Bank"

As if there weren't already enough bad banks, many have quietly but forcefully advocated the creation of a so-called bad bank. In this proposal, bad debts would be collected from sick banks, transferred to this new institution, and then financed by the taxpayer. The good debts, on the other hand, would remain with the banks in question, enabling them to issue new loans—and probably another round of bad debts—in the future, all of which merely perpetuates and deepens the global debt trap.

Here's an apt response to this proposal given by Professor Niall Ferguson, an economic historian at Harvard University.

The bad bank already exists. It's called the Federal Reserve. And since September of last year [2008] it has been acting particularly like a bad bank. Do we need another bad bank to take the pressure off the Fed, so that it doesn't become too obvious that the Fed has become a dumping ground for toxic assets? The problem with a separate bad bank is the problem of valuing the assets that it would buy up. Nobody knows what these assets are worth any more. If the banks are effectively insolvent, then it would be better if they went into government ownership.[6]

We would like to expand on the thinking behind the path to liquidation described earlier.

There are vast numbers of banking managers who seem to have plenty of experience creating bad banks on their own without any help from the government, and who seem almost predestined to head up a new bad bank. They are in the prime of life. Perhaps this is why the idea is so popular.

In the United States, Charles Prince of Citibank would surely be an ideal candidate. In Germany, Herr Georg Funke of Hypo Real Estate might view concerns about his pension claims worth 560,000 euros as less burdensome through this innovative career path. Fred Goodwin of the Royal Bank of Scotland would help to give the team a multicultural edge. And don't forget Peter Wuffli, who so adroitly transformed UBS into the world's largest bad bank, even winning the title of "Banker of the Year" along the way.[7]

CHAPTER 3

The Great Money Game

Warning: Reading On May Seriously Damage Your Faith in Government

To truly understand the present crisis, one must understand a few fundamental principles in relation to money. What is money? How did it come into being? What characteristics must it have? And what role does the government play in all of this?

Before you read our answers to these questions, we would like to issue a warning. There is a grave risk that your view of the world, perhaps dearly held and entrenched by decades of government propaganda, will not survive the shock. And when you know the answers to these questions, you may very well feel a pressing need to buy gold. Last, if you then also consider, even momentarily, the wrongs of the present global currency system, this impulse will probably grow into an irresistible urge.

Salt, mussels, and cigarettes. What is money and how did it come into being?

A Good Idea

The popular textbook definition of money: "Anything that performs the functions of money is money. Money has three distinct functions: a medium of exchange, a store of value, and a unit of account." Ideally, money fulfills all three functions.[1]

It is highly probable that money emerged spontaneously on open markets. Voluntary exchange is the starting point of any emerging economic life. It is the basis for the creation of wealth and civilization. The free exchange of goods and services allows for the emergence of an economy based on the division of labor, which, in turn, is a precondition for the emergence of widespread prosperity. Without free exchange, specialization is impossible. Without free exchange, economic activity is limited to meeting one's own immediate needs.

Each individual has very different abilities and the world is blessed with a myriad of resources that are, by their very nature, unevenly distributed. From this initial starting point, the need and advantage of specialization and the distribution of labor are self-evident. A task that one person may find very easy because of individual talents and abilities, another may be unable to achieve even with the greatest of effort. Similarly, while some regions are blessed with easily accessible resources, such as, say, salt deposits, others may have easily extractable mineral ore. What could make more sense, then, than to organize a bartering system that brings incalculable benefits to all concerned?

Direct Exchange

This bartering system presumably began as direct exchange—salt traded for metal, jewelry for fur, spices for weapons. However, direct exchange is subject to severe constraints. It only functions when parties to the exchange meet at the same location, and can offer precisely the goods in precisely those quantities that the other party wishes to acquire at that particular time. And it was these obvious limitations that generated both the driver and the pathway for a transition to indirect exchange.

Circular Exchange

With indirect exchange came the introduction of an intermediate step. Instead of one's own goods being exchanged immediately for the desired goods, a good of a third kind is accepted provisionally, which, in turn, can then be exchanged for the goods actually desired—provided by a different trading partner, at a different location, and at a different point in time. What may appear complicated at first glance, entailing additional effort, is, in fact, an ingenious, not to say revolutionary, idea: circular exchange.

Circular exchange works best when the exchange medium has some particular characteristics. It should be as widely accepted as possible, facilitating quick and rapid exchanges for the widest possible range of goods. This opens the field to even the most specialized, least salable goods, which, in turn, encourages equivalent specialization in the manufacture of those goods.

The circular exchange is also the essential precondition for the emergence of a society based upon the division of labor, in which each individual develops and uses his own strengths to his personal advantage. Only in this way can a differentiated and efficient economy emerge.

Money—A Salable Good

A good is salable if it is frequently in demand by large numbers of people. A basic foodstuff like corn is a case in point. Plus, it boasts another critical property: it can be subdivided at will—down to a single grain—without loss of value.

Another key: some goods are very durable, sometimes virtually indestructible, and this, too, is an advantage that should not be underestimated. Still other goods are valuable in small quantities. Their advantage is that they can be easily transported.

All of these properties—plus others—contribute to the salability of specific goods. For a medium of exchange, what goods should one choose, then, from among all those that boast these characteristics to varying degrees?

The answer to this question was presumably arrived at by our forefathers on the basis of trial and error. For the purposes of our inquiry it does not really matter what particular goods were selected at the end of this free market process. What is important is that they established themselves as generally accepted means of exchange as a result of decisions taken freely by a multitude of independent participants. These goods are termed—in accordance with the preceding definition—*money*.

History Reveals Many Different "Monies"

In the past, a wide variety of goods have been used as money across various cultures. The economist Murray N. Rothbard, whose observations on the emergence of money we have followed here, cites tobacco in Virginia during the colonial period, salt in Abyssinia, cattle in ancient Greece, nails in Scotland, copper in Egypt, plus corn, glass beads, and mussels in various regions at various times.[2]

In Germany, cigarettes became the most common means of payment following World War II, and a second government bankruptcy, before a new government put an end to this free—nay, forbidden—market.

It is worth mentioning another, completely different type of money at this point. A type of money that falls completely outside the scope of the alternative forms described earlier. A type of money that is neither a salable good nor embodies the promise to deliver any. A type of money that is not a valuable good in any sense.

This curiosity did not emerge from freely operating markets, mind you. Rather, it owes its status as money entirely to government decree. It is money only because the state—with its monopoly over the use of force—has declared it to be such, compelling citizens to use it whether it's in their interest to do so or not.

We are, as you already suspect, speaking of the national currencies that are now ubiquitous across the globe. And in its current free-floating form, it is a unique type of money that has only existed for not quite yet 40 years—since August 15, 1971, when President Richard Nixon declared the end of the Bretton Woods system. Even now, nearly four decades later, few seem to recognize that this particular incarnation of money is the antithesis of the money that emerged from free markets. Its value and acceptance are based exclusively on faith in the state—and the threat of legal force.

Gold and Silver Win the Day

Meanwhile, across large parts of the world and the among the most varied of cultures, two goods have emerged as victors in the natural selection process for the most durable, fungible, and transportable medium of exchange—goods that proved themselves to be clearly superior and most preferred above all others: gold and silver.

In *What Has Government Done to Our Money?* Rothbard writes:

This process: the cumulative development of a medium of exchange on the free market—is the only way money can become established. Money cannot originate in any other way, neither by everyone suddenly deciding to create money out of useless material, nor by government calling bits of paper *money*. For embedded in the demand for money is knowledge of the money prices of the immediate past; in contrast to directly used consumers' or producers' goods, money must have preexisting prices on which to ground a demand. But the only way this can happen is by beginning with a useful commodity under barter, and then adding demand for a medium for exchange to the previous demand for direct use (e.g., for ornaments, in the case of gold). Thus, government is powerless to create money for the economy; it can only be developed by the processes of the free market.[3]

He goes on to stress:

Money is not an abstract unit of account, divorceable from a concrete good; it is not a useless token only good for exchanging; it is not a "claim on society"; it is not a guarantee of a fixed price level. It is simply a commodity.[4]

The key difference between this and other commodities lies in its use, in the first instance, as a means of exchange. In the second instance, however, *it continues to remain in demand on the basis of its intrinsic characteristics as a valuable commodity.*

The Price of Money—The Precondition for Efficient Economic Activity

The invention, or use, of money goes far beyond resolving the limitations of direct exchange. Money fulfills a further, extremely important function, which may also be viewed as a side effect of its use, and, to some extent, an unintended consequence.

When using a commodity as money, all exchanges are initially transacted in money. This automatically establishes monetary prices for all exchange relationships. And with the aid of these prices, it is, of course, easy to directly compare the prices of the most heterogeneous goods. Instead of one cow worth two pigs or three axes or a sickle valued at two sacks of corn, standard prices exist for all goods.

Prices are the common denominator of all goods and services. Prices are the necessary precondition for profitability calculations. Without prices, it is, needless to say, very cumbersome for individuals to make rational decisions regarding the profitable exchange of goods. Prices as a common denominator for all goods and services are an essential precondition for the emergence of efficient economic structures.

Monetary Prices Must Be Market Prices

Even at this point in our argument it should be clear that monetary prices must equal market prices for efficient economic activity to occur.

Why? Most people prefer a better supply of material goods to an inferior one. If one takes this fundamental truth as a starting premise, the essential problem of social organization consists in maximizing economic production—and therefore opportunities for consumption—under the limiting condition of resource scarcity.

In other words, answers must be found to the following questions: How must the available and, unfortunately, ever-scarcer resources be utilized to guarantee the most abundant production of goods? How can a structure of production be found that is suited to satisfying the most urgent material human needs in each situation? Which needs are the most urgent? Which are less urgent and must therefore be passed over?

From the almost limitless multiplicity of production processes and the many combinations of factors of production, which make the most economic sense? Which technologies should be employed? All of these questions—and many more—can only be answered if calculations of efficiency and profitability are applied.

Even communism seeks, albeit unsuccessfully, to solve this fundamental problem according to the maxim "to each according to his needs." However, socialist economists overlook an essential problem that their system cannot solve: without market prices, efficient economic activity is impossible.

The calculation of profitability and efficiency must be based upon market prices in order to create an economic structure of production that solves the problem formulated earlier—maximizing production in the face of scarcity. Only those market-based calculations allow for the rapid, flexible, and efficient coordination of supply and demand. And it is only that coordination that produces an optimum structure of productive capacities, for example, the manufacture and distribution of the appropriate number of automobiles with the specific colors, features, and options to meet the demand for each.

In contrast, an economic system that, in the absence of market prices cannot calculate profitability and efficiency, will fail miserably in the task of allocating supply and demand. Consumers wind up with virtually no variety and no choices, for example, two-stroke East German Trabants that are inferior, scarce, costly, and virtually all the same.

A very ingenious, but uncomplicated, proof of the inferiority of planned economies was presented by Ludwig von Mises as early as the third decade of the last century. Unfortunately, socialist experimenters—then as now—were not open to rational economic argument. And the few economists among them who did acknowledge the problem persisted in the argument that, once communism reached an advanced stage, it would create a new type of human being and eventually solve this problem. In other words, "one had to have faith." And unfortunately, it was this irrational faith in communism's ability to overcome economic laws that prevailed, ultimately causing untold hardships for billions of people around the world.

Fractional Reserve Banking—The Heart of the Inflationary Evil

Can it be right to lend more than one owns? Common sense would seem to dictate the answer: no, of course not.

What one does not own one can—and must—not lend. Throughout history, Greeks, Romans, and jurists of medieval Europe all shared this reasonable view.

But there always were—and still are—influential interest groups that see things entirely differently, seeking repeatedly to persuade governments of their era to throw out this basic principle. They did everything in their power to gain the ability to lend more than they owned, ultimately succeeding in pressing home this demand—a demand that in earlier times had been branded as deception. Thus emerged the system of fractional reserve banking, which is currently practiced all around the world.

What Is a Bank?

Picking up from where we left off regarding the history of money, as precious metals became more widely used as a currency in free markets, and as this enabled flourishing trade and business, certain practical needs also emerged: money had to be securely stored and it had to change hands as easily and as safely as possible.

Thus, in the late sixteenth and early seventeenth centuries, a large number of banks were founded in the important trading centers to the south and north of the Alps to help meet these needs. They were essentially money warehouses, holding the precious metals in safe custody on behalf of their clients. At the same time, rapid growth in trade generated the need for traders or trading companies to settle their accounts on a regular basis, and the banks took on this task: they allowed the trading companies to pay for goods by means of simple bookkeeping entries, without the need for the gold to even leave the warehouse.

This period also saw the growing use of banknotes. The money warehouses simply issued a certificate representing a defined quantity of stored precious metal—a warehouse receipt, if you will. These receipts were, in essence, nothing other than banknotes. With larger sums in particular, they had—and continue to have—the great advantage of portability, relieving traders of the cost and inconvenience of transporting heavy precious metals from place to place. In short, the banknotes greatly facilitated trade.

The creation of money warehouses and the use of warehouse receipts for settling payment transactions represent the birth of banking and banknotes. This eminently sensible and practical system was then expanded modestly. For example, the banks offered a new service whereby they would interact with one another on the client's instructions, transferring gold from the client's bank account to the banks of the client's trading partners, either physically or by means of simple bookkeeping entries. Thus, the first checks and bank deposits emerged.

At this early stage, the emergence of banknotes, checks, and bank deposits in no way affected another critical aspect of the emerging financial system: the money supply. Rather, the facilities we described so far were merely proxies for money. In other words, they represented a claim to a specific quantity of precious metal, held by the bank in physical form. It was not until the introduction of fractional reserve banking that rapid and significant growth in the money supply—a kind of counterfeit money, if you will—became possible. And it was this expanded kind of money that opened the floodgates for modern forms of inflation.

Ingenious Idea or Brazen Deceit?

As long as the warehouse owners—whom we shall now call *bankers*—fulfilled their duty, they caused no harm and provided services in the free market that rendered trade significantly easier.

It apparently did not take very long, however, for the newly established bankers to discover an intriguing temptation in their money warehousing functions: normally, only a small portion of the precious metal with which they had been entrusted was physically transported or earmarked for delivery. The lion's share of the metal remained in long-term storage.

Some of the less scrupulous among the bankers—yes, they existed back then, too—must have asked themselves the alluring question: What is to prevent us from issuing multiple bank notes for the same gold in storage? Why not put out a bigger supply of bank notes than the actual supply of gold? We could then use that extra money to finance business transactions, and no one need be the wiser.

At the time, however, any bankers thus tempted would likely have been cut off at the pass—prevented from yielding to this temptation by the prevailing mercantile principles of morality, propriety, and ethics of that era. For one thing, the owners of the gold would have been unlikely to consent to this kind of double-dipping usage of their money—at least not without some kind of compensation, given the substantially greater risk exposure that it implied. For another, they would have abhorred the uncertainty: Does the gold securitized by a particular banknote actually exist? Or not?

In principle, therefore, this concept—today called *fractional reserve banking*—runs absolutely counter to the interests of the bank depositor and provides exclusively for the enrichment of the banker. And it is precisely for this reason that it was almost invariably regarded as criminal—an early form of double-leveraging that was not only regarded as immoral by the Church but was also widely forbidden throughout much of the long history of finance.

None of this, however, has prevented the overwhelming majority of contemporary financial theorists and economists from treating fractional reserve banking, the foundation of the modern financial system, as the most normal thing in the world.

A more detailed treatment of this material falls outside the scope of this book. But if you are among those who have been swayed by the many decades of government justifications for their manipulation of money, and if you remain skeptical about our observations, then we recommend a more detailed study of this extremely important topic.

The state monopoly over money, which is ultimately behind the universal introduction of fractional reserve banking, has already caused great misery around the world. It is here that the true roots of the global debt trap are to be found, a crisis that could reach its sad climax in the next few years. In the public discussions that take place in the media about the causes of the present crisis however—and possible measures to resolve it—this pivotal issue is barely ever mentioned.

In his 2006 book, *Money, Bank Credit, and Economic Cycles,* Jesus Huerta de Soto documents numerous historical examples reaching back to antiquity, demonstrating quite conclusively that repeated attempts made through the ages to introduce fractional reserve banking were, in most cases, rebuffed.

Today, in contrast, the entire world lives under a government monopoly over money whose fiat currencies (currencies not backed by a physical commodity) can be created by central banks at will, with the aid of a banking cartel dependent on those same central banks.

Indeed, it is largely thanks to fractional reserve banking that all modern banks are ultimately vulnerable to a panic run on their deposits, just as soon as the number of bank clients losing confidence—and acting on their fears—reaches critical mass. The quintessential dilemma of fractional reserve banking is therefore quite obvious: it is simply impossible for any bank to give all customers all their money back at the same time. Therein lies the fundamental difference between the pure money warehouses of old and the fractional banking system of modern times.

Most economists would argue, of course, that, without fractional banking, economic growth would be too slow, profits would be too small, and many of today's modern financial institutions could not survive. Perhaps. But given the speculative bubbles and busts we have just witnessed and given the sick, global debt trap we are now ensnared in, a more stable, balanced, slow-growth approach is precisely what most financial doctors should be prescribing.

The great Achilles' heel—and ultimate Armageddon—of the modern banking system comes, undoubtedly, with the threat of a national or international run on the world's largest banks. Science fiction? Absolutely not!

The U.S. banking system came close to that moment in September of 2008 in the wake of massive runs—mostly by institutional customers—on banks like Washington Mutual Bank and Citigroup. This is what prompted then-U.S. Treasury Secretary Henry Paulson to drop to his knees and beg Congress to rush to the rescue with emergency legislation—the Troubled Assets Relief Program (TARP)—to infuse $700 billion of capital into America's largest banks. And this is what also prompted Congress to dramatically raise FDIC insurance coverage limits on consumer bank deposits—from $100,000 to $250,000—while providing unlimited coverage to business checking accounts!

Germany faced a similar Armageddon at approximately the same time, as the German chancellor Angela Merkel stood before the cameras and, with panic etched on her face, announced a state guarantee for all bank deposits.

How much these federal guarantees will ultimately cost taxpayers—and how much time they will buy us before the next panic strikes—remains to be seen.

But ultimately, they do little more than prolong the fiction and conceal the true causes of the banking crisis, the global debt trap, and inflation—not only the fractional banking system per se, but more importantly, the rampant abuse of that system by current monetary policy.

Politicians from all corners of the world meet for crisis summits with much ado, always with an eye toward grandiose announcements intended to consolidate confidence or pacify panic. Here in Germany, politicians do the same, creating so-called high-carat working groups. And everywhere, governments seek measures that are supposed to alleviate the effects of the recession and prevent the crisis from coming to a head.

Throughout these deliberations, however, great care is taken to never mention the true causes of the crisis, which lie in a monetary and fiscal policy that overleverages the fractional banking system. Nor is there any discussion of the true solution to the problem, which is neither new rules nor more government oversight, but merely the return to serious and prudent monetary and fiscal policy—or, in an ideal world, the abolition of the state's financial monopoly based on its current system of central banks and fractional reserve banking.

Free market solutions to the global debt trap naturally conflict with the centrally planned economies that created the debt trap in the first place. Thus, although politicians routinely profess their commitment to the free market, any discussion of the natural corollary to free markets—a reduction of their power—is strictly taboo. It is rarely considered by any major political party.

Excursus: The Ethics of Money Production

The precise reasons behind this truth can be found in the book *The Ethics of Money Production* by Jörg Guido Hülsmann, published in 2007. This book contains all you need to know about the how, where, when, and why of money production and monetary systems presented in a very readable manner.

Professor Hülsmann espouses the free market with no ifs or buts, together with its underlying principles of freedom of contract and the right to private property. He presents the lies of popular propaganda used by monetary policy makers through the ages and lays bare how the state impinges upon the property rights of its citizens, in more or less subtle ways, through the exercise of monetary coercion and manipulation. He also points out that a radical change of direction is, in principle, possible at any time, but also diametrically opposed to the egotistical interests of the political class. This important book on the centerpiece of state power is essential reading for anyone who wishes to understand the causes of the present crisis in detail.

Key Communist Demands Have Already Been Fulfilled

It is not by chance that in the *Communist Manifesto*'s list of 10 "despotic inroads on the rights of property and on the conditions of bourgeois production"—demands made by Karl Marx and Friedrich Engels to enforce the communist seizure of power—we find the following:

> Centralization of credit in the hands of the state, by means of a national bank with state capital and an exclusive monopoly.[5]

This important demand by the preachers of a world communist revolution has long been achieved in our world of central banks. The same applies to their demand for a "heavy progressive, or graduated, income tax."

In 1975, the top income tax bracket in Germany was taxed as much as 56 percent, but it did not become payable until earnings reached 5.9 times the level of average earnings nationally. In 2007, the top income tax rate *seemed* to be lower, at only 42 percent (not counting "solidarity tax" and a wealth tax), but it became payable at a meager 1.9 times average income.

In the United States, the highest *federal* income tax bracket—35 percent (at the time this chapter was written)—is not as onerous. But when you add state and local income taxes to other tax burdens, it is not very different from Germany's. In other European countries that have a semi-socialist tradition, the so-called progressive nature of the taxes has traditionally been even steeper. And in Japan, in addition to income taxes of up to 50 percent, inheritance taxes are among the highest in the world.

In sum, in most developed countries, it has never been as difficult to become prosperous—or build wealth—through honest work as it is today.

Global Monetary Orders Come and Go—The Fall of the Berlin Wall

Nothing is forever. Anyone with a superficial acquaintance with history knows this truth, but only a small minority truly take it to heart. The majority can simply not imagine radical change and upheaval. They prefer to settle in with what they think is a comprehensible and comfortable past, and then extrapolate it into the future. They imagine that tomorrow will be more or less like today, that history's multiple episodes of the rise and fall of nations simply do not apply.

Nor does one have to delve into ancient history for a relevant example. Quite the contrary, not long ago, most of our German readers have had the opportunity to witness a similar change of historic dimensions from the comfort of their armchairs. Some may be glad they were not directly affected by the historic upheaval, while others may take pride in their active participation. We are talking, of course, about the collapse of the Soviet Union, the disintegration of the Eastern Bloc, and the fall of the Berlin Wall.

For nearly a half billion people, almost everything that had previously been perceived as immutable reality changed in a single stroke. Literally overnight, apparent certainties became obsolete, turning life destinies of countless individuals upside down and inside out, forcing them to face a dramatically changed reality, adapt abruptly, and forge radically new plans.

The nearly universal, blind assumption that citizens of the West will be spared a similar fate is, in itself, a reason to question that view. Nor can anyone know with certainty whether they will be among history's winners or losers when the chips are down. It is precisely for this reason that it makes sense for everyone, including the reader, to consider whether there might not be some sensible steps to take to protect oneself from the twists of economic fate. Read on for some telltale clues.

Did the Collapse of the Soviet Union Really Come as a Surprise?

For the overwhelming majority of observers—both in the East and the West—the collapse of the Soviet Union came as a complete surprise. That is to be expected. But given their training and philosophy, what is truly astonishing is that it was equally unexpected by virtually all Western economists. Over the course of decades, they had not only gotten used to the idea of socialist economies, they even began to believe the statistics issued by communist governments that almost invariably painted a picture of rising prosperity. And despite obvious, gaping holes in those statistics, critical analysis of official Eastern Bloc growth rates were either very rare or denounced as politically biased. Critical discussion of glowing official stats in the face of visibly deteriorating living conditions was equally scarce.

These unfortunate omissions do not mean, however, that the collapse was *truly* surprising. Western economists in particular could—and should—have known better. After all, Ludwig von Mises, cited earlier as the original thought leader in the Austrian School of economics, had published a brilliant analysis as far back as the 1920s. His thesis: the long-term self-destruction of centrally planned economies like the communist nations directly or indirectly under the yoke of the Soviet Union.

And yet, the ossification around dearly held—or at least customary—patterns of thought was simply too comfortable, too tempting, and again, career risk played a role: it was well known that no economist or political scientist was ever fired for failing to predict a momentous upheaval.

Economic history, too, is the history of change. It offers multiple examples of rise and fall in which fiat currencies and currency systems play a prominent role. The German people can look back over their recent history and see no fewer than three major episodes of paper currency turned into confetti by the governments of the day. Yet, despite this direct experience, faith in the stability of the financial system remained unbroken until just recently, the underlying reason why our words of warning, embodied in the subtitle of *Das Greenspan Dossier*—"How the U.S. Federal Reserve Jeopardizes the Global Monetary Order"—were met with great skepticism.

Following the great debt crises of 2008 and 2010, however, it's quite apparent that our entire world is already a very different place. What until recently was the preserve of a small minority in the financial industry has found its way into the mass media. As we wrote in the 2009 German edition of this book, "even an ignominious end for the euro—predicted by its critics from the very start—is suddenly no longer rejected as crazy talk, and correctly so, in our opinion."

The Great Experiment in Global Fiat Currencies

The present global currency system, to which many economists apply the term the *dollar standard,* owes its emergence to a broken promise by an American president: on August 15, 1971, President Richard Nixon declared to the world that his nation's previous promise—to convert U.S. dollars into gold at the rate of $35 an ounce—would no longer apply. In other words, he abandoned the convertibility of the dollar into gold, ending unilaterally the once-sacrosanct agreement signed at Bretton Woods, dismantling the international currency system that had prevailed since the end of World War II, and opening the path to a far more volatile world.

Thus began one of the greatest economic experiments since the introduction of communism in Russia: for the first time in history, the entire capitalist world was to be based on a purely fiat currency system.

Since that fateful day, the prosperity and adversity of the world's currencies has rested largely in the hands of politicians and bureaucrats. The disciplining mechanism that previously checked inflationary policies was gone. And it should come as no surprise that, all around the world, unbridled inflation was unleashed, the supply of money and credit has often exploded, and economic imbalances have reached unprecedented levels.

Clearly, the global economy has lacked any built-in homeostatic mechanism to control or offset emerging imbalances. And clearly, the end result has been the global debt trap from which painless escape is now impossible.

No one can pinpoint precisely when we will witness the endgame of this unlimited money supply explosion and debt orgy. But when lying sleeplessly at night, any thinking economist, no matter how sanguine, must know that the so-called global monetary order is essentially unrealistic and unstable—that sooner or later, it will come to an unpleasant end. The global debt trap—demonstrated by the banking crisis of 2008 and the sovereign debt disasters of 2010—make one thing crystal clear: The question is no longer *whether* a collapse will come, but *when and how* it will strike.

In this sense, the pattern is, indeed, comparable with that of Soviet Union. Let no one be fooled: when making future plans in this environment, you must expect the unexpected.

We Should Insure Ourselves Against These Major Risks

Many economists and stock market insiders are in closer agreement to the nexus of our arguments than they would have you believe. But they rarely discuss it. And if pressed, the most they will concede is that, although a collapse is possible, it is too far away in time to be relevant to your present decisions or plans. Even the real estate bust and recent sovereign debt disasters have done nothing to fundamentally shake their capacity for intellectual entrenchment.

We do not deny that the issue of timing is debatable. Nor do we rule out the possibility that it may take more time to reach the endgame of the global debt trap. But should you really rest your entire financial future on the hope that their guesses may prove to be right?

We are of the opinion that you should not. Rather, you should take precautions starting immediately. You should assume that, by their very nature, collapses come with little or no advance warning. They *will* catch most observers by surprise.

That's what you need insurance for, broadly defined as a contingency plan, a hedge or an alternative safe haven for your money. You need to safeguard against catastrophic risks that pose a potentially fatal threat to your wellbeing and lifestyle. It is the prudent thing to do even if the probability of the feared events is relatively small. If the event does occur, however unlikely, it would dramatically affect your life situation.

Insurance was invented to protect you from this eventuality. For risks that may cause an acceptable, absorbable degree of harm, you probably do not need insurance. But for risks that have the potential to destroy your life, you must not be left uninsured. And this rule applies all the more if the costs of safeguarding against the risks are low.

If the global currency system were to collapse, it would bring with it considerable losses in the value of assets—losses that could transform a relatively carefree retirement into an impossible nightmare, losses from which a recovery could be extremely difficult. It follows that prudence would demand that you safeguard yourself against this eventuality to the best of your ability. The price of this insurance policy is small—merely the opportunity cost for any money spent on the premiums. Nothing more.

Is it not astonishing, then, that most people—at least in Western countries—have no insurance against a currency catastrophe? That they stumble starry eyed into the future, without giving a thought to their personal future? That they trust that everything will somehow turn out well? That they rely on their government, of all things, and on its promises of payment? That they believe the government will actually fulfill its clearly unsustainable promises to make all debt payments and fully fund Social Security, Medicare, and government pensions? That they allow the entire destiny of their wealth to be based on the assumption that this extremely unstable financial system will persist?

All Major Periods of Inflation Took Place in Times of Fiat Currencies

This naïve faith becomes even more incompressible if one studies the history of the major inflationary times, for all such periods took place in times of discretionary paper (or fiat) currencies. The renowned Swiss professor Peter Bernholz published a very important economic history on this subject in 2003, titled *Monetary Regimes and Inflation*. In it, he comes to the following conclusions, important for all of us:

> The political system tends to favor an inflationary bias of currencies.
> All major inflations have been caused by princes or governments.

All hyperinflations in history have occurred during the 20th century, that is, in the presence of discretionary paper money regimes, with the exception of the hyperinflation during the French Revolution, when the French monetary regime, too, was based on a paper money standard.

Monetary regimes binding the hands of rulers, politicians and governments are a necessary condition for keeping inflation at bay.

Hyperinflations are always caused by public budget deficits, which are largely financed by money creation.[6]

The results of this economic history could hardly be more unambiguous. There could be no clearer indication of the very high risk of a coming period of hyperinflation. Or could there?

Alan Greenspan Understands the Connection

Perhaps you are skeptical of the authority of Professor Bernholz. If so, then read the following sentences from former Federal Reserve Chairman Alan Greenspan, until recently so adored by the media.

This is the shabby secret of the welfare statists' tirades against gold. Deficit spending is simply a scheme for the confiscation of wealth. Gold stands in the way of this insidious process. It stands as a protector of property rights. If one grasps this, one has no difficulty in understanding the statists' antagonism toward the gold standard.[7]

The end of the Bretton Woods exchange rate system marked the end of what was at least a semi-realistic monetary and fiscal policy. From that day forward, the floodgates were opened to a highly dubious accumulation of debt. And around the world, politicians have repeatedly exploited this change to usher in inflationary policies.

Therein lie the origins—and consequences—of the global debt trap. And that's why, in mass democracies with a financial system based on fiat money, all roads ultimately lead to inflation and the collapse of the financial system. That is the sad quintessence of the twentieth century characterized as it was by inflation and hyperinflation.

Since the End of Bretton Woods, Debt and the Money Supply Have Risen Dramatically

The great advantage of a currency backed by gold lies in the fact that citizens are protected from the threat that Greenspan described so lucidly, that is, the greediness of politicians. Politicians are, by their very nature, vote maximizers. Their overriding goal is to obtain or retain power—be elected or reelected—and the simplest way to achieve this goal is by showering short-term benefits on key groups of voters. Unfortunately, to the degree that self-interest is a measure of reason, it is actually rational for politicians to ignore the long-term consequences of their policies and concern themselves strictly with the next election.

No one who has understood this system of incentives can be surprised by what has happened since the dismantling of Bretton Woods. Against this backdrop, the unusually high rate of growth in the global supply of money and credit was to be expected, while any hope for a return to prudent monetary and fiscal policy was, unfortunately, wishful thinking.

One interesting question does emerge. The end of the Bretton Woods dates back to 1971. But in many parts of the world, the start of the great orgy of debt accumulation did not begin until the 1980s, about a decade later. Why?

The reason: some things just take time. Economists sometimes speak of institutional inertia. We would like to express the concept a little more clearly. It simply took a few years—and the apparent success of this experiment in the United States—before politicians in Europe and elsewhere realized that they, too, could now pursue entirely irresponsible policies, the long-term consequences of which they would not be held accountable for.

Keynes provides the appropriate and often-cited calendar quote in this regard: "In the long run, we are all dead." Our response: "Yes, but our children or our children's children live on."

What Lies at the End of This Road?

In his monumental work, *Human Action,* Ludwig von Mises addresses the question as to what would lie at the end of this great inflationary road. He assumes that there are no natural limits to credit creation, which would *necessarily* give rise to deflation. The central banks are, in principle, able to facilitate a continuation of inflationary booms through repeated injections of new liquidity.

Nevertheless, with each new round of monetary manipulation, the economic imbalances become greater. This means that the price of a return to prudent policies, although theoretically possible at any given time, grows increasingly larger with each cycle, and thus, increasingly improbable. In recent decades, we have already come a long way down this path. The imbalances and risks are already enormous. What, then, awaits us at the end of the road?

Ludwig von Mises provides an answer:

If the credit expansion is not stopped in time, the boom turns into the crack-up boom; the flight into real values begins, and the whole monetary system founders.[8]

Flashbacks to the hyperinflation of the German Weimar Republic? We're afraid so.

CHAPTER 4

The Road to (Hyper)Inflation

Will the bursting of the real estate bubble lead to a deflationary endgame? Or will the printers of money with their so-called rescue packages and unaffordable economic stimulus programs prevail, producing rampant inflation? That is the decisive question for investment success over the coming years. So it behooves you to become familiar with the arguments behind both scenarios, and this, in turn, is not possible without clearly defining the terms.

Today, the terms *inflation* and *deflation* are generally used to refer to a rise or decline in price levels measured by a basket of consumer goods. Although technically accurate, the problem with this definition should be clear: it describes only one of many symptoms—namely price changes in a basket of goods that can be manipulated at will. However, the underlying cause of these price changes remains—intentionally—unclear. Plus, the composition of the consumer basket, along with the methods for measuring their price changes, leave an extremely broad latitude for generating politically desired results.

In contrast, the classic definition of the terms inflation and deflation, which has now largely fallen into disuse, begins not with the symptoms but with the cause. *Inflation (deflation) is an increase (decrease) in the supply of money and credit.*

Let's first explore the latter.

The Deflationary Scenario

The direct consequence of speculative bubbles that burst is, of course, none other than a price collapse in the object of that speculation. If these are contained in the consumer basket, and if they cheapen the basket overall, then economists who base their definition on consumer prices will speak of deflation.

Bursting speculative bubbles also are deflationary in classical definition: they lead to an increase in the demand for cash and a decrease in the supply of money and credit. Cash and equivalent—including cash in circulation, federal funds, money market funds, and other short-term instruments—are viewed as havens in times of great uncertainty in the financial markets, and they are thus in greater demand.

But the demand for credit shrinks as the risk appetite among businesses and private investors declines, and as the value of credit collateral, such as equities or real estate, also goes down. At the same time, the supply of credit also shrinks, as banks pull back from lending in the downward phase of the cycle, imposing more stringent credit requirements.

In the wake of bursting speculative bubbles, monetary stimulus experiments also fail to achieve the desired effect. To describe this pattern, Keynes coined the term *liquidity trap*—the failure to take into account the impact of speculative bubbles and their collapse.

Consumers Are Massively Indebted, if Not Excessively in Debt

Real incomes have hardly risen for years, if at all.

An extremely important source of consumer finance was the mortgage equity withdrawals referred to earlier. With the aid of mortgage loans, homeowners converted their price gains into cash and spent it on consumer goods. Now, in the wake of falling home prices, this source of credit has dried up.

It is the *reverse wealth effect,* whereby falling property values (and stock prices) can lead to falling consumer spending and rising savings rates. At the same time, we see:

- Globalization, particularly the investment boom in China, has led to excess production capacity and probably also to overinvestments in the consumer goods sector. This, in turn, puts downward pressure on consumer prices, especially during the downward phase of the business cycle. At the same time,
- Chronic unemployment in the labor market makes significant wage increases, such as we saw in the 1970s, rather unlikely.
- Plus, large numbers of banks have their backs to the wall or are even de facto bankrupt, making a decline in lending almost unavoidable.

Huge Sums in Bad Loans Must Be Written Down—Deflation Is Only Plausible in a World Unable to Print Money

All of these pressures lead to deflation arguments, which certainly do have a certain validity. But that's assuming a world without the ability to run its money printing presses and to incur gigantic levels of government debt. However, in our world—characterized by the government monopoly of money, fiat currencies, unfettered politicians, and central bankers committed to inflation—things are very different indeed.

As we can now witness the world over, almost all politicians, economists, central bankers, and opinion leaders seem convinced that the cause of the Great Depression of the 1930s was not the credit-driven boom and speculative bubble that preceded it in the 1920s, but rather, inadequate government stimulus *after* the bubble burst. Propelled by this theory, they are now doing everything possible to prevent deflation and create inflation.

Why? Because politicians prefer an inflationary crisis to a deflationary one. Inflation masks the reality of the losses incurred. Also, inflation is less blatant and more subtle, with true causes that are harder for the public to discern, making it easier for politicians to find scapegoats and cover up their own failures.

Politicians also find it easier to gather support for—and from—a consuming public addicted to the "buy now, pay later" syndrome. They maximize votes for the near term, while gambling callously with the public's long-term welfare. The devil may care, but they don't.

Keynesian Interventionists Control Policy and Debate

Most policy think tanks and university-based research, often government financed, is firmly in the hands of Keynesian interventionists. They are not grounded in empirical evidence supporting the benefits of free markets. Nor do they pay much heed to the obvious pitfalls of government-planned economies. Instead, the interventionists believe they can produce better results than free markets. And never before in modern times have we seen this ideological bent drive policy to the extent that it has in the wake of the 2008 banking crisis or the 2010 sovereign debt crisis.

Gigantic rescue packages have been decreed with the overt and deliberate goal of socializing losses—losses that the financial sector amassed entirely due to miscalculation, failed speculation, and poor decision making. On both sides of the Atlantic, giant banks and insurance companies are nationalized; massive deficit-busting stimulus packages are enacted; and entire nations are bailed out.

Bernanke's Inflationary Keynote Speech

Further such measures are almost certain to follow, especially given Fed Chairman Ben Bernanke's strong penchant for intervention. In his keynote speech titled "Deflation: Making Sure 'It' Doesn't Happen Here," dating back to November 21, 2002, he proposed unconventional monetary policy measures in the event that policy makers should one day come to the conclusion that a deflationary crisis was looming.

Since then, we have repeatedly pointed out that this speech is essential reading and should be taken very seriously, for even back then, it mapped out the path that policy has now followed—not only in the United States, but throughout the world.

All means are being applied in an attempt to avert the end of the great accumulation of debt that began in the early 1980s. We proceed from the assumption that this policy, which ultimately destroys the value of money and, with it, the welfare of broad swaths of the population, is indeed feasible. At the same time, we see no reason to doubt the core message of Bernanke's speech, which reads as follows:

> But the U.S. government has a technology, called a printing press (or, today, its electronic equivalent), that allows it to produce as many U.S. dollars as it wishes at essentially no cost.[1]

In a society burdened with excess debt to this extent, the principal threat is debt deflation, which would trigger a deflationary depression.

What does this mean for you as an investor?

As long as recessionary forces in the economy prevail, despite an extremely inflationary monetary and fiscal policy, there will be little or no consumer price inflation. The deflationary forces from the bursting of the speculative bubble and the bad investments made during the upward phase of the cycle—in particular in the financial sector—could ensure falling prices. Only after this natural correction process is choked off by government intervention will the consequences of the inflationary policy manifest itself in rising prices.

While the deflationary phase persists, investors are best protected in the havens of government bonds. Here they can avoid asset losses and even achieve price gains. However, as soon as the inflationary phase begins, bonds become major losers. In this phase, it is gold and other select commodities that are the main beneficiaries.

Stocks can, admittedly, also rise during periods of inflation, but only at disproportionately low rates in comparison with gold, commodities, or strong currencies not affected by inflation. In the corporate sector, meanwhile, inflation leads to an overstatement of corporate profits, and undermines corporate assets. Furthermore, the history of financial markets demonstrates that equities are often extremely undervalued in regard to P/E ratios and book value toward the end of a period of high inflation. Why? Because periods of high inflation are not times of prosperity. To the contrary, many segments of society are impoverished, and stocks are actually very cheap relative to other assets. As we explain later, that's what happened at the end of the inflationary 1970s and even after the hyperinflationary 1920s in Germany.

Looking ahead, the coming months and years promise to be extremely tense. The risks are exceptionally high, and there is far more at stake than mere money. The reason: historically, even economic crises of lesser dimensions have often had undesirable political consequences.

In the light of the considerable insecurity and dangers that exist, it is essential to stay regularly informed, at a high level, regarding current trends. Above all, one must remain extremely flexible and keep an open mind in order to react rapidly and in an unconventional manner should the circumstances dictate.

The Wise Men of Economics (the Wise Careerists) . . .

Every year the German Council of Economic Experts presents its Annual Report, and 2007 was no exception. These professorial policy advisors, unjustifiably elevated by the media to the position of economic wise men, travel to Berlin especially for this event, to present themselves before the largely uncritical press and to oblige their clients. There they stand, enjoying the limelight and the proximity to power, showering their audience with what they clearly believe to be irrefutable wisdom.

What's most ironic is that even now, when the utterly absurd miscalculations of this motley crew of experts should be clear to everyone, the media *continue* to applaud these same prophets of prosperity, who continue to spread their bankrupt theories, utterly devoid of insight about the crisis.

Why? That is our rhetorical question to the editors of leading newspapers. In particular we ask: What drives those publications, professing to favor free markets, to this curious mode of behavior? What self-interest leads to the strange filtering out of extremely important topics, which ultimately serve to undermine faith in the press—a press which has a key role to play in democracy as the fourth estate?

At the very minimum, we direct this question to the German print media. At least they enjoy the necessary freedom to decide for themselves whether they wish to give their readers the same conformist standard fare that is already the preserve of German state television . . . or . . . whether they wish to replace this theater of the absurd with reality shows that pull no punches? Do they think their readers can't handle the truth? Do they fear a reader rebellion if they tell their readers that the emperor of monetary policy has no clothes? Or are they simply heeding the cynical sales maxim that "bull sells!"—in the sense of both bullish and bull manure?

On the subject of state-run television, we have noticed that, in Germany, the pundits are quick to deride, and rightfully so, China's state-controlled media. But they dare not use this same expression to characterize Germany's state-run television stations ARD and ZDF. At least in China, the ground rules are obvious, and there's no believable pretense of objectivity. The ground rules, or factual constraints, that govern the print media in the West are, unfortunately, much harder to fathom.

With this backdrop, we now return to the 2007–2008 Annual Report by the German Council of Economic Experts. Two quotations should suffice to illustrate the tenor of this comprehensive work:

> The real estate crisis will not lead to a recession in the United States.
> The risk of a slide into recession in 2008 appears . . . extremely small.[2]

Of course, we, too, have made forecasts errors over the years. This is normal and cannot be avoided. We make statements of probability, not certainty, while the economy and society are, in many ways, unpredictable. However, in 2007, the imbalances and risks were all too obvious. To have simply overlooked them appears to us to be almost impossible. Nonetheless, these sentences are right there in the 2007–2008 Annual Report. The fact that this erudite committee never forecast a recession speaks volumes, in our opinion.

Perhaps the true wisdom of these experts lies not in forecasting the economy but in the furtherance of their own careers. We see nothing reprehensible in this as such; indeed, we hold ambitious people in high regard, inasmuch the desire to get ahead is an important engine of competition and capitalism. But if this aspiration is pursued through political favoritism instead of honest competition in free markets, then it leaves a nasty aftertaste. For this reason, we are dispensing here with official language and, with a nod to George Orwell, will speak not of "wise men of economics" but instead of wise careerists.

We ourselves clearly pointed out the threat of a recession emanating from the United States at the turn of the year 2007–2008 in our publications, which certainly did not find their way into the centers of political power. For example, in an article in which we criticized the 2007–2008 Annual Report, our headlines were: "Our Indicators Increasingly Point Toward Recession," "Index of U.S. Leading Indicators on Course for Recession Once Again," and "Is the Recession Imminent?"

Claus Vogt wrote:

The economic situation has come to a head. Consequently the risk
of a painful cyclical slump has risen significantly. Please be sure to
review your portfolio structure now, as to whether it really does
match your individual risk tolerance level, even in the event that a
normal cyclical slump should occur. Bear in mind that, in the past,
the Dow Jones Industrial Average has always fallen during a recession, without exception. On average, the loss was 36 percent; and
in other market sectors or countries, it was significantly worse.
Realistically speaking, you must therefore factor in price losses of
at least 30 to 50 percent. At the same time, because of the bursting of the real estate bubble, the huge economic imbalances that
we have discussed here repeatedly, and the enormous quantity of
derivatives that the financial system is still weaving and spinning,
there is a considerable risk that it will exceed a normal recession
or a normal slump.[3]

In this way, we unambiguously prepared our readers for the coming calamity and saved them from disastrous losses—at a time when the
wise careerists were unable to detect a single hint of a looming recession.
Such far-reaching, yet politically incorrect, insights and forecasts, such as
a warning of imminent recession and diagnosing its causes in monetary
policy, are not to be expected from a top committee of policy advisors.
The wise careerists are professors, part of the economics industry. Their
university careers depend, to a large degree, on never talking out of turn,
never straying too far from the herd or prevailing academic fashion, always
swimming with the mainstream.

Those who wish to make a career in policy advice know the importance of espousing a basic position that is essentially friendly toward
the government and politics, that does not question the primacy of
politics demanded by almost all politicians. Political intervention in
the economy and society, they insist, must be applauded; otherwise,
one stands no chance of pleasing the powerful. It follows that you cannot expect too much from a committee on government dole. Not even
the forecast of an otherwise obvious recession. And certainly not an
explanation of its causes in the failures of fiscal and monetary policy.
Or can you?

Bad at Economic Forecasting,
Good at Script Rewriting

The 2007–2008 Annual Report is also a classic illustration of another important insight into the work of the wise careerists. Consider a further quotation:

> With a . . . neutral real interest rate of 2 percent, it is clear that American monetary policy was too expansionary in the period from 2003 to 2005.[4]

We would agree 100 percent. It is precisely this irresponsibly lax monetary policy that has received the severest of criticism in our writings. Unfortunately, the wise careerists waited two to four years before they had the courage to utter this insight in public. We suspect they were politely waiting for the key figure responsible for this lax monetary policy, former Fed Chairman Alan Greenspan, to resign. Diplomacy reigns supreme.

But they weren't done. A little further on, the Annual Report turns to the monetary policy of the European Central Bank (ECB). On this subject it reads:

> In the EU, there is a slightly expansionary-to-neutral orientation of monetary policy. . . . All indicators therefore lead us to conclude that monetary policy has headed towards a neutral orientation this year.[5]

In the first nine months of 2007, to which the gentlemen are referring, the euro zone money supply grew by a resounding 10.9 percent, a double-digit figure that, in the days of the old German Bundesbank, was considered an untenable, irresponsible state of affairs. But the EU luminaries succeeded in digging up indicators that enabled them to depict monetary policy as "slightly expansionary to neutral."

How times change! And how nimbly politicians switch yardsticks! What was yesterday considered irresponsible and dangerous now enjoys broad support and pseudoscientific justification.

Is this cavalier attitude toward monetary policy merely a monetary fashion trend? Or is it a more permanent fixture? Right now, for all practical purposes, it's the latter. The newfangled monetary credo of this era seems to be that nearly all economic problems can be readily solved simply by resorting to money printing presses manned by bureaucrats who assume no responsibility for the consequences. Speculative bubbles, rising commodity prices, increasingly unfair wealth distribution, and the destruction of incentives for economically rational behaviors such as saving are ignored or even encouraged. And in a more advanced stage, the complete collapse of the monetary system, the destruction of the economy, and, when carried to an extreme, the unraveling of society itself—all seem to be risks that our leaders embrace without more than passing concern.

Yet, strangely, connecting the dots to these outcomes is apparently taboo among adherents of this new economic religion—a cult that rivals communism by virtue of its monstrous absurdity. Its supreme leaders—central banks, idolized by contemporary economists like golden calves—behave like they're the ultimate solution to problems they themselves create.

Prominent among the Greenspan worshipers is a German economic luminary, Bundesbank president Axel Weber—the man who, in his own words, emulates Alan Greenspan. On August 2, 2008, he was quoted in the press with the following assessment of the situation at the troubled IKB Industriebank:

> The problems at IKB are specific to that institution. . . . In addition, the exposure of German credit institutions to the U.S. housing market are manageable and limited, overall.[6]

Weber went on to reject the comparison made in some media reports between the present situation and the banking crisis of 1931 as "entirely erroneous."

So there you have it: "Entirely erroneous." Well, we now know whose assessment of the situation was truly erroneous.

In light of such monumental miscalculations—and an almost absurd understatement of the risks created by monetary policy makers lauded as luminaries in the media—how can we *not* fear for the future?

How can we *not* be deeply worried that entrusting responsibility for monetary policy to such experts will lead to catastrophe?

Were our forefathers not correct when they transformed gold and silver into money, relying on elements that cannot be created by politicians and their handpicked experts?

Clearly, a long-lasting solution—one which helps us escape the global debt trap and consistently avoids catastrophes like the sovereign debt crisis—is to be found only in the introduction of a sustainable global monetary order, including the abolition of central banks and the state monopoly over money. We are pragmatists. We know this cannot be achieved overnight. But it can be achieved in stages over time.

Consider this: the twentieth century was not only the century of devastating wars, but also the century of devastating financial destruction, including hyperinflation. The state's monopoly over money, which is, of course, an invitation to such follies, is the key to explaining this catastrophic balance sheet. And yet it is also for this reason that the truth about central banks is an utterly taboo subject.

Nonetheless, we must give Mr. Weber credit for firmly opposing political attempts to sell German gold reserves. In doing so, he ensured that Germany will continue to enjoy a favorable starting position in regard to monetary policy when a new global monetary system is ultimately in place, whenever that day may come.

That it could all be different is demonstrated in the following article, which we published in March 2007 in the German monthly, *Smart Investor*.

Does the bursting of the American housing bubble threaten the global economy? . . .

We are currently experiencing the classic echo bubble in the equity markets, which now appears to be coming to an end because so-called carry trades (printing presses for money initiated by central banks) are coming unglued as interest rate differentials between currency zones decline. A noteworthy result of these carry trades was the collapse of what was once the strongest currency in the world, namely the Swiss franc, which is now among the weakest. At the same time, almost nothing has changed in the economic structure or economic trends of Switzerland that could remotely justify this nosedive. But in our current age, speculators from all corners of the globe have taken control of the financial markets. They borrow huge sums from banks at absurdly low interest rates (1 or 2 percent for Swiss francs) only to exchange them for U.S. government bonds, for example. Profit margins of several hundred percent are the rule.

This will come, as come it must: slowly but surely the world is heading for the greatest financial crisis of all time. The basis for a turn for the worse could be an economic downturn in the world's largest economy, the U.S., which we expect will come at the end of this year or the start of next. There, the gigantic housing bubble triggered by the irresponsible and lax monetary policy pursued in the '90s by the maestro of the Federal Reserve, Alan Greenspan (now one year into retirement) could burst. It followed, as surely as night follows day, that, in the wake of this monetary policy, the American consumer is burdened with debt as never before, and their savings rate (–1.4 percent) has gone negative. As if this were not enough, U.S. banks have run their reserves down to their lowest level in 17 years. All the criteria for an enormous financial crash are there. All that's missing is the trigger. . . .

This was all financed by Asia, with China at the head, and Greenspan was not bashful in telling the American public that they were doing something valuable for the global economy by absorbing Asia's savings quota through their insatiable consumption. This position can hardly be surpassed in terms of cynicism, for it is saying, in effect: if you, fellow Americans, drive a gas-guzzling, mortgage-financed luxury car through gridlocked streets to buy your groceries at the supermarket, then you are doing something positive for the common good, the economy and the maintenance of the American workforce. And moreover, through your generosity, you are solving the poor Asians' problem with their high compulsory savings rates.

In February of this year [2007], the first mortgage chickens came home to roost, namely in the subprime mortgage field. These are mortgage loans given to borrowers who, based on standard industry criteria, were known to be bad debtors even at the time the loans were issued. The second-largest financial services provider to specialize in this risky area, New Central Finance Corporation, admitted that there were irregularities in the balancing of these loans. Provisions had to be drastically increased. The British bank HSBC also made known that it had been forced to increase provisions for losses from its mortgage business by 20 percent, to $10.6 billion. The tip of the iceberg?[7]

Why the U.S. Mortgage and Foreclosure
Crisis Is Not "Over"

Nine months after we published the preceding article, in December of 2007, the recession that the wise careerists had been unable to see began in earnest.

Meanwhile, the subprime mortgage crisis spread to prime mortgages; the prime mortgage crisis set off a chain reaction of failures in the U.S. banking industry; and these, in turn, struck Spain, Ireland, the U.K., Eastern Europe and even supposedly strong economies like Germany.

Indeed, the rot of bad mortgages has been so vast that, despite the greatest outpouring of government aid in the history of the world, it continued to fester and deepen long after the wise careerists in governments officially declared the debt crisis "over."

The most critical measure of the crisis is the percentage of homeowners that are late in making their mortgage payments—the mortgage delinquency rate. But even as government officials were declaring the crisis over, if you had asked them for an estimate of how much the delinquency rate might rise, the most they would be willing to admit to is one or two percentage points.

"Subprime mortgages?" they'd respond. "Sure, subprime mortgages will go bad, of course. They were on the margin to begin with. But prime mortgages? Heck no! They're solid. You'll never see that $10-trillion market experience similar difficulties."

By 2010, however, the delinquency rate on all U.S. mortgages, including all *prime* mortgages, had soared to a level that was actually *higher* than that of subprime mortgages at the time government officials first began making such declarations.

According to the Mortgage Bankers Association (MBA), at the end of the second quarter of 2010, the delinquency rate on all U.S mortgages for one-to-four residential properties was 9.85 percent of *all* loans outstanding. In other words, nearly one in ten mortgages was delinquent—an astronomical level.[8]

Moreover, this figure reflected strictly mortgages with at least one payment past due. It did not include loans in the process of foreclosure. According to the MBA, the percentage of loans undergoing foreclosure was an astoundingly high 4.57 percent. Thus, if you combined the loans in foreclosure plus loans past due, the all-inclusive bad mortgage rate was 13.97 percent.[9]

How much money did that involve? According to the Federal Reserve's Flow of Funds, at the end of the second quarter of 2010, the total amount of home mortgages outstanding was $10.644 trillion.[10] With 13.97 percent of those going bad, that meant that $1.487 trillion in U.S. mortgages were still in distress even *after* Bernanke's Federal Reserve had pumped in a similar sum by buying up mortgages securities.

Some political leaders and industry apologists sought to argue that, perhaps, most of the homeowners were only slightly late in their payments and could be kept in their homes with larger, more expensive government bailout programs. But those arguments were full of holes—four to be precise.

First, even the largest and most expensive government mortgage bailout programs of the 2007–2010 period were dismal failures. *Safe Money* editor Mike Larson provides the facts:

> Washington claimed the Home Affordable Mortgage Program (HAMP) would save nearly 3.3 million homeowners by giving them loans with more favorable terms. But less than one-tenth that many—a mere 295,348—were actually helped. Officials also swore the government's Home Affordable Modification Program (HAMP) would help up to five million homeowners secure new loans owned or guaranteed by Fannie Mae and Freddie Mac. It actually helped less than 5% of that number—around 220,000. They said the FHASecure program would help 500,000 families refinance—but it was canceled after helping only 3,900 mortgages. Washington's Hope for Homeowners program, originally billed as the ultimate hope for nearly six million homeowners who may face foreclosure, helped precisely *zero* homeowners. There were only 326 applications for the program and not a single one received a new mortgage or even modification of an existing one. The HUD Implementation of Recovery Act included $13.6 billion for the Department of Housing and Urban Development. But foreclosures exploded 673 percent after it was signed into law by President Obama on February 17, 2009.
>
> Can Washington really be this incompetent? According to the Special Inspector General of the Troubled Asset Relief Program (SIGTARP), the answer is a resounding "yes!" SIGTARP says the government's mortgage programs are a disaster.[11]

Second, it was simply *not* true that most homeowners were "only slightly late" in their payments. According to the MBA, the percentage of loans that were *ninety* days or more past due or in the process of foreclosure was still an incredibly high 9.11 percent.

Third, there has emerged in America an entirely new phenomenon called *strategic defaults*. These are defaults by homeowners who *can* afford to make their payments but deliberately cease doing so strictly to save the money or spend it on something else. Worse, this strategy, although of highly questionable ethics, is entirely rational. The homeowners are under water in their mortgage with little hope their homes will appreciate in value; they know that banks can often take two years to repossess their homes; and they know that by stopping their mortgage payments they can live rent free, saving very substantial sums. So they are defaulting en masse even if they still have their jobs and income.

Fourth, as we review the final galley proofs of this book, we cannot resist inserting this last and most shocking new wrinkle to the U.S. mortgage crisis—the breakdown in foreclosure procedures that has prompted attorneys general to investigate the industry in all 50 states, and which is giving millions of U.S. homeowners another excuse—plus a legal weapon—for defaulting.

Thus, now, you can see, in the brightest of lights, the full scale of the Armageddon brought about by the wild monetary expansion engineered by Greenspan. And now, you can also see the true genesis of even wilder inflationary escapades under Bernanke. Most important, it is obvious that the path to mortgage mayhem and the road to inflation are interlinked.

All this is why, for a number of years now we have been recommending that investors exercise extreme care in the management of their assets, making sure that they include large cash positions. Admittedly, this ultra-conservative approach—in an era of artificially low interest rates—cannot deliver high rates of return. However, most of those who venture far afield—such as entrusting their money to highly speculative hedge funds—must expect a sorry end. The no-free-lunch axiom also applies to the management of assets. Rather than pursuing better returns on your money, seek instead the return *of* your money, devoting your energies to finding a safe escape from the still-vulnerable American asset bubble in the not so unlikely event that it will again come crashing down.

Escaping the Global Debt Trap—Inflation Forecast

The title of this book embodies our core argument that a great portion of the globe is entrapped in the snares of massive debt, from which we believe there is only one likely escape: high rates of inflation in the coming years and even the possibility of hyperinflation.

Never forget that all historic periods of very high inflation had the following two primary elements in common: fiat money that could be multiplied at will along with dramatic increases in the level of government debt that is overwhelmingly monetized, that is, financed, with the newly created money.

This combination, always so disastrous in the past, is now present. For this reason, there can only be one outcome, in our view: currency devaluation.

This forecast is supported by another lesson from the history of the financial markets: once the inflationary path has been embarked upon, a change of direction is unlikely. Indeed, the political justification for taking the inflationary road is, in essence, that there is no other alternative. Their line-in-the sand posture is that turning back from that path and seeking an alternate one, would, almost by definition, immediately trigger precisely the crisis they are seeking so desperately to avoid. Not only would they have to face the prior imbalances that had been swept under the rug by the first rounds of money printing, but would now have to face the additional problem of inflation itself.

What are inflationists likely to do in that situation? They will tell us that the only possible response to any new crisis is a political one, namely still *more* money printing and still *more* inflation. This is the inflationary vicious cycle in which we have found ourselves repeatedly and is the underlying driver of speculative bubbles. This is the persistent consequence of the global debt trap.

At this point, however, we must make a few important qualifying comments: inflation does not fall from the skies; it doesn't just happen. Inflation is the result of entirely deliberate political decisions. For this reason, in principle, the alternative always *does* exist. But because the path of least resistance is to inflate still further, the politicians almost invariably opt for this path, and it's this path that we expect will prevail in coming years.

An Exception: How Paul Volcker Brought 1970s Inflation to a *Temporary* End

A peak at a prior dramatic episode can be very enlightening: at the end of the 1960s, the course of global monetary and fiscal policy was on an inflationary course, emanating then, as it does now, from the United States And in the 1970s, currency depreciation, as measured by consumer prices indices, reached a peak annual pace in excess of 10 percent in the United States. Even in more conservative Germany, we saw peak CPI inflation of 7.1 percent.

But as we approached the end of the decade, the inflation began to fuel widespread discontent among investors and even the general population. A broad political consensus emerged that inflation could not be allowed to slip further out of control. The immediate reason: the U.S. government bond market was facing imminent collapse, putting the financing of the U.S. government and its access to new credit at risk. Domestic and global bond investors—the bond vigilantes of that era—went on a buyer's strike. They refused to buy long-term U.S. Treasuries, virtually shutting down the market for U.S. government securities.

New York Times columnist Paul Krugman, who argues repeatedly for even more deficit spending to spur the U.S. economy, continually asks, "Where are the so-called bond vigilantes that everyone seems so afraid of?" For an answer, he need only look back to the late 1970s and early 1980s.[12]

Under intense attack from the bond vigilantes, President Jimmy Carter appointed Paul Volcker to the post of chairman of the Federal Reserve, giving the new Fed chief carte blanche in the mission of combating inflation, with little immediate concern for the consequences. Volcker responded by drastically raising interest rates, slapping stiff controls on consumer credit, and, inevitably, driving the U.S. economy into a tailspin.

This decision, although appropriate at the time, was part of what cost Carter the presidency in 1980. Voters never forgave him for shock to the economy delivered by the drastic interest rate rises necessary for curbing inflation—a double-dip recession from 1980 to 1982. In other words, Carter paid the political price for the errors in monetary and fiscal policy of his predecessors, while his successor, Ronald Reagan, reaped the benefits of Carter's tough decisions.

During that period, Paul Volcker once invited the editors of the *Wall Street Journal* to a meeting in his office. He informed his guests of his intention to bring inflation to an end. Ironically enough, he asked the journalists to support him. He said he knew how easy it would be to tear into his policies journalistically and fan the flames of popular discontent. He stressed that, although his was the correct path in the long term, it would be very painful—and therefore unpopular—in the short term. He argued that this anti-inflationary policy was urgently needed and, quite clearly, in America's best long-term interests. He appealed to the editors' reason, to their patriotism, and they listened. His policies received the support he sought in the financial press.

This episode makes four things clear.

First, it demonstrates that monetary policy makers cannot claim ignorance. Whether they're lighting bonfires of inflation or snuffing out its flames, they know exactly what they're doing. They know that inflation does not fall from the skies, but is largely their own creation—something they have the power to start *and* to end.

Second, it shows that a return to a realistic monetary and fiscal policy, no matter how rational it may be in the long term, is tantamount to political suicide. In other words, it can only be implemented by the rare politicians who place— or are forced to place—the welfare of their country ahead of their own.

Third, it illustrates how the introduction of a staunch anti-inflationary policy ultimately requires the support of the media to help keep public discontent within certain bounds.

But most important of all, it shows that none of this can happen until politicians feel they have no other choice—until we see the kinds of high inflation rates that precipitated the bond market collapse of the late 1970s and early 1980s.

Reliable Information and the Black Swan

In light of the preceding, our inflation forecast is, in essence, largely a political one. And since it's driven less by predictable economic forces, it's a forecast that's somewhat more difficult to make than the forecasts we made in *Das Greenspan Dossier*. At that time, it was clear that, no mat- ter what politicians or central bankers did, the housing bubble would burst with predictable consequences. The outcome was inevitable. Only the timing was an open question.

In contrast, our current inflation forecast comes with no such inevitabil- ity. It's contingent upon future political decisions. Furthermore, there is, of course, always the risk of an unpredictable dramatic upheaval—war, natural disaster, epidemic, or revolution—the now-famous *black swan events* to which Nassim Taleb devoted his book. Such events can change the course of history in a single stroke.

For you, the reader, this entails a not-so-small degree of uncertainty, leaving you no choice but stay as well-informed as possible. The path we're on is clearly inflationary. But that does not mean you can sit back complacently—and assume blindly—that no one will ever rebel against the trend, that no anti-inflationary changes of course are ever possible.

In the light of the experiences of recent years, it should be abundantly clear, however, that the early warning signs of such a policy shift will not come from heeding the words of the so-called wise men of economics. Neither can sales brochures disguised as research reports produced by Wall Street marketing teams (dubbed "research departments") show you the way. You will have to make the effort to seek the advice of a nearly extinct species—truly independent analysts equipped with sound common sense.

Better yet, you can use your own common sense. You could hardly do worse than the so-called councils of experts of central governments. If the experience of recent years leave some issues in doubt, this is certainly not one of them. That's one trap we trust you will not fall for again.

In early April 2009, for example, alert German readers might have spotted an analysis in the leading German newspaper the *Frankfurter Allgemeine Zeitung,* with the following bold headline: "Investors carefree about inflation. Inflation of 2 to 2.5 percent expected."[13]

This statement was supported by a graph. It showed that inflation forecasts, which had been 2.6 percent in 2004, had fallen below that level in April 2009. At the same time, a detailed report was carried elsewhere about the risk of deflation detected by one of the so-called wise men. But we see no reason to take this deflation forecast any more seriously than the "no recession" forecast from the same wise careerists quoted earlier.

We even expressly warn investors against extrapolating from trends that apparently point toward declining inflation. Yes, commodity price levels could always fall in the short term because of a global recession, but even in that scenario, a path has been clearly set for inflation. Too much focus on short-term price declines is another classic trap into which you should not fall. Be careful: it's the value of your hard-earned money that's at stake.

The problem: you will only know this for sure in a few years. Only time will tell whether our inflation warnings are justified. But by then, it could be too late. If you don't take protective action now, you will have already been caught among the millions of guinea pigs in this great inflation experiment.

The Specter of Deflation?

Consider once again the extreme consequences of deflation, and you will see how unlikely it truly is at this juncture. In a deflationary scenario, the extreme debt burdens that nearly all economies have been shackled with in recent years could no longer be serviced. The excess debt of federal governments, local and state governments, corporations, and households would suddenly loom far larger and more onerous. The economy would sink immediately into a severe depression; social chaos would be rampant. What politician is ready and willing to voluntarily go down this road?

The ultimate dilemma: in theory, debts can of course be paid off. But in practice, as soon as they are, they set off a sharp *decline* in the supply of credit, bringing equally sharp declines in demand, consumption, and prices—in a word, *deflation*.

But right now, and as far as the eye can see, there is an almost universal, deeply entrenched consensus among politicians, their central banks, and their economic advisors that *deflation must not be allowed to occur under any circumstances*.

In other words, they're effectively taking the position that the gigantic debt mountain is *never* to disappear. They want every penny from repaid loans to be rolled back immediately into new loans. They don't want to reduce debt burdens. Quite the contrary, they want to maintain the status quo of the mass indebtedness. They want perpetual refinancing. They want never-ending new lending. They want to perpetuate—and even deepen—the global debt trap.

Of course, for loans to be repaid, somebody has to save. But alas, despite lip service to the contrary, no politician really wants people to save money. They want them to borrow and spend. They don't want debts to be paid down, let alone paid off. And so they proceed to deliberately make savings unattractive, even penalized. They punish savers with nominal interest rates near zero, with inflation-adjusted interest rates *below* zero, and, to add insult to injury, with income taxes levied on those miserable yields.

Meanwhile, they give cheap money and tax incentives to borrowers—even to the point of spurring a mini-boom and bust in home sales by granting new homebuyers tax credits. Result: a mini-boom in U.S. home sales and housing starts through April of 2010, followed by a mini-bust that promptly erased the earlier gains.

The bottom-line questions are:

- Why should anyone in his right mind save in this day and age? Does the government itself ever save? Of course not. Worse, the government deliberately punishes those who do and lavishly rewards those who don't.
- How can they so easily forget that saving is the source of all capital, the engine of economic growth and, ultimately, prosperity itself?

It's all quite simple: The wellspring of wealth creation is abstention from consumption—saving. The money saved finances investment. Good capital investments then produce profits, which, in turn, foster higher levels of consumption.

This is, and always was, the formula for prosperity, the secret of success behind the rise of nations. Those who deviate from it—seeking instead to create wealth out of thin air—will destroy wealth and render societies impoverished. The classic case is quantitative easing.

Quantitative Easing, or "Look Mom, No Hands! We're Printing Money!"

Three of the most powerful central banks in the world—the U.S. Federal Reserve, the Bank of Japan, and the Bank of England—have publicly espoused a policy of *quantitative easing*.

The European Central Bank (ECB) is following a similar path, but differs in that it has still not *publicly* professed this creed; clearly the inhibition level is a little higher in Continental Europe than in the rest of the world. Nevertheless. it is probably only a matter of time before the ECB bureaucrats cross the same monetary frontier.

Most people, unfortunately, don't have the faintest idea of what quantitative easing really means. They do not understand the phrase. They are certainly unaware of its true implications. They probably presume a complex concept that justifies the comparatively high salaries of the central bankers who pursue it.

The term was obviously chosen as an unmitigated euphemism with the exclusive purpose of concealing a simple reality—a truth that would be far easier for people to understand but far more difficult to accept. This is why the term is rarely ever translated into an English that the average American would understand. And in Germany, the press doesn't even bother to translate the English into German. Why should they? If the goal is to conceal the truth, why not do so with a foreign phrase that is even more incomprehensible?

Regardless of the language, what central bankers really mean by quantitative easing is nothing more and nothing less than running the printing presses to create paper money.

And beyond the use of fancy language, what the monetary policy makers in Japan, the United Kingdom, and the United States are really doing is openly and blatantly singing the praises of those printing presses. This is not new. A gifted soloist—U.S. Fed Chairman Ben Bernanke—was the first to raise his voice above the throng, with the now-infamous phrase ". . . the U.S. government has a technology, called a printing press . . . that allows it to produce as many U.S. dollars as it wishes at essentially no cost."[14]

Bernanke left us no doubt that inflation is always feasible in countries with fiat currencies. And he made it abundantly clear to everyone that he's the man to turn that feasibility into actuality.

In principle, a central bank can purchase any security or any commodity. There are, admittedly, a few legal limitations, but they are hardly worth the paper they're printed on.

This unbridled money printing parallels out-of-control federal budget deficits in two ways: first, the urgent goal of financing the federal deficits is one of the key reasons politicians are so quick to unleash the printing presses. And second, like the federal deficits, all forms of principles and promises fall by the wayside just as soon as the need arises.

Consider, for example, the European Stability Pact, which forbade and forswore annual budget deficits higher than 3 percent of GDP. And consider how quickly—and universally—those limits have been shattered, how easily those rules became paper tigers, and how conveniently they were overridden precisely when they were needed the most.

Indeed, as fate would have it, the EU Commission published its forecast for national debt just as we were proofreading this passage for the German edition of this book in May 2009. See for yourself the thoroughly alarming development.

The average national deficits of all 27 EU members was 6 percent in 2009, rising to 7.3 percent in 2010—more than double the caps. And that was *after* averaging in the supposedly more disciplined countries and *before* new weakness in the European economy!

What did the Commission do about this blatant breach of its own hard and fast rules? Did it insist that the agreement be adhered to? No chance! Rather, it moved to reassure its colleagues in the member states with the pronouncement: "The countries concerned need not fear any imminent enforcement proceedings."

Shocking.

Even more shocking, however, has been the rush by the U.S. central bank to buy $1.7 trillion mortgage-backed securities and Treasury bonds, plus hundreds of billions in U.S. government bonds, with other central banks following their lead.

What happens when a central bank buys bonds or other securities? It pays for them, of course. It transfers the money straight into the seller's account.

Where does the central bank get the money? Does it have the money in its coffers or borrow it? Neither! It merely creates the money out of thin air. Science fiction? If it weren't happening before your very eyes, you might certainly think so. But it's fact.

Wouldn't you love to pay for things without having the money—and without ever having to borrow it or pay it back? Wouldn't you like to play with money that did not previously exist? In other words, wouldn't you love to operate your own, personal, legally sanctioned counterfeit money machine? Sounds both fantastic and impossible, doesn't it? Yet, that's precisely what our central banks do.

The Mafia is undoubtedly green with envy.

Why are average citizens like us never allowed to run our own money printing presses? The reason is both obvious and rational: anyone in any economy who takes or seizes ownership of goods without providing something in return is doing nothing less nothing more than *stealing*. But alas, that privilege is reserved for the government, and the handy mechanism by which this is done is provided by the central banks: quantitative easing.

As George Bernard Shaw said, "If the governments devalue the currency in order to betray all creditors, you politely call this procedure *inflation*."

U.S. Central Bankers Have Finally Lost All Inhibitions—The Turning Point

March 18, 2009, marked a turning point in American monetary policy and, therefore, presumably for the global monetary order at whose center the

U.S. dollar still stands. It was on this notable date that the Fed announced it would begin buying longer-term Treasury securities, heralding the direct monetizing of government debt—the final transition to direct inflation of the economy.

Again, exactly what does this mean?

To answer this question, one has to consider it in a meaningful context; in other words, by starting with the original fundamental problem of all governments, whether they enjoy democratic legitimacy or are outright dictatorships. No government can earn money on its own, or create wealth. Rather, it must persuade or coerce its citizens or subjects, by whatever means, to give them money, which they can, in turn, redistribute—either to government officials or to society.

The desire quickly emerges to pay out more money than one has. Most people know this impulse, of course, but, in contrast to governments, they do not have access to the legal means.

What Can a Government Do If It Wants to Spend More than It Has?

Answer, it must get the money by following any of several possible well-trodden paths known around the world and throughout the ages.

1. Tax increases. Government leaders recognize that this path is less popular and brings with it the danger of invoking the resistance, wrath, and rebellion of the population, or, in democracies, elections that kick them out of power.
2. Wars of conquest—unfortunately, a path that has been taken far too often in history, and fortunately, a barbaric form of money creation no longer readily available to Western democracies.
3. Borrowing the money. In earlier times, kings who lived beyond their means went into hock with the banks. Their modern-day successors raise the money on the financial markets. The obvious disadvantage: The loans must be repaid, with interest. The not-so-obvious limitation: ultimately, if debts get out of hand, credit ratings will fall, interest costs will surge, the bond vigilantes will attack, and further borrowing could become impossible.
4. Running the money printing presses. In earlier times, they sometimes tried to skimp on the gold content of coins. Then, with the advent of

paper currency, printing up excess quantities emerged as the new, far more powerful mechanism. And today, the state-sponsored creation of money has been elevated to an even higher high-tech plane—electronic transfers from the bank accounts of central banks to the bank accounts of private-sector institutions.

From Now On the American Government Will Pay with Freshly Printed Money

This fourth pathway is the one the U.S. government pursued in 2009 and 2010—with a vengeance. The U.S. Treasury issues bonds—IOUs—which it hands off to the Federal Reserve Bank. The Federal Reserve, in turn, transfers money to the government's bank account, money that previously did not exist, money that the central bank simply creates in the form of an electronic book entry. Then, the Federal Reserve does the same—in even larger quantities—for government-sponsored (and now government-owned) agencies such as Fannie Mae and Freddie Mac, buying their mortgage-backed securities and other agency bonds.

This newly created money does not represent real wealth. No new goods are created. No new services are rendered. This lack of substance behind the money, however, does not stop the government from using it to pay its bills, meet payroll, or subsidize moribund banks.

So mark March 18, 2009, as a date to remember. It represents a decisive break with previous monetary policy. It's a day that will probably go down in financial history as being every bit as important as August 15, 1971, when Nixon dismantled the system of fixed exchange rates under the postwar Bretton Woods agreement.

Now, here we are, a few decades later, and again the U.S. government has taken a *further*, decisive step along the inflationary road paved by Nixon and others since. The final levees containing inflation have been breached. Brace yourself. And be sure to buy gold.

Importantly, the U.S. Federal Reserve is no trailblazer in taking this step. Japan's central bank took a similar path in the early 1990s. And in the present economic cycle, it was the father of all central banks, the much-venerated Bank of England, that made these methods seem respectable. But because the U.S. Fed has been entrusted with the responsibility for the U.S.

dollar—the world's primary reserve currency since World War II—it's the Fed's transgressions that are, of course, the most decisive ones.

And if you're expecting the European Central Bank (ECB) to stem the flow of paper money, don't hold your breath. ECB bureaucrats have, up to now, always found ways of staying more or less in step with American inflationary targets. No wonder. They are almost all unabashed fans of Alan Greenspan.

Indeed, the best that inflation-fearing Europeans can hope for is that the ECB will be deadlocked, unable to achieve a consensus among its member governments, all of which want to have their say. However, as we've seen, the ECB is no more a bastion of stability than the Fed. And as we've further seen, virtually no central bankers are monetary guardians, but the precise opposite. They collaborate with the most highly indebted nations; they are in cahoots with the inflation mongers.

Even the once-honorable Swiss National Bank has joined their ranks with increasing zeal. How? First, it sold the majority of Switzerland's gold reserves. Then it began to sell its own currency, with the declared aim of weakening it.

In sum, we repeat a fact that you must not forget in the coming years:

Inflation doesn't just happen. It doesn't fall from the skies. Inflation is man-made. It is the result of conscious political decisions.

Is Zimbabwe the True Trailblazer?

As early as 2004, we referred to the role of Zimbabwe as a monetary policy outsider. "Their 'courageous' unconventional (monetary) measures will certainly make the hearts of those vocal groups of unconventional central bankers, particularly in the USA, beat faster,"[15] we wrote.

Since then, that country, the successor to what was once the jewel of the British Crown in Africa, has suffered a breathtaking economic collapse with unbridled hyperinflation. "One thing leads to another" is the most uncommon common denominator we can find to describe the extreme despair and human tragedy that it has wrought.

In February 2009, Zimbabwe, the poster child for nations in decline, knocked nine zeros off its currency, the Zimbabwe dollar. Unfortunately, in a nation where zeros rule—zero responsibility and zero accountability—the government and the central bank continued on their path of destruction, unchallenged.

The governor of Zimbabwe's central bank, who explicitly invokes God's authority for his actions, gave an interview to *Newsweek* magazine in 2009. We would not dare withhold from you the most interesting passage: it expresses succinctly not only the personal view of that country's rampaging autocrats, but also the worldview of most modern central bankers:

> **Question:** "Your critics blame your monetary policies for Zimbabwe's economic problems."

> **Answer:** "I've been condemned by traditional economists who said that printing money is responsible for inflation. Out of the necessity to exist, to ensure my people survive, I had to find myself printing money. I found myself doing extraordinary things that aren't in the textbooks. Then the IMF asked the United States to please print money. I began to see the whole world now in a mode of practicing what they have been saying I should not. I decided that God had been on my side and had come to vindicate me."[16]

European Currency Reform—A Fictional Retrospective on the Expropriation of Savers

From the Reichsmark to the Gold Euro

Few savers of modern times—whether living in the United States or in Germany—were aware that, almost one hundred years ago, on the fourth of August of 1914, another new experiment was conducted on a monetary system: Germany summarily annulled its obligation to exchange its banknotes for gold. From that day forward, German citizens could no longer cash in their paper money for their beloved, reliable gold marks.

Less than 10 years later that same saver would have to pay one trillion— one thousand billion—marks for just one of the former gold marks: in 1923 the German economy had collapsed, and on November 15, 1923, the first German currency reform took place. For one trillion reichsmarks, each citizen received one rentenmark.

June 1948 brought a second currency reform in Germany. The German Bundesbank was founded, and the deutschmark replaced the reichsmark.

The Bundesbank was given nominal independence, meaning it was supposedly not bound by directives from the federal government or other institutions.

Then, although Germany's citizens were comparatively fond of the deutschmark, they had to exchange them *again* in 2001 in accordance with the dictates of still another monetary experiment—the euro.

For citizens of the East Germany, which had fallen into the hands of socialists after World War II, there was still another currency reform. But because of the policies of Helmut Kohl, geared toward his reelection and to which longer-term considerations fell victim, East Germans got off very lightly indeed. Instead of being forced to accept the market price for East German marks, they were able to exchange their "confetti money" for deutschmarks at a preferential rate that was economically absurd.

The European Central Bank, the central bank of the euro zone, was supposedly independent according to law. It did not use its nominal independence, however, to pursue a policy that was truly independent from the demands of the United States. The ECB even managed to trump Alan Greenspan's lax monetary policy: at times, the euro-zone money supply actually grew at an even faster clip than the United States's.

Now let's take a leap of faith and move from fact to fiction: fast forward to August 2014. You are an economic historian of that time, and you write the following report:

As the months go by, the population begins to rebel. They have been rocked from one financial, economic, and currency crisis to another. At first, they watched passively as central banks ran the money printing presses (quantitative easing). But they soon began to lose their patience as the consequences struck—prices first going up at double-digit rates, then *truly* skyrocketing, and ultimately setting off one national labor strike after another, paralyzing the entire economy.

The rapid money supply growth in the United States that began under Alan Greenspan's stewardship in the 1990s accelerated visibly, destroying global confidence in the U.S. dollar, the world's leading reserve currency and the anchor of the global discretionary paper money system (fiat money). Global investors became less and less willing to put their savings into U.S. government securities.

And as soon as the U.S. Treasury tried to lure domestic savers by offering higher interest rates, the resulting credit squeeze triggered a collapse in the global economy, and a depression began. Across the world, both in academic circles and among the policy makers, the reintroduction of monetary stability was suddenly up for discussion. The demand for the introduction of the gold standard (sound money) again became respectable.

It is at this juncture that European governments decided to undertake a *further* experiment to restore the faith of their citizens in the financial system: they created the gold euro. And this new currency ended the 100-year-old experiment with discretionary paper money that began so spectacularly in 1914.

The exchange rate of the gold euro was 1:100. In other words, for one hundred euros you got one gold euro. Only now do economists and historians begin to recognize the profound effect that the earlier retreat from sound money—and the introduction of state-sponsored counterfeiting—has had on the course of history. Only now is there finally a broader understanding of the true toll that inflation has taken on the economy and society.

In Zimbabwe, by 2008, the rate of inflation had reached the unheard-of pace of 65 plus 107 zeros. But in Europe, fears of a Zimbabwe-type outcome—where even veteran mathematicians had trouble keeping track of all the zeros—are ended.

The return to economic reason is complete. With the gold euro, the foundation for sound money, a central demand of classic liberalism, has finally been restored.

Could this really happen? Yes. In fact, in our book *Das Greenspan Dossier: How the US Federal Reserve Jeopardizes the Global Monetary Order,* we pointed out the inevitability of this outcome—the reintroduction of gold. And, at the same time, we made a plea for that reintroduction.

Even some who spoke approvingly of our book found it strange, even regrettable, that we considered this "monetary madness." After all, the great economist John Maynard Keynes himself saw it as a relic of a bygone age, and many economists agreed with Keynes's view that the first global economic crisis was, to a large extent, due to the "draconian constraints" of the gold standard that prevailed at the time.

European central bankers were so eager to sell their gold reserves that an international agreement had to be reached that allocated an annual quota for gold sales to each country, allowing them to exchange their gold reserves for paper money and interest-bearing government securities without having a major impact on the market. Under pressure from the public, however, this policy was reconsidered in Germany as early as 2008 when the German central bank decided *not* to exhaust its selling quota, suspending its gold sales instead.

Astonishingly, the country with the highest gold sales in 2008 was a country that did not belong to the euro zone and whose currency had been regarded as one of the soundest in the world since the end of World War II: Switzerland. It was Switzerland of all countries that topped the list, with 125 metric tons in gold sales. Switzerland's central bankers should write a new textbook to explain their policy to their people. The most apropos title: "How to Ruin the Reputation and Stability of a Currency Previously Regarded as a Global Haven."

It seems interesting to us that the U.S. government has stuck by its policy of *not* selling a single gram of its state-owned gold reserves. This has not prevented it, however, from recommending other countries do precisely that.

But it was the United Kingdom, under Chancellor of the Exchequer Gordon Brown, that gave gold investors the greatest gift imaginable: he sold off half of the United Kingdom's gold reserves at the turn of the century, thereby achieving the remarkable feat of selling when prices were at their lowest. This low point, which marked the end of a 20-year slide, is known among analysts as the "Brown bottom."

Meanwhile, the biggest seller of gold was Russia, while the biggest extractor of gold was China, at 300 metric tons. China does not publish figures on its national gold reserves.

In Germany, a rethinking of monetary policy began in the years 2009 and 2010. At that time, the respected chief economist at Barclays Germany, Thorsten Polleit—along with Guido Hülsmann of the University of Angers, France—were publicly recommending a return to the gold standard, while a similar recommendation was made by Joseph Salerno of the Mises Institute in the United States.

The fact that their recommendation was quoted in the German magazine *Der Spiegel* and the fact that the article bore the title "The Curse of Cheap Money" marked a turning point in public attitudes.[17]

CHAPTER 5

How Could It Have Come to This?

The following quotation is from a speech by St. Louis Fed President William Poole at Truman State University in early 2008. For many years, Poole was a member of the Federal Open Market Committee (FOMC) at the Fed, and was therefore among those we call arsonists of monetary policy.

> I must say that I am a bit troubled that I hear loud claims that the FOMC did not tighten policy enough, and soon enough, in 2004–2005 to choke off the bubble in house prices and unwise lending in the subprime mortgage market, developments that are at the root of today's problems. I do not recall many loud and insistent voices for tighter policy at that time. Policy makers are not clair-voyant. I wish I had seen these unfortunate developments in the housing market in their early stages, but I didn't.[1]

I suppose we must believe Mr. Poole when he says he was too ignorant to recognize the all-too-obvious problems in the U.S. housing market.

But to believe that he was also unable to see the far more significant excesses in the credit markets, a core area of monetary policy, is more difficult. Nonetheless, we must ask: How much of that admitted ignorance is disclosed on the résumés of central bankers, and how much additional ignorance is acquired with years of central bank experience?

In any case, Poole was quite right when he said that monetary policy makers and central bankers are not clairvoyant. It is precisely for this reason that we are confirmed opponents of the state monopoly over money and the whole concept of the central bank. The central bank's Central Committee, manned by individuals of the caliber of Mr. Poole, is entrusted with the daunting task of setting the precise interest rate at any given time for extremely complex modern economies, and then to set that interest rate by decree.

The present authors do not presume to have this uncanny ability. Poole clearly doesn't, either. However, this obviously did not prevent him from joining a committee responsible for state-controlled price-fixing of interest rates. The critical issue here is not the acumen and know-how of one William Poole or any other specific monetary policy maker. It is the theoretical—and practical—impossibility of achieving the task that central bankers pretend to strive for.

It is widely accepted that there is a tried and tested method for determining the appropriate price and properly allocating supply and demand for any good or service—the free market. It's also widely accepted that there is a tried and tested method for utterly ruining an economy—centralized state control. Yet for the most important price of all—the price of money—there is no such recognition.

It is for these simple reasons—reasons even Mr. Poole could probably grasp—that we criticize so sharply the concept of government money price-fixing—manipulating interest rate levels. And it is why we plead so vehemently for free credit markets. Federal Open Market Committee members are as incapable of determining the correct interest rate as Central Committee members are incapable of price-fixing thousands of commodities, goods, or services. All that central bankers really seem to know with certainty is the salaries they are willing to accept to undertake this impossible task. They apparently have little concern for the ultimate price they are willing to make the public pay to help them further their careers.

Richard Fisher, as president of the Federal Reserve Bank of Dallas, is another participant in this monetary price-fixing. According to press reports, he admitted in March 2008 that the Fed had kept interest rates too low for too long. To err is human was the implication, mimicking Poole's earlier admission that monetary policy makers are not clairvoyant. But by the time Fisher confessed this obvious truism, it was far too late. The damage to the economy had long been done—the largest speculative bubble of all time had already burst.

No matter how tardy, any such recognition and appeal for moderation by any central banker can be a welcome ray of hope. But alas, appearances can be deceptive, and Fisher himself promptly offered the following exculpation for the monumental failure for which he was jointly responsible: he insisted that it was very tough to raise interest rates rapidly even when it was necessary to do so.

I beg your pardon. If central banks are truly independent, why on earth should it be so difficult to do what's necessary for the health and stability of the economy? And why is it so much easier to lower interest rates with equal or greater speed even when it is *not* necessary to do so?

From a purely operational point of view, exactly the same levers are pressed to either lower or raise interest rates—levers that Fisher and his colleagues obviously master like virtuosos when they think it's time to cut rates. Clearly, central bank bureaucrats have the power to raise interest rates. It's not the power that's lacking—it's merely the courage to act independently.

In 1979 and the early 1980s, Fed Chairman Paul Volcker showed quite clearly how this works: You let the market determine the appropriate level for interest rates. You allow interest rates to rise to whatever level is necessary to restore balance to the supply and demand for money and credit. And then you let reason return to the global economy, providing a stable environment for growth for years to come.

Unfortunately, however, Volcker's tough policies came with a high price: his term was not extended. The Greenspan era began. And the West embarked on a trajectory that culminated in the biggest economic catastrophe since the Great Depression.

Despite this lightweight connect-the-dots exercise, it seems that some Federal Reserve officials cannot muster the strength to undertake it. Or, they conveniently forget that Volcker ever existed. In a March 4, 2008, speech, Fed governor Frederic Mishkin, for example, said, "There is little the Fed can do to influence the headline inflation rate."

What? The same people doing the most to *create* inflation now maintain that they cannot do much to influence it? Their memory failures are exceeded only by their spineless audacity.

Mishkin goes on to observe that: "the recent observations on core inflation suggest that higher energy costs and the lower exchange value of the dollar may have been sources of upward pressure on core inflation."[2]

Of course. But why it always assumed that rising energy costs and a falling dollar are some kind of extra-terrestrial events? They are not. They are, themselves, also caused by lax monetary policy that's fully within the control of the authorities.

Inflation—in all its aspects—is always a *monetary phenomenon*. Rising prices are the result of inflationary policies, not the cause. Is it really possible to become a central banker without having learned this basic fact? And to remain a central banker while publicly declaring that two plus two equals five?

These official pronouncements are after-the-fact rationalizations by the perpetrators of monetary policy failures—all made even after witnessing the financial catastrophe that those policy failures have caused. They should suffice to demonstrate that everyday political life can hardly be beaten for sheer entertainment value. But it's not a laughing matter. These individuals hold positions of great power. Even now, they have a tremendous influence over the course of economic events. They hold the fate of billions of people in their hands.

We have pointed out again and again that the creation of speculative bubbles through monetary policy is tantamount to playing with fire—an extremely dangerous game guaranteed to end poorly. And now, sure enough, the whole world has been ablaze.

So what is to be done to prevent these arsonists from setting new global fires? They protest their innocence. They play dumb while knowingly continuing down their wayward path. They spill oil on the burning fire, doing everything to increase the money supply and keep short-term interest rates at zero.

The next new weapon in their arsenal: don't be surprised to see them engineer a kind of below-zero interest rates in the form of a cash tax designed to compel citizens to spend their money without delay.

But no matter which bigger guns they come up with, everything points to an all-out war on our society's long-term welfare through the deployment of ever-bigger weapons of mass fiscal and monetary destruction. We live in very unsettling times indeed.

Worse, as often occurs in wars, the gigantic government manipulations and market interventions since the onset of the debt crisis also reveal elements of corrupt favors for old friends. *Daily Reckoning* editor Bill Bonner, known for his insightful and caustic commentary, has coined a perfectly apt term for these processes—*the war on bear markets*. It is none other than the logical extension of the ongoing war against common sense and against the basic rules of serious economics that has been raging for decades—the war in which Alan Greenspan was a leading combatant.

The U.S. government clearly expressed its dissatisfaction with the price level of risky—perhaps even worthless—bonds, real estate, and stocks. So it decided to do something about it. It eschewed half measures. And, in concert with the unconventional monetary policy measures threatened by Bernanke several years ago, the government also launched a series of other unconventional measures.

These measures underscore the truth in Bonner's comments. Their new battle cry—war on bear markets—is, in many respects, so loud and clear, it even drowns out any reverberating echoes from the war on terror.

Yet the similarities with the war on terror are striking: The campaign now underway will cost trillions of dollars. It will prove to be a long-drawn-out enterprise whose consequences are unforeseeable. And it is unlikely to have the desired result. Instead, one can expect any number of unforeseen consequences and side effects.

Bottom line: Get ready for an interesting future, full of surprises.

We commented on the start of the war on terror project in October 2001 as follows: "War economies are inflationary. . . . War economies also entail turning away from free markets." Both observations apply equally to the war on bear markets.[3]

We Are No Clairvoyants, Either

Our readers know us—and not only in matters of monetary policy—as implacable voices in the wilderness. We write relentlessly against the cancer-like growth of the state and adhere steadfastly to classical liberal positions. In doing so, however, we sometimes feel like Don Quixote, tilting at windmills, for over the years we have, unfortunately, succeeded in changing nothing.

Of course, we are no clairvoyants, either, and cannot tell the future. Our forecasts, too, are sometimes prone to error. This makes us relatively modest in our claims and protects us from the hubris that is all too widespread among (monetary) policy makers.

The world is, as everyone knows, a very complex place in which chance also plays a major role. History, which historians like to reconstruct as a logical, even inevitable process is, in fact, a sequence of events greatly influenced by unforeseeable random events and coincidences.

Social systems—and along with them, economic systems—are not, statistically speaking, subject to standard normal distribution. They do not adhere to linear patterns. Rather, again and again, they display major fractures and fissures. They cannot be distilled into computer models. They repeatedly deliver humbling lessons to all those who dare hold themselves out as prognosticators.

The book we mentioned earlier, Nassim Taleb's *The Black Swan,* is entirely devoted to this idea, and to the principle drummed into every student in every elementary course on logic—that it is very risky to extrapolate from the particular to the general. However, few people seem to be receptive to these basic insights.

Instead, mathematically oriented forecasting models have been ubiquitous in the economic sciences. Indeed, it was based on these models that major banks built their modern portfolio theories and risk control strategies—most of which have now failed so spectacularly. After only one and a half years of crisis, they were in ruins. But any hints of fixing what broke are conspicuous by their absence.

True, it is impossible to know the future. But it *is* possible to recognize systems that are obviously flawed or unsustainable over the longer term. Putting this recognition into practice is the alpha and omega of successful stock market trading. Indeed, the famous speculator George Soros, who has, in the meantime, become a fan of regulation, addressed this topic exceptionally well in his underrated book, *The Alchemy of Finance.*

His main argument: The stock market bubble that began to develop from 1995 onward was a classic example of a system that was clearly unsustainable. Based on absurd assumptions by market participants, it was destined to sooner or later collide with reality and shatter into pieces. The real estate bubble that ensued shared the same destiny. The foundation upon which it was built was clearly not sustainable over the long term.

Thus, in both cases, it was easy to predict their unpleasant end and, at least in part, to predict the consequences.

A further, albeit longer-term, example of unsustainable experiments is the fully discretionary global paper money system (fiat money system) that began in 1971. Its unpleasant end is still to come. We consider the probability to be very high that this end will be visited upon us in the coming 5 to 10 years at most. And intertwined with the fiat money system is the ever-increasing level of government debt—a further example of a system that cannot last.

We repeat: one need not be clairvoyant to recognize all of this. Nor must one be an economics professor. Indeed, the latter qualification would appear to be more of a hindrance than an aid to recognizing these negative trends of epic proportions. And topping the list of qualifications needed to achieve this state of blindness would probably be long experience as a policy maker or a central bank bureaucrat.

Moral Hazard, an Invitation to Dance on the Rim of the Volcano

Bernanke's Transformation from Paul to Saul

You have already read earlier in this book how the Federal Reserve promoted what Charles Prince so aptly described as a dance atop the volcano of the financial markets. This set of problems is tackled by central bankers in their soapbox oratory under the rubric of *moral hazard*. Even Ben Bernanke once fancied himself in the role of a responsible monetary policy maker, warning of the dangers of setting a false course toward moral hazard.

Bernanke has addressed this topic publicly on several occasions. He has pointed out that it was not the task of the central bank to protect speculators from the negative consequences of their actions—from losses and, in certain circumstances, from bankruptcy.

On the basis of statements like these, an uninformed observer might well have gotten the entirely false impression of this man's fundamental convictions in relation to monetary policy. Was this really the same man who acquired the nickname "Helicopter Ben" because of his unabashed public praise of the printing press for creating money? Could this be the same person who made the infamous antideflation speech? Had he undergone a transformation from the Saul of monetary policy—the man who said throwing money to the people from helicopters was essentially correct—to a Paul, advocating a return to halfway responsible monetary discipline? After he had secured the goodwill of the powerful through his utterly inflationary speeches and arrived at the helm of the Fed, did he decide to become a second Paul Volcker?

Earlier, Greenspan had undergone a reverse transformation. He began his first term at the Fed espousing free markets and sound money but ended it as the torch bearer of uninhibited opportunism. Was Bernanke now undergoing a similar transformation in reverse? In short, was Bernanke transforming himself from a wanton opportunist to a prudent statesman?

For a short moment in time, Bernanke was almost able to give Fed watchers that impression. But then the initial consequences of the bursting housing bubble became visible, and we saw the first signs of the inevitable credit crunch that it triggered. Suddenly, Bernanke's moral hazard warnings fell swiftly by the wayside. In a knee-jerk reaction to events, he promptly dropped his soapbox oratory and slashed interest rates. Blow by blow over the ensuing months he implemented the very same "unconventional monetary policy measures" he had originally espoused—none other than the uninhibited use of the printing press.

By this point, even among the few naïve enough to believe Bernanke's moral hazard speeches, all illusions were surely shattered. And once again we saw the great wisdom and experience contained in the counsel: "not by your words but by your deeds shall ye be judged." And the message of his deeds is unmistakable, as follows:

> Monetary stability and the value of the dollar do not interest me.
> Nor do I care about what befalls holders of U.S. government bonds.
> The fate of future generations means even less to me.
> Our sole concern at the Fed is our friends on Wall Street who are now in need.

As you can see in Figure 5.1, Bernanke did absolutely the same thing as his predecessor Alan Greenspan. He talked the moral hazard talk but walked the monetary easing walk. He slashed interest rates even lower than Greenspan ever did.

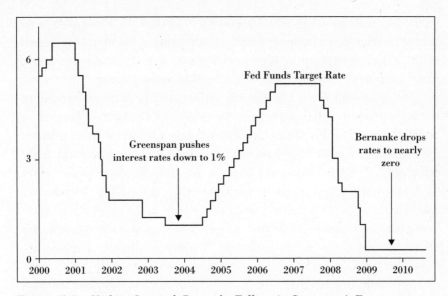

Figure 5.1 Nothing Learned: Bernanke Follows in Greenspan's Footsteps
SOURCE: Federal Reserve.

British Soapbox Oratory

The governor of the Bank of England, Mervyn King, did even better. On October 9 he gave a speech to the Northern Ireland Chamber of Commerce and Industry that clearly rejected the moral hazard policies that had become legendary in the Greenspan era—the "Greenspan put" in which monetary aid was granted for large-scale speculators who had gotten into trouble. The paper contains the lines:

> [T]he provision of such liquidity support undermines the efficient pricing of risk by providing ex post insurance for risky behavior. That encourages excessive risk-taking, and sows the seeds of a future financial crisis.[4]

This unambiguous statement demonstrates that central bankers know only too well what they are doing.

But then, just two days later, the plight of Northern Rock, a major U.K. mortgage bank, became known. For the first time in decades, an incredulous public had the chance to experience—or see on their TV screens—a bona fide run on the bank. Savers, fearful for their deposits, stood in long queues at the bank counters to salvage whatever was left. "*If you panic, panic first,*" goes the concluding sentence of *Das Greenspan Dossier*.

And what did Mr. King and his colleagues do? Without ceremony, the paper quoted earlier headed for the shredder—the fate of all soapbox policies. King and his colleagues immediately proceeded to do exactly the opposite of what they had described in the paper as correct monetary policy. And at least until 2010, it was impossible to deflect them from this path—the very same path that they themselves described as mistaken.

What do we learn from this? Simply that liars and opportunists are ubiquitous—as far as the eye can see. "When a reputation is ruined, it's ruined for good," as the German poet Eugen Roth once said.[5]

And until at least 2010, the Bank of England has followed the path trod by Ben Bernanke with utter consistency, in accordance with the preceding maxim.

Unconventional monetary policy measures and quantitative easing—the unrestricted use of printing presses—are the engines that have driven their policies. And in this case, those policies came with the unrestrained purchases of newly issued gilts—U.K. government bonds—by the Bank of England, paid for with money hot off the electronic printing presses.

It's as simple as that. The government issues a bond, but does not sell it to the public in the open market. Instead another agency of the government, the central bank, comes along and snaps up the bond, paying for it with money that did not previously exist. In short, the government counterfeits the money. Then it uses this newly created money to pay its bills.

This point is too important to avoid repeating: the money does not have to be earned and saved, it is simply created. In this way, the government can obtain goods and services without providing anything in return. If you remove the *newspeak* and use plain English, then it is clear that a type of legalized, government-sanctioned fraud is being committed. Suddenly, much more money is in circulation than before, although the quantity of goods has remained the same.

Why, then, is the printing of money forbidden to everyone except the central bank on pain of severe penalties?

Blackberries of Monetary Policy

Clearly, the "unconventional monetary policy measures" that Ben Bernanke once spoke of only in theory are now being put into practice. But instead of the helicopter—cited originally by Milton Friedman as a metaphor for an extremely lax monetary policy—technical progress today allows for other possibilities, which can go beyond this diffuse form of monetary carpet-bombing.[6]

Consider, for example, the idea of the cash tax, once floated by Irving Fisher and discussed in a Fed strategy paper as an "unconventional measure."[7]

From our perspective, the cash tax equates to the introduction of a kind of *yogurt money*—a product with a use-by expiration date, forcing its holders to spend it as quickly as possible. According to the theory, this increases the speed of money circulation, stimulating the economy and generating inflation.

We wonder: Could Bernanke and Company be considering replacing the helicopter with these new devices? If so, perhaps they should be called monetary Blackberries: every citizen would effectively receive such a device from the government. Perhaps they would have to stand in line at City Hall and pay a fee for it. A central computer would capture all the data and transactions, and the freshly printed money could be paid to the right person in the right place and at the right time, without fear of collateral damage.

These mini-money machines would replace the government consumer vouchers already tested in Japan. And, at the same time, represent a further step along the road to serfdom—on the road to mass surveillance. Far-fetched? Perhaps. But no more far-fetched than the extreme measures taken so far. And not so far-fetched that it does not set the hearts of government inflationists racing.

Bernanke, Geithner, Gross, and President Obama—The Fish Stinks from the Head Down

From the arguments we've presented so far, it should be abundantly evident that the government's monetary and interest rate policies could never pass a simple smell test. And because the fish stinks from the head down, it is worth examining some of the key U.S. decision makers in the current situation a little more closely.

In the final analysis, we are at a dramatic historical turning point—one that may rival the collapse of the Soviet Union in its scale and extent. It therefore cannot do us any harm to look a little closer at some of the most important actors.

Let's begin with Ben Bernanke, who, as Fed chairman, fills, by far, the most important office in regard to economic policy. Right at the apex of the U.S. housing bubble, in the summer of 2006, Bernanke provided some notable and memorable commentary on the processes at work in the housing market. He said that the sharp rise in housing prices merely reflected the economic strength of the United States. And one year later, at the start of the current crisis, the same Ben Bernanke estimated the banking sector's writedown requirement resulting from the crisis would be "up to $100 billion," which turned out to be a mere fraction of the actual total.

Are You Genuinely Clueless or Are You Lying?

Bernanke is regarded as an intellectual heavyweight. But to quote Forrest Gump, "Stupid is as stupid does." Great intellect is no insurance against stupid actions, no guarantee against miscalculations and incorrect forecasts.

Nor does above-average intellect square with Bernanke's statements about the housing bubble. We find it utterly impossible to believe that even halfway sensible people with a rudimentary economic education— not to mention access to one of the biggest research departments in the world—were not in a position to recognize the largest speculative bubble of all time. Central bankers not only have hundreds of economists at their disposal, but they also have access to the most up-to-date macroeconomic statistics in the world. It is simply not conceivable that this giant speculative bubble, so obvious to anyone with eyes to see, could have escaped the notice of the central bank bureaucrats with their incomparable research resources.

There must be another explanation, which boils down to one simple two-word sentence: Bernanke lied.

He lied just as surely as his predecessor, Alan Greenspan, did, as evidenced by minutes of the Federal Open Market Committee.

Why Do They Lie?

The obvious moral of Aesop's "The Boy Who Cried Wolf" is that even when liars tell the truth, they are never believed. But what's not obvious is that the world's leading central bankers are vulnerable to the same fate. The best solution: Stuff your ears with bee's wax to mute their siren songs. Then judge them strictly by their deeds.

Still, this leaves a further, unanswered question: *Why* did Bernanke lie? Was it calculation, opportunism, wishful thinking, or mere character weakness? We have a hard time coming up with a plausible answer; his motives are, of course difficult to discern from the remote position of a Fed watcher.

But in light of his academic career, we can come up with only one possible argument: intellectual vanity. Bernanke built a large part of his academic career on the question of the cause of the Great Depression of the 1930s, and his answer directly contradicts that of the Austrian School. He proceeds from the assumption that the speculative bubble of the 1920s played no significant role, and that the decisive factor was the government's inadequate fiscal and monetary response to the bursting of the bubble.

Instead of clinging to his failed theories, one would at least expect the minimum intellectual integrity to recognize that they failed and to renounce the flawed monetary policies that are predicated upon them. Unfortunately, the opposite is the case. Not swayed by reality, Bernanke continues to pursue the agenda he has expounded again and again in recent years, continually seeking the solution to the problem in the unrestrained use of the money printing presses.

Thus, one of the most powerful positions within the political realm—the chairmanship of the world's most powerful central bank—remains firmly in the hands of someone who, from the perspective of the Austrian school, helped create the foundations of the current crisis and the alarming moral decline of the financial industry.

Yet, at the same time, from the perspective of those in power, Bernanke is the perfect man for this role in these times: from relative obscurity, he vaulted masterfully into the chairmanship of the Fed. And with a speech now legendary among his critics, he drew the attention of the powerful in Washington, staking his claim to high office.

It was November 21, 2002—in the final phase of the bear market and economic weakness triggered by the bursting of the technology bubble.

That was the day he gave the speech we told you about earlier—under the title of "Deflation: Making Sure 'It' Doesn't Happen Here."

This was no soapbox speech. Neither was it everyday monetary policy propaganda. No, the man taking the lectern was a diehard inflationist with a programmatic agenda. Here, for once, plain language was spoken on the nature of monetary policy; the customary cloak of euphemisms, lifted. We've cited it here earlier. Now let's examine it in greater depth:

> But the U.S. government has a technology, called a printing press (or, today, its electronic equivalent), that allows it to produce as many U.S. dollars as it wishes at essentially no cost. . . . We conclude that, under a paper-money system, a determined government can always generate higher spending and hence positive inflation.[8]

With this speech, Bernanke staked out a position as an unrestrained inflationist with a degree of clarity seldom heard. He was, and remains, an expert on the 1930s, and continues to stubbornly advance the position that the misery suffered at that time could have been prevented through the spirited use of the printing press to create money.

What politician could resist songs with such a clear pitch as this one? An academic luminary claims to know the recipe for preventing a nascent global economic crisis. And this recipe entails no bitter medicine for politicians, but rather, the sweet, reality-blurring remedy called *inflation*. What better credentials for promoting your career in policy and for becoming the government's favorite?

But not content with this, Bernanke had another moment of glory on the occasion of Milton Friedman's ninetieth birthday. In this regard, the reader should be aware that Friedman, together with his co-author Anna Schwartz, had postulated the theory that it was too *little* inflation of the economy by the central bank that triggered the Great Depression.

In his speech, Bernanke went as far as to make a promise that, in our opinion, he will someday learn to regret. He uttered the following, very distinctive words:

> I would like to say to Milton and Anna: Regarding the Great Depression, you're right; we did it. We're very sorry. But thanks to you, we won't do it again.[9]

By "we," he meant central bankers.

At the time Bernanke gave this promise, he had already broken it from the perspective of the Austrian School of economics. Remember: this school holds the view that it was the inflationary monetary policies of the 1920s and the speculative bubble that they triggered that were the true causes of the Great Depression—not the monetary policy response to the bursting of the bubble.

But at the end of 2002, the Federal Reserve, to which Bernanke belonged as a governor with voting rights, was already in the process of inflating the economy to an extent never before seen, and blowing up the next speculative boom—the giant housing bubble and the echo bubble in the stock market. The consequences of this entirely deliberate course of action, defended again and again by Bernanke as the answer to virtually everything, have, in the meantime, led to a crisis that has long since been described as the worst since the 1930s.

Our message to Bernanke is simple: We are sorry, but you've done it again. You are the ringleaders, creating the theoretical breeding ground upon which the politics of this catastrophe could thrive. And even now, your intransigence leaves us speechless.

We are sometimes asked what Bernanke *should* do in the light of the situation we now face. The correct—and admittedly oversimplified—answer is this: he could tell the people the bitter truth and announce an immediate change of direction.

The crisis is inevitable no matter what he does. But ultimately, the longer the Fed seeks to prevent it, the longer it will prolong the agony. The only responsible monetary policy—assuming the free-market solution of abolishing the state monopoly over money and the central bank system is unattainable—is *not* to inflate the economy. Rather, it is simply to control the supply of money and credit by letting the market determine the correct level of interest rates, as Fed Chairman Paul Volcker demonstrated in 1980. Unfortunately this will not gain you many friends in the short term, certainly not among politicians. What's a person to do, if he wants to become the darling of the people and of the powerful?

Timothy F. Geithner Caused the Crisis, Too

America's central bankers are the fathers of the speculative bubble of recent years in regard to monetary policy, and therefore, also of the consequences when it burst. We cannot stress this extremely important point too often, as it is consistently absent from a media that are generally supportive of Washington and Wall Street. The main perpetrator, Alan Greenspan, is already in retirement, and can leave to historians to determine what the verdict should be about his legacy—the assessments of his few contemporary critics or those of his vast army of disciples.

More to the point, many of his followers are not yet in retirement. They are still in exalted positions. Case in point: U.S. Treasury Secretary Timothy F. Geithner. In October of 2003, Geithner became president of the Federal Reserve Bank of New York, the branch directly responsible for the Fed's all-important open market operations. He was also vice president of the Federal Open Market Committee, the Federal Reserve's primary decision-making committee. Thus, Geithner played a pivotal role in the bubbles, and in the murky, extremely questionable rescues of its primary casualties—Bear Stearns and AIG. Now this man is Treasury secretary in the Obama administration. Is this cause for optimism?

Bill Gross Calls on the Government to Guarantee Rising Bond Prices

A very different man is also worthy of mention in this context: Bill Gross, managing director of Pimco, one of the world's largest fixed-income fund families. He is no policy maker, but he and his employer have been major opinion leaders.

His analyses of the capital markets have always interesting and informative. During the long boom years of the past, he was a committed defender of relatively free markets, accurately describing the otherwise taboo topics of the government's money monopoly and central banking system. At the same time, however, he has also been a toothless critic within the system, never questioning the frontiers that system prescribed for itself—even when the sinister excesses and misuse of this system were almost impossible to overlook.

Moreover, as the debt crisis evolved, Gross deviated further and further from the course he had held before the crisis. From our perspective, he reached his nadir of reason in his monthly "Investment Outlook" of February 2009. In it, he actually called upon the government to prevent the market from finding a price for specific investments, and instead to effectively *guarantee* rising prices. He specifically mentioned municipal bonds, commercial mortgage-backed securities (CMBS), and corporate bonds. We quote:

> [T]hey should recognize that supporting critical asset prices such as municipal bonds, CMBS, and even investment grade corporate bonds is a necessary step towards eventual economic revival.[10]

A financial expert of this caliber, who has so much to thank capitalism and the free market for, should know that, from a free market perspective, it is both damaging—and utter madness—to artificially support prices. He should know that anyone seeking to prevent the market from determining prices will simply delay needed market corrections. The price signals emanating from the market are the decisive mechanism promoting an efficient economic system. As long as no one knows who holds which securities and what price can be obtained for them on freely operating markets, confidence cannot be restored to the financial markets in any sustainable manner. The market's unforgiving value determinations are an absolutely essential precondition for a healthy market, including true assessments of the financial health of all players. Why should we trust our money to someone who's afraid of the market's judgment of its creditworthiness?

When banks go bankrupt and are no longer creditworthy, we must accept this fact and replace those institutions with others as painlessly as possible. Remember: not every bank participated in the dangerous madness that led to trillion-dollar losses. There were also prudent bankers who did nothing of the kind.

If anything, the government's role should be strictly to assist in facilitating a trouble-free transfer of the business—from those institutions driven to bankruptcy by incompetence, greed, and miscalculation to those whose managers have made more prudent decisions. The cloaking and concealment of the truth through price fixing by the government is utterly unjust and sends entirely the wrong signals. It rewards the bad and penalizes the good. It prevents a performance-related correction process and merely delays the inevitable adjustments.

As we said, we greatly value Mr. Gross's work. But we have selected him here as a particularly prominent example of a very misleading public discourse about a crisis, which, in itself, has gone entirely astray. Our criticism applies exclusively to his published appeals to the government to prevent a free-market solution to the crisis. But, in those appeals, Gross is representative of an attitude that prevails in the media, in Washington, and even on Wall Street.

Barack Obama Berates the Equity Markets

No one knows how Obama's policies will change in the time remaining in his presidency. But we do know this: despite growing resistance from Congress, he and his administration have run up, by far, the biggest deficits and accrued the largest debts in American history, other than during major world wars.

What can we expect from him next? We can only judge based on what he has given us so far: at each stage of this crisis, aggressive government intervention has been the first, immediate, knee-jerk response—to rescue failing auto manufacturers, to prop up housing markets, to use Fannie Mae and Freddie Mac as instruments of the state to manipulate mortgage markets, to extend unemployment benefits, and more.

Further, Obama has repeatedly given us very important indications of his fundamental economic convictions: when the equity markets responded to his economic stimulus package with heavy share price losses, he could do little more than indulge in market-bashing. When markets responded negatively to other policy initiatives, speculators and short-sellers were blamed.

In this we see an important indicator of Obama's fundamental view of the world—or at least an indicator of a limited respect for free market mechanisms—a mechanism that will ultimately obey its own laws and not be influenced by official pronouncements. Sooner or later, the markets will administer a harsh lesson and teach some humility to those who fail to grasp this fact. Markets give no quarter. Entirely unemotionally and with no regard for the individual, they find the right price—even when the most powerful man in the world considers that price to be incorrect.

These Men Are Supposed to Save the World?

So there you have it: Three men who are fully committed—politically, financially, and personally—to perpetuating the global debt trap at virtually any cost. With the preceding anecdotal comments, we hope we have succeeded in making clear that, despite their experience and intellect, they have neither the means nor the caliber to extricate us from the global debt trap without serious pain. They all adhere to the false doctrine that presumes the ability to prevent the inevitable—to sidestep the consequences of the debt trap simply through government intervention and money printing.

Instead, we fear that their obstinate adherence to failed methods and false theories ensure that the current crisis will worsen—so much so that it would justify a comparison with the collapse of the Soviet Union. We hope for the best. But for the sake of prudence and the protection of our families, we must also prepare for the worst.

It gives us no pleasure to see our contemporaries lose their money or their jobs through their faith in false financial prophets. More than ever, our greatest concern is for the future of our children and grandchildren. We draw heavy criticism for our views. Yet it is through precisely these no-punches-pulled warnings—the ones that draw the most venom—that we have helped prepare many of our readers for these catastrophes. They are not ensnared in the global debt trap. They have not been among those making bad investments and holding unrealistic expectations.

Needless to say, however, it's an understatement that, as bearers of bad news, we are not always welcome everywhere. Regrettably, the victim's scorn is not always directed against the perpetrators. We hope, through this book, to make a further contribution to directing that scorn and contempt toward those who truly deserve it.

Merkel, Köhler, Steinbrück, and Others: A Sobering Look at Germany's Saviors of the World

Government Experiments

We still don't know exactly what Barack Obama stands for. He may not find out himself until the next wave of the debt crisis strikes. But do we know any more about what physicist Dr. Angela Merkel stands for? After many years as Germany's chancellor, she remains an astonishingly blank political canvas. In recent years, she has focused on areas that allow her to present herself as a do-gooder and world savior; and this strategy has allowed her to largely evade day-to-day political decision making.

She is a leader of a grand coalition of tax raisers. She is the mother of the greatest tax increase in the history of the German Federal Republic, following the rise in the value added tax: Mrs. Merkel has "blessed" Germany—a country which had long suffered an unbearable tax burden—with an *additional* massive tax increase. This must go down in history as her greatest political achievement. Measured by her actions, Merkel therefore stands for higher taxes. Period. This will probably be her government's most significant—and saddest—legacy.

Perhaps one should view this massive tax increase as a logical progression from Merkel's previous activities and successes. Before the reunification of Germany, Angela Merkel was secretary for Agitation and Propaganda at the Academy of Sciences in East Berlin. According to her own assertions, she was a "cultural representative." In 1990, she made the seamless transition to a similar role, this time as undersecretary in the Federal Press and Information Office, the West German euphemism for an essentially similar, albeit less extreme, agenda—agitation and propaganda.

That she is no more up to the job of handling the crisis than her coalition partners is beyond question in our view. The speed at which her grand coalition has thrown all principles of budgetary policy out the window is as breathtaking as their handling of the banking crisis, which trampled virtually all free market rules. Money suddenly seems to have no meaning any more. But thanks to a new law that mandates new savings targets, everything is supposedly going to be better *after* 2020. Let that one melt on the tongue—"after 2020"!

What value can this law possibly have? It conjures the image of an advanced stage alcoholic who swears by his latest New Year's resolution—never to touch a drop after 2020. He may even achieve this goal—simply because he may never live to see the day.

The reality: any laws defining savings targets that do *not* go into effect for many years hence are not worth the paper they're printed on. Everyone knows this. But our politicians can do no better than make hollow promises about the future that will not, of course, fall on them to implement, but to their unknown successors.

It is the theater of the absurd at its finest. With it, we careen down the road to serfdom at an ever-faster pace. Soon we will be able to predict, with greater precision, when East German conditions will arrive in today's Germany. Based on the developments under Mrs. Merkel's stewardship, we are tempted to describe her as the cynically planned revenge of Erich Honecker and the old East Germany.

The German President and the Monster

In summer 2008, no less a personage than the German president, Horst Köhler, was given the task of propagating his version of the credit crunch among the people. As we have come to expect from politicians, he did not address the origins of the crisis in monetary policy, but joined in the populist search for scapegoats.

Of course, one can rightly point out that Germany has had to endure far worse presidents than Horst Köhler. He was very much the one-eyed king in the valley of the blind. He can hardly be mistaken, however, for a defender of free markets. Certainly not with his résumé!

Horst Köhler was not just any old-guard bureaucrat. An economist by training, he moved on a fast track toward the lofty heights of the bureaucracy. From secretary of the Ministry of Finance, he became president of the German association of savings banks, and then president of the European Bank for Reconstruction and Development—all at a time when Europe had long been fully reconstructed and enjoyed an enviable level of development.

His next post was managing director and chairman of the executive board of the International Monetary Fund (IMF). The IMF is an institution that promotes the theory and practice of government control over the economy around the world, in particular the notion of the state monopoly of money. Through the sale of its gold reserves, it clearly demonstrates what type of organization it is.

This is the man who was Germany's president for six years, from July 2004 until May 31, 2010.

During one of his many public appearances, Herr Köhler offered the following insights into the debt crisis, inspired by none other than a trip to the zoo.

It must by now have become clear to every responsible-minded person in the industry that the international financial markets have become a monster, a monster that must now be caged.[11]

There followed a list of demands that can only be characterized as the knee-jerk response typical of politicians and bureaucrats: more and tougher *regulation*. Of course, the only rational demand would have been to delve in to—and combat—the true origins of the crisis. But that, as we know, is not the tried and tested route of government bureaucracies. Instead, these perpetually seek to expand their size and scope—more laws, more regulations, more supranational bureaucracies, more ministries and departments, more civil servants—all at the taxpayer's expense of course. Yes, there it is again: the road to serfdom—the road that most politicians and bureaucrats seem to find in their sleep, that preserve jobs in the short term, but leads to catastrophe in the long term.

Returning to Köhler's "monster," let's give him the benefit of the doubt and see today's financial markets from his perspective—as a monster. If that's the case, then what about those whom Köhler termed "responsible-thinking" people who profited from the monstrous growth? Did they not grasp the nature of what they were dealing with? Instead of viewing it as a monster, why did they see it as a unique opportunity to line their pockets with practically no risk?

How, then, should one describe the period before the great crisis? Instead of viewing it as a monster, it must be viewed as the biggest bank heist of all time, albeit a legally sanctioned one. All the actors, whether responsible or irresponsible, behaved not only legally within the rules laid down for them by the central banks and other supervisory authorities, but, from their perspective, they also behaved rationally in nearly all respects.

Quite simply, they attempted to maximize their personal benefits within the applicable rules. Whom can we blame for that? Every decision maker in the world of the government-protected banking cartels—whether forward-thinking or not—was exposed to practically irresistible incentives to take ever-greater risks with other people's money. The central banks had made it clear to them again and again, in unmistakable terms, that when the chips were down, they could rely on the government for bailouts. Who could resist an offer like that?

Charles Prince, former CEO of Citibank, vividly expressed this very important point just a few weeks before the onset of the crisis. On July 9, 2007, he uttered a few sentences in an interview that will probably make him immortal in the history of the financial markets—presumably for reasons other than those he had imagined. He said:

> When the music stops, in terms of liquidity, things will be complicated. But as long as the music is playing, you've got to get up and dance. We're still dancing.[12]

At that time, Citibank shares were trading at $51.60. By the end of February 2009 they had fallen to $1.40, and the U.S. government owned 36 percent of the bank. In other words, the frenzied dancer Prince, who had since been fired, had helped ruin the biggest bank in the world. And in the process, he himself became a millionaire one hundred times over. Many of his colleagues did the same, though seldom to the same outrageous degree.

In Figure 5.2, you can see the stock chart of Citibank since 2006. The arrow shows when Charles Prince, then CEO of Citibank, told the public that he deemed dancing on the rim of a volcano to be a good thing. His aptitude to do this risky dance de facto bankrupted his bank—but not him, of course.

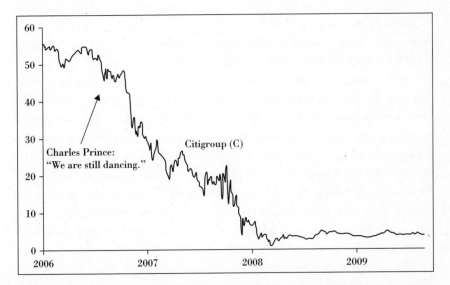

Figure 5.2   Charles Prince's Last Dance as Citibank CEO (Citigroup Stock Price)

With the preceding quote, Mr. Prince put the rules of the game in a nutshell, rules that every thinking participant—whether responsible or otherwise—knew inside out: the incentive to take part in the high-wire, leveraged dance on the rim of the financial volcano was huge. It was actively promoted by central bankers following the bursting of the stock market bubble in the year 2000, and made irresistibly attractive. As long as the bets turned out good, billions could flow into the pockets of the wildest of dancers. And even if the bets backfired, they could still count on billion-dollar settlements and central bank rescues. What about the losses? The dancers seemed to have little concern there, either. Any losses fell on the shoulders of shareholders, especially hapless average investors, and ultimately, the taxpayers as well.

One question remains open, however: What sort of music drove Germany's regional state banks—along with its building and loan associations—to *their* wild dances? We are unable to discern monetary incentives in Germany that are so ubiquitous in the United States. Nor can we see what drives state bankers. Perhaps the Olympian spirit reigns in bureaucratic circles—it's all about participating, even if there is little or no chance of winning.

Once again: it was the central bankers and their political masters that facilitated and promoted the attitude laid bare so publicly by Prince. Again and again, they offered a redemptive hand to speculators disguised as bankers, and from 1998 onward, even to high-risk funds.

Obvious signs of great moral hazard, so disastrous in the long term, were, as in the United States, always defended with the argument that they were necessary to prevent much worse from occurring. And this flawed incentive was entirely understood by all participants. The topic was discussed within the universities as it was within the central banks. And whether the band leaders were Bernanke at the Fed or King at the Bank of England, they repeatedly and specifically said, in their official pronouncements, that they must do everything to *avoid* the moral hazard. Once again, the biblical adage applies: "Ye shall know them by their fruits." In other words, judge them not by their words, but by their deeds!

Of all people, is it conceivable that former German president Horst Köhler failed to comprehend these simple relationships? In any case, he deliberately skated over them when filing his defense, and presented the populist and demagogic demand that the monster be caged with new laws and regulations.

At the same time, it is clear that this short-sighted appeal for a strong government cannot achieve the desired result as long as the Frankenstein monster makers themselves are allowed to continue to run amok, unhindered.

Western governments and their institutions—particularly their monopoly over paper money and their central banks—bear direct responsibility for this economic disaster of epoch dimensions. So it should come as no surprise that the servants of those same governments are now attempting to divert attention with vivid images and easy scapegoats. That tactic lays the groundwork for still further laws and even more government.

The sequence of events is clear: first, the government creates the institutions that produce the enormous problems. Then it creates new institutions to solve these very problems—a vicious cycle. There it is again, Hayek's road to serfdom, which can now be traveled even more quickly in the wake of a crisis caused by the government in the first place.

"Top Economists" Applaud

Consider this news headline in the wake of the government's giant rescue package for sinking economies: "Top economists hail the rescue package, saying 'resolute government intervention required.'"

It does not matter precisely to whom the headline refers. It could be almost any contemporary economist with a media presence or active in policy advice. What is important in this report is that none of those named, not a single one, saw the crisis coming.

It should logically follow that if someone is unable to recognize the obvious signs of an impending crisis, then he is also likely to lack an understanding of its origins—particularly the monetary forces that ruined the financial system and triggered the worst crisis since the 1930s. Nevertheless, the journalists maintain that they are top economists. What qualifies someone as a top economist in those journalists' eyes? A professorship? A job as a policy advisor in the bureaucracy or a central bank?

We find it striking that all of the major figures referred to in this article have been conspicuous for their ignorance and miscalculation both before and during the crisis. Yet they praise the various rescue packages in unison and demand the resolute intervention of the government. On what basis are these demands made?

What predestines the luminaries to be able to appraise the situation better now than they could before and during the crisis? How can they fathom the consequences of the rescue packages when they were unable to recognize the causes of the crisis?

Why don't otherwise critical journalists also raise these questions? And why don't they cast at least some doubt on the pronouncements of these top economists?

We regard this public spectacle—along with the mendacious treatment of the crisis—at times with amusement, but always with grave concern.

Politics Can Seriously Damage Your Finances, Your Health and, in Extreme Cases, Our Democracy

Fiscal Enabling Acts

Science has proven that smoking is bad for your health. And anyone who has somehow not yet gotten the message can read it on every pack of cigarettes.

Yet history also has proven that too much power in the hands of the government can be fatal to the financial health of its citizens. But there are no such warnings on thousands of investments that fall victim to the booms and busts that government creates. And there are certainly none that warn you about the perils of the government's monopoly itself.

If this crisis—and the entire twentieth century—taught us nothing else, it's the perils of excessive power in the hands of government. But with modern propaganda—including the government's monopoly on education— our leaders have so far succeeded in consigning this simple truth to near obscurity. The growing size and power of the government is less and less frequently viewed as a threat to the individual. Instead, the government's oversized role has been repackaged and marketed as a benign fatherly function—our savior from cradle to grave.

In Germany, the cancer-like growth of government has gained greatly in momentum in recent years, particularly since the reunification of West and East Germany. Plus, the EU bureaucracy also continues to grow unabated, still another layer of government power.

Even in the United States, which traditionally benefits the most from free markets, every crisis is promptly used as an excuse to further strengthen or expand the role of government.

Indeed, the global debt trap—and the series of crises it has engendered—has opened the door to government intervention in America that a short while ago would have been unthinkable. The enormous sums that the government is pouring into the economy—plus the manner in which these new laws have been fast-tracked through the U.S. Congress—must surely give cause for grave alarm. Yet, many people still seem to be unaware of the grand scope of this drastic expansion of government power.

Yes, in the United States in particular, there are vocal critics, with some echoes of those critics in Europe. However, they have so far been unable to alter the course of events. On October 3, 2008, they were unable to stop then-President Bush from signing the Troubled Asset Relief Program (TARP) into law, giving the U.S. government virtually a blank check to bail out not just banks but almost any corporation. And 137 days later, they could not stop President Obama from signing the American Recovery and Reinvestment Act, by far the largest government stimulus package in history, again granting broad powers to the government to intervene in the economy. Nor could they do anything about a series of similar interventions and rescues by the United Kingdom and the European Union.

Later, in 2010, when Greece was near bankruptcy, there were some feeble European attempts to resist intervention, but all resistance was overwhelmed by the bailout bulldozer: on May 2, 2010, euro zone countries and the IMF agreed to a $150 billion loan for Greece plus, seven days later, a $1 trillion European Financial Stability Facility. Each of these measures merely plunged governments deeper into the global debt trap and gave them license to intervene more broadly in their economies.

Each of these are what we call *fiscal enabling acts*.

What's most shocking to us is how quickly governments can override popular concerns to pass these new laws and then, as soon as they become a fait accompli, how readily those popular concerns seem to fade.

What both leaders and followers seem to forget is that there were no fewer than three Enabling Acts in Germany during the crisis years of 1919 to 1924, through which the German Reichstag ceded power to the German government for "a limited period of time." These efforts were not exactly a ringing success, but they were important milestones along the road to dictatorship and into the abyss.

The endpoint of these legislative initiatives was the Enabling Act of March 23, 1933, the "Law to Remedy the Distress of the People and the

Empire," which established the Nazi dictatorship. In common with many other laws and state interventions in the natural course of events, this law achieved the precise opposite of what its name suggested.

Keep this important historical precedent in mind when assessing the many fiscal policy initiatives and enabling acts that have already been passed in response to the debt crisis—not to mention those which remain to be passed in the future. Laws on the promotion of welfare or the relief of distress are generally just as ineffective as the use of the printing press to create money. If this were not the case, then every country in the world would have passed similar legislation long ago. And Zimbabwe would be the richest country on the planet.

The Supplementary Financial Market Stabilization Act—The Road to Arbitrary Expropriation

In Germany, we call our Supplementary Financial Market Stabilization Act the *Finanzmarktstabilisierungsergänzungsgesetz.*

Try saying that. If you can, you will get an excellent phonetic impression of what is to be expected from federal governments.

Nonetheless, we still live in a democracy (barely), where at least laws have to be passed to allow the state to plow ahead with its massive interventions. The text of these laws is publicly available, so you can find out what is coming your way. And these laws all have names like the Supplementary Financial Market Stabilization Act, which serve to conceal the lawmakers' malicious intent in a thoroughly Orwellian manner.

Finanzmarktstabilisierungsergänzungsgesetz is not only a verbal monstrosity, which in its own way shows how bad things have gotten in the land of Goethe and Schiller, it's also monstrous in its content. It is a Frankenstein that breaks through a critical barrier that was supposed to protect citizens from the over-reaching hand of government. It is a law that tramples property, and therefore freedom. It is a breach in a dam that can and will serve as a model for future government attacks on property rights.

The unvarnished name of this law should be "The Expropriation Act." Read for yourself the sorry highlights of this bill in their original form, and you will see how Germany's "grand coalition" of tax raisers and debt creators handle property rights. . . .

Article 3. Act on the Rescue of Enterprises to Stabilize the Financial Market (Rescue Takeover Act)

Section 1. Expropriation to Safeguard Financial Market Stability. (1) To safeguard financial market stability, expropriations may be performed in accordance with this Act. . . .

Section 2. Act of Expropriation. (1) The expropriation shall be effected by issue of an Ordinance of the Federal Government without the consent of the Bundesrat [Federal Council]. . . .

Section 3. Procedure. (1) The Federal Ministry of Finance, as the expropriation authority, shall be responsible for the implementation of the expropriation procedure. . . .

Section 4. Compensation. (1) Compensation shall be paid for the expropriation. Any person whose right is prejudiced by the expropriation and thereby suffers pecuniary prejudice may demand compensation. . . . (3) The compensation shall be based on the current market value of the expropriated object. . . . The administrative bodies of the enterprise concerned shall be obliged to provide the expropriation authority with the documents necessary to determine the value of the enterprise and to provide information. . . .

Section 5. Legal Protection. (1) Upon application, the Federal Administrative Court shall rule in the first and last instance on the validity of ordinances under Section 2. . . .

The government supposedly expropriates "only for the benefit of the public," of course. But look again at the precise terms used: *expropriation, act of expropriation, expropriation procedure,* and *expropriation authority* are terms that require no further explanation. The government expropriates, and, in the process, maintains that it is preventing greater harm to the general public. Yet, the veracity of the latter point is subject to no public scrutiny.

All under the rubric of "ensuring the stability of the financial markets"! All a result of the global debt trap that the governments themselves helped create in the first place!

But what exactly is this "financial market stability" that is supposed to be secured through expropriation? And what will prevent the government's claim to "secure the stability of the financial markets" to be used as a rationale for just about any attack on property rights? It is here that we can see the great danger of this unprecedented law.

Who or What Truly Threatens the Stability of the Financial Markets?

Based on the underlying logic of this act, virtually anything could be deemed a threat to the stability of the financial markets. Take rising interest rates, for example. A spike in interest rates would certainly have dramatic negative consequences in an absurdly overindebted society. So doesn't that mean that expropriations would again be required?

Rising commodity or precious metal prices could also be viewed as a threat to the stability of the financial markets—even a threat to social harmony. And there again, the government could use it to justify expropriations.

By definition, falling stock prices also undermine financial market stability, don't they? Does that also lead to more expropriations?

And what about analysts or authors who rail against these laws, seeking to protect their readers from the worst consequences of government insanity? Do they also threaten the stability of financial markets? What might their fate turn out to be? Indeed, wasn't a German finance minister who accused economists of causing great damage with their talk of a crisis? Perhaps we, ourselves, as authors of *Das Greenspan Dossier*, are also to blame for the crisis, from the government's point of view? Will more politicians use its critics as handy scapegoats to divert attention from their own responsibility? Is it becoming all too easy to hold short-sellers, bears, and other critics responsible for the collapsing stability of the financial markets? And what or who will prevent the concept of expropriation from spilling over into the realm of ideas?

Why You Should Be Afraid of This Government

This is why the new German law scares us. In recent months and years we have always stated—clearly and unambiguously—who we believe actually threatens the stability of the financial markets. It is, without doubt, the government deploying its monopoly over money and its central banks. But this simple truth almost never appears in public discussion. Coincidence?

Compared to what it could soon become, the crises flowing from the global debt trap are still comparatively minor, and already the new laws have broken in to dangerous new ground. Ironically, however, governments around the world are doing everything possible—and we mean *everything*—to transform the global debt trap into an even larger disaster. And to the degree that the government interventions succeed in the short term—creating a false boom with more speculative bubbles in stocks, commodities, or emerging markets—they will transform it into a massive crisis of truly epoch proportions.

The German expropriation act has the potential to go down in history as a milestone along the road to serfdom already embarked upon. And remember: the German people are not traveling this road for the first time. Be afraid. History proves that terrible laws are often the precursor to terrible times.

The Rats Abandon the Sinking Ship

From the late 1990s until the onset of the housing bust, Federal Reserve Chairman Alan Greenspan enjoyed a reputation as an infallible maestro, and his fan club was huge. He was even regarded as a messiah of monetary policy by people who could and should have known better. Only a small minority remained immune to this rare form of mass indoctrination.

A key figure among the indoctrinated was former U.S. Treasury Secretary Paul O'Neill, who, on September 17, 2001, commented on the interest rate reduction just announced by the Fed with a sentence bristling with stupidity: "Greenspan always does the right thing."[13]

At the time, Greenspan critics were few and far between, and our forecast—that Greenspan's policies would lead to catastrophe and that he would go down in history as one of the worst central bankers of all time—was largely ridiculed.

But times change, and with them the thought processes of large numbers of people. Slowly at first, then with increasing momentum, the fog of mass delusion clears. In Greenspan's case, this process did not begin until his retirement, and then only very tentatively.

A turning point of sorts was marked by an article that appeared on August 8, 2007, authored by economist and Nobel Prize winner Joseph Stiglitz. Stiglitz was an economic advisor to the Clinton administration and chief economist at the World Bank. As such, he has naturally adopted positions on economics and monetary policy that we do not share. From our point of view, he belongs to the overwhelming majority of Keynesian economists who dominate in the universities, politics, policy advice, and the mass media. Thus, we believe that his views can be a good bellwether for following changes in the consensus view on economic policy—clearly definable fashion trends, which politicians closely follow in order to represent opinions most likely to command a majority following.

In Stiglitz's August 2007 article, bearing the headline "America's Day of Reckoning," he suddenly begins to adopt relatively critical positions in relation to monetary policy—positions that begin to approach ours. The main problem: the period the professor criticizes does not begin until 2001, which is far too late. One must go back much further to properly explain the global debt trap and all of the current difficulties it is causing. But Stiglitz's own past stands in the way, for until 1999 he was a member of President's Clinton's Council of Economic Advisors. If, during this period, he uttered even the hint of criticism for Greenspan's policies or issued even faint warnings about the huge speculative bubbles it was creating, we would be quite surprised. Certainly, no such commentary has made it into the public domain.

But now, starting in the summer of 2007, the time appeared ripe for economists of his ilk to start publishing critical opinions about Greenspan's work. After all, by this time he no longer held any public office. We fully share Stiglitz's conclusion, even if we cannot condone his long period of silence and complicity. He writes:

> There is an old adage about how people's mistakes continue to live long after they are gone. That is certainly true of Greenspan.[14]

And we ask: Where were you, Mr. Stiglitz, when these mistakes could still have been corrected?

Fast forward to today, and not surprisingly, here's what we discover: *In surveys asking respondents to name the principal guilty parties behind the debt crisis, Greenspan now ranks among the leaders.*

Our response:

> We demand the ultimate "Cash for Clunkers" program. But not for cars! For central bankers and politicians!

After all that has been said up until now, it is absolutely clear that the global debt trap—and the long chain of linked crises it has created—is not the result of a failure of the markets, however construed. It is the result of monumental failures of monetary policy.

Despite any propaganda to the contrary, there can be no doubt about this simple truth. How, then, could all the government rescue measures so far, none of which address the cause of the problem, possibly achieve the hoped-for effects? And how is a repeat of this sad and dangerous crisis to be avoided?

Simply put, the entirely false political maxim for handling the crisis reads, "The market has failed, so all kinds of political interventions in the market must now be enacted."

And behind this public hogwash is the credo, albeit never publicly stated, which goes like this: "Losses caused by grossly imprudent decisions by banks, insurers, and other companies not need be borne—as originally envisaged and provided for in law—by those who consciously took those risks. Rather, they are the responsibility of the disinterested general public."

You, dear reader, along with your children and your neighbors—citizens who had no direct involvement, who did not assume the risks, who may have even been among those warning *against* those risks—are asked to foot the bill instead. The fact that, despite this scandalous injustice, the population is *not* rising up in revolt is an unfortunate miracle—and leads us to doubt the workings of society's fourth base of influence, the press.

From our point of view, this gross injustice, an injustice that represents a further step along the road to serfdom as it tramples the principles of the market economy, can only be brought to an end by radical means. We call it the ultimate Cash for Clunkers program—for central bankers and politicians.

In the United States, owners of older, supposedly less fuel efficient, cars were given a cash incentive to trade them in for new cars with better fuel efficiency. In Germany, car owners were offered an even bigger incentive—a 2,500 euro "scrappage premium" to trash any car nine years or older.

Now, what we need is a similar program for scrapping central bankers, politicians, and large swaths of the government bureaucracy, but *without* any obligation to purchase replacements.

All joking aside, in others words, if incentives are the game of choice, then any such incentives must be geared toward the reintroduction of the market forces in the economy.

What we need to create prosperity and put the crisis behind us is not more government, more laws, more regulations, more politicians, more secretaries of state, more bureaucrats, more central bankers, more subsidies, or more rescue programs (which merely rescue the politicians that create them). No. These merely plunge us more deeply into the global debt trap or a subsequent inflation trap.

What we need is precisely the opposite—less government, fewer laws, fewer regulations, fewer politicians, fewer secretaries of state, fewer bureaucrats, fewer central bankers (ideally none), fewer subsidies, fewer rescue programs, less debt, and less inflation.

We need to return to the kind of liberal, free market principles that, for example, helped turn West Germany, devastated by World War II, into a land of economic miracles. We need to refocus on the notion that prosperity is created by companies and their employees, not by politicians and their central bankers. They can only redistribute wealth created by others, either openly through taxation and appropriation or more furtively through inflation.

If we want companies to continue to create prosperity, then we must permit an economic system that follows the rules of successful business; in other words, free market rules. Within this framework, the regulatory power of the state monitors and enforces adherence to those free market rules.

At the present time, however, Germany is regrettably in the process of transforming what was once an economic miracle into a eurocratic, performance-inhibiting, socialist country. And, unfortunately, other major Western powers, including the United States, are following a similar path.

As Figure 5.3 shows, one of the last growth industries left seems to be the state. Laws, regulations, rulings, and other legal actions are growing like weeds. Unfortunately, this is not the way to prosperity, but to serfdom.

We argue, with no ifs or buts, for the abolition of the government's monopoly over money. We seek for the denationalization of money, to use the phrase coined by Hayek. With near-certain probability, this measure would lead—as it nearly always has done throughout history—to the introduction of a currency backed by precious metals, whose volume could not be increased at will through the interplay of politics and central bank manipulations. Only realistic, sound money can keep the cancer-like proliferation of the state at bay. Only this kind of money can ensure that negative economic trends and imbalances of the scale we now see cannot return.

With this measure, politicians would be deprived of the opportunity to live beyond their means, to steal from future generations, to feed the high lifestyle of their voters, and to systematically weaken the economy's foundation strictly for purpose of winning the next election.

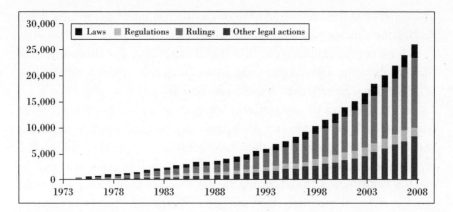

Figure 5.3 Law, Regulations, and Rulings Growing Like a Cancer
SOURCE: European Union.

In essence, the result of the analysis we have presented here is this: monetary policy is not the solution it purports to be. It is the problem.

Yes, we know that by making this demand we have no chance of landing a lucrative contract in government. Fortunately, our independence gives us the freedom to express, with clarity and force, demands that are highly unpopular among politicians.

Do these demands make us hopeless idealists, voices in the wilderness fighting a losing battle? Or is there hope?

History teaches us that, at critical junctures, incredible things can and do happen. The peaceful end of the Soviet Union and their communist satellite states, including the reunification of Germany, is an excellent example. We ourselves did not consider it possible that we would see a reunified Germany in the twentieth century. But great crises always bring with them great opportunities. They prepare the ground for revolutionary changes—both for the better and for the worse.

We consider the probability very high that the global debt trap will ultimately drive us to a dramatic deterioration of the current crisis. The grand rescue programs offered by the governments of the United States and Western Europe are merely a continuation of the same policies that gave us the crisis in the first place. Even if they succeed in the short term, the very most they can deliver is still another speculative bubble similar to the one that followed the government's response to the stock market bust of 2001. But that merely delays the day of reckoning a little further while making the existing problems that much worse.

Like cash for clunkers, the best that these rescues can achieve is time shifting—bringing demand and some growth forward in time, at the expense of demand and growth that would have come later.

If our forecast of a significant intensification of this crisis proves correct—much as our forecast of the current crisis contained in our book *Das Greenspan Dossier* did—then large areas of the world could become breeding grounds for revolutionary change. With this book we wish to make a contribution to debunking the lie that has been heard again and again over recent months—that there is no alternative. And unfortunately, this particularly powerful breed of political rhetoric is being used to rationalize and justify virtually anything.

However, we nurture the hope that, at decisive forks in the road, this will change. And we further hope that our book can make a contribution to ensuring that, at those critical junctures, the correct path—the free market path—will be taken, advancing the freedom of the individual and leaving the road to serfdom behind. Unfortunately, the warnings in *Das Greenspan Dossier* went unheeded. We hope that our new warnings in *The Global Debt Trap* will be accorded a better fate.

Our greatest hope is that, this time around, our forecasts will actually prove to be incorrect. But, alas, that outcome is highly unlikely, in our view.

We would expressly point out that hope alone is not an appropriate basis for investment decisions. While always hoping for the best possible scenario, you must always prepare for the most probable. It is in this spirit that we wrote the concluding part of this book, which presents our assessment of the various investment classes and presents you, the investor, with possible ways of handling the crisis.

CHAPTER 6

What Can You Do Now?

Forecasting in Difficult Times

The bigger the crisis, the greater the government reactions to it. This factor alone makes it very difficult to make predictions in times of great upheaval. Who can claim to know which political interests will achieve the upper hand and—as history teaches us—succeed in putting entirely idiotic, even criminal measures in place? The essential foundations of a free society are private property and clearly regulated property rights. Again and again, governments have come into power that do not respect these foundations, and that have expropriated property from their citizens.

There are two variants of this: forcible expropriation and subtle expropriation. Forcible expropriation, that is, what the law defines as robbery when perpetrated by anyone other than a government, can be found in the history books as frequently as subtle expropriation, that is, what the law defines as counterfeiting when practiced by anyone other than a government. Forcible redistribution was—and is—the motto of socialists and communists, while expropriation by inflation is has been inscribed on the banners of the Keynesians.

Both variants of expropriation are a clear and present danger for a society based on private property. The former variant, forcible expropriation, has historically been accompanied by inhumane levels of brutality. From an economic point of view, it makes little difference whether the protagonists called themselves communists, Stalinists, socialists, or National Socialists: their concept of the economy entails the broad abolition of private ownership and the creation of a centrally planned economy directed by the state. Today's central banks are, to some extent, consistent with this approach. Like a foreign substance derived from a planned economy, they have penetrated the economic body and have interfered with the free market.

Less obvious, but no less ominous for prosperity and freedom, is the second variant—subtle expropriation, the protracted road to serfdom taken by the interventionists who find their justification in Keynes's theories. In contrast to communist revolutionaries, who quite consciously and purposefully seek to achieve their ideal vision of an economic system with one stroke—and by way of corpses or gulags—the interventionists are often entirely unclear as to what awaits them at the end of their chosen road. They justify each individual step as merely a temporary corrective measure—a little push to help put market forces on the right course (right as they define it). But they are unable and unwilling to forecast the cumulative impact of a long series of these interventions on the complex interplay of free markets. Nor can they measure its impact upon the interplay of millions of individuals, each with different abilities, desires, and goals.

We repeat: the key prediction of this book is that by perpetuating and deepening the global debt trap, governments are guaranteeing a further dramatic acceleration of the global financial and economic crisis over the coming years. As a consequence, we regard it as highly probable that the next decade will see very acute changes and upheavals.

Never forget the obvious sequence of events we introduced at the outset: strictly speaking, these exceptionally turbulent times—culminating in the near meltdown of global financial markets in 2008 and the sovereign debt crisis of 2010—began with the bursting of the biggest stock market bubble of all time in the year 2000. At that time, the equity markets underwent a break, a turning point with far-reaching consequences, as the Nasdaq lost three-quarters of its value.

Subsequently, a few indices—including the widely watched but unrepresentative Dow Jones Industrial Average—achieved new highs during the four-year cyclical bull market of 2003 to 2007. But many key stock markets, notably the Nasdaq, along with many individual stocks did not. And in real terms, adjusted for inflation, all broad market indices, *including* the Dow, remained significantly below their all-time high of 2000.

Thus, we were and remain convinced that the year 2000 was the top—a key turning point in global equity markets, with far-reaching consequences. In addition to the bull and bear markets that generally follow the business cycle and are relatively well known (but almost never taken into account) by investors, there is also a much longer cycle that lasts around 10 to 20 years.

This longer-term cycle begins with extremely low valuations based on fundamental analysis, with measures like price-earnings ratios in single digits and dividend yields of more than 6 percent. In this phase, stocks in general are unpopular as an investment class—small wonder, given that in the earlier years, stocks would have delivered no gains and even abundant losses. Nonetheless, stock prices rise and climb the proverbial wall of worry, often extending those gains for many years, despite continuing low popularity ratings as an investment class.

At some point, however, mass psychology undergoes a dramatic shift, and it soon seems as if nothing in the world is more desirable than stocks. Even as the fundamental valuations reach unattractive levels, new investors flooding onto the market pay little heed. It is the last hurrah of a boom whose days are numbered.

Stock prices are perhaps the best barometer for the general mood of the nation. Times of falling share prices, or when share prices have already fallen, are bad times—in every respect. Social unrest and wars also correlate strongly with severe share price declines. In this sense, the study of the stock market must go far beyond an analysis of how to make money and delve into the realm of the social sciences. It is primarily—but not exclusively—on the basis of these relationships that we make our forecast of social unrest and international tensions—two outcomes that must be expected as a consequence of the global debt trap.

Tough Times for Legends—"In God We Trust; All Others Pay Cash!"

During the Great Depression, this slogan was frequently seen in restaurants in Nebraska. Warren Buffett reminds us of its significance in his March 2009 comments, as follows:

In God we trust; all others pay cash! . . . The watchword throughout the country became the creed I saw on restaurant walls when
I was young.[1]

The Oracle of Omaha then gave his Berkshire Hathaway shareholders
a further forecast:

We're certain, for example, that the economy will be in shambles
throughout 2009—and, for that matter, probably well beyond—
but that conclusion does not tell us whether the stock market
will rise or fall.

In the autumn of 2008, the world was full of investors dissatisfied
with the performance of their portfolio and they therefore changed brokers,
switched investment advisors, or perhaps even took their portfolio into
their own hands. Some even went so far as to exchange their entire portfolio
for shares in Buffett's Berkshire Hathaway, selling for $147,000 each, in the
hope that they would finally put an end to worries about the management
of their assets.

By March 2009, however, the result would have been very disappointing:
Berkshire Hathaway shares had lost more than 50 percent of their value.
The outcome was similarly disastrous for anyone buying the shares in
euros. And if investors had sold their gold to buy Berkshire Hathaway—or
used gold as their benchmark—then the total loss (plus lost opportunity)
would have been about 75 percent!

Figure 6.1 shows the stock price of Warren Buffett's Berkshire Hathaway.
Buffett is undoubtedly one of the best investors of all times. But still he lost
more than 50 percent in just a few months when the crisis hit.

Of course, Warren Buffett and his team are only people—albeit exceptionally rich ones. And people make mistakes now and again. They, too, will
sometimes experience the same disappointments as every small investor the
world over. In this particular case, however, the moral of the story is that
the stock market can deliver unpleasant surprises even to the most successful
investors and speculators. And it is the stock market—not some pundit on
TV—that is the only final arbiter of who's a successful investor and who is
not. The price of a share or the level of a stock index ultimately reflect millions of individual opinions. And, in the final analysis, it is the majority of
these opinions that, in each case, determines the direction of the share prices.

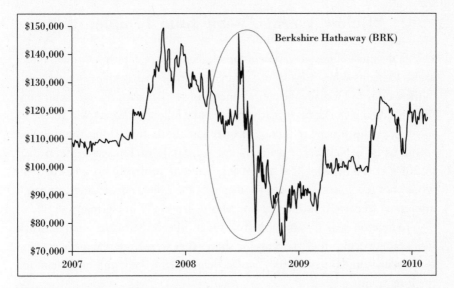

Figure 6.1 Even Value Investors Can Lose More than 50 Percent in Just a Few Months (Berkshire Hathaway Stock Price)

For example, Warren Buffett increased his holding in the oil giant Conoco Phillips. He bought shares in the group for $7 billion when the price of crude oil was at the record level of approximately $150 per barrel. Following his purchase, there was a dramatic drop in crude oil to under $40 in the space of a few short months; and as Conoco Phillips share prices shadowed the oil price plunge, the $7 billion investment was suddenly worth only $4.4 billion.

This did not alter Warren Buffett's conviction—well substantiated and shared by us—that energy prices will rise in the long term. "But so far I have been dead wrong," Buffett admitted to his shareholders. He also spoke of his purchase of shares in two Irish banks, which had simply appeared to him to be cheap based on his valuation methods. In the meantime they became significantly cheaper, and Buffett has had to write down 89 percent of this investment. These examples demonstrate how unusual times have become—so unusual that even the tried and tested methods of the most successful stock market speculators of all time no longer function.

Moreover, Buffett was certainly not alone in the apparently unlimited ability that investment icons had in losing money in years like 2008.

"Below Average"—Sir John Templeton

One of the most famous investment fund legends, the Templeton Growth Fund, is also losing its shine. It is one of the largest actively managed investment funds in the world, and it made the entire concept of stock market mutual funds popular around the world, particularly in Germany following World War II.

It was the superstar among investment funds for a long time, linked to the name of another legendary investor, Sir John Templeton, who died in 2008 at the near-biblical age of 95. There is probably no investor who would not recognize Templeton's image, as the fund's advertising campaign attempted to carry it into every household, especially in Germany.

Templeton was a value investor, much like Buffett. He scoured stock lists of the world's stock markets for shares that were undervalued according to standard fundamental analysis. He then bought them and held them for the long term.

According to the Templeton Growth Fund's prospectus, it ". . . allows continuous wealth building while attempting to avoid sharp fluctuations. Thanks to this strategy, the fund has been one of the most successful of the last 50 years over the long term." That's what the advertising said, and for quite a while, it was true. But those times are past. Morningstar has long since withdrawn its highest rating for the fund, downgrading it to below average. What's ironic is that Sir John Templeton himself—who no longer had anything to do with investment decisions—had long been warning, unambiguously, of bad times ahead.

In the short period between mid-2008 and March 2009, Templeton Fund investors lost about 60 percent of their money. So it should come as no surprise that they began to exit the fund *en masse*. They realized, although far too late, that even the successors of a mythical figure like John Templeton are no protection against serious losses.

What about investors who believed the industry credo that "share prices always rise in the long term"? They are slowly realizing that "long term" may perhaps be too long for their own individual circumstances.

For example, those who invested in S&P 500 stocks at the turn of the century, falling for the industry's false promises of long-term growth, face losses even at the peak of major rallies and wipeout losses when the market approaches its trough. Even at the close of the decade, when the S&P 500 was near a major rally peak, they were in the red.

The Best Advice for Investors: Self-Reliance

We would expressly advise investors against entrusting responsibility for their assets to a fund or a broadly diversified holding such as Berkshire Hathaway or Templeton Growth Fund. Indeed, the advice we gave in 2004 continues to hold true:

- First and foremost—self-reliance. Investors must take matters into their own hands, accepting full responsibility for the results.
- Second, if you use mutual funds, pay very careful attention to the costs.
- Third, stay flexible. This is obviously not an environment for buy-and-hold strategies. You must monitor your investments—including mutual funds—at all times. If the performance is bad, don't let broker commissions or tax considerations get in your way. Riding out major losses is rarely the correct decision!
- Fourth, don't hesitate to make radical changes in your portfolio. When recession looms, act swiftly to dump all investments that may be vulnerable.
- Fifth, if you follow advisors, make sure they are willing and able to forecast recessions and bear markets. They are hard to find, but do exist. Examples: Mike Larson's *Safe Money Report* in the United States, and Claus Vogt's *Sicheres Geld* in Germany. Both have demonstrated that it *is* possible to predict downturns with ample time for investors to prepare for them.

Earlier, we chose the example of Warren Buffett to illustrate a key principle—that value investing, no matter how sound, can make you money only with an economy enjoying long-term growth and a stock market enjoying a long-term bullish trend, such as we witnessed between 1982 and 2000. But in secular bear markets, which can last 10 to 20 years—or even more—it's a mistake to assume than it can do more than help you *lose* less money than you would have otherwise, not exactly a worthy goal.

The big picture view that most investors have missed in recent years is that a secular bear market does not preclude intermediate recoveries that can last for months or even years, such as during the cyclical boom from 2003 to 2007. And what can be especially deceptive is that, during such intermediate periods, the rise in share prices can be massive. Yes, with a continuing appraisal of the markets, investors can participate in those rallies moderately. But they must not lose sight of the long-term risks.

Nor can they afford to forget history. In the 1970s, for example, U.S. investors suffered a long-term bear market against the backdrop of stagflation in the real economy; and in real, inflation-adjusted, terms, they could have lost over 70 percent. Similarly, since 1990, Japanese investors suffered an even longer bear market, with stocks returning to levels of the early 1980s, leaving investors empty-handed after nearly three long decades. If they bought at the very beginning of Japan's 1980s bull market, they'd be at breakeven. If they bought almost any time thereafter, they would be deep in the red.

How do you grow your wealth during such periods? It's certainly not by buying and holding diversified mutual funds as many would have you believe. It must be through the application of an active and flexible strategy using a consistent method.

Consider, for example, a major bank stock that traded above $20 per share, which, at the height of the banking crisis, fell to $2 per share, a 90 percent plunge from peak to trough. From that low point, if the share price climbs, say, 20 cents in a single day, the media could trumpet it as a 10 percent surge, and brokers could lure investors to buy more. "Don't miss the start of a new bull market," they say. Or "Use this is as your big chance to average down—dramatically reducing your average entry price," they argue.

However, we are of the opinion that as long as the bear market remains intact, each sharp recovery in share prices should be used as a *selling* opportunity—to get rid of remaining positions. And instead, investors should seek an entirely new investment strategy within the framework of a long-term bear market.

Yes, "Buy the big dips" was the correct investment strategy during the bull market of 1982 to 2000. It is not the correct strategy now. Through our writings and our publication of *Das Greenspan Dossier,* we showed early on that it was possible to recognize the great turn that occurred in 2000—the transition from a long-term bull market to a long-term bear market. Similarly, we proceed from the assumption that our arsenal of analytical instruments will also help us detect the *next* transition—back to a bull market that should occur at some point in the future. We won't pinpoint it precisely. Nor do we have to, because the next bull market is also bound to last for many years.

Let's now review the prospects—and the best tactics—for each major investment class, beginning with stocks themselves.

Stocks

Stocks During Periods of Hyperinflation

The rise of the United States to a superpower was one of the greatest success stories ever. But as you can see in Figure 6.2, the stock market did not accompany this impressive achievement by smoothly rising year for year. No, there have been long periods, lasting 15 to 20 years, when the stock market was going nowhere and even declining. These long-term trends are called secular bear markets. The one we are currently experiencing started in 2000 and can easily last another decade.

Since stocks are tied to hard assets with real value, they've often been recommended by Wall Street as a hedge against inflation. The theory is that when the book value of corporate assets rises, so will their shares. This makes sense. But unfortunately, no matter how eminently reasonable it may sound in theory, it's flawed in practice: the history of financial markets shows that equity investments can offer little or no protection against inflation.

Consider, for example, the price trend of German shares during the hyperinflation that occurred in the early 1920s. In Figure 6.3, you can see the trends for producer prices, subsistence costs, the U.S. dollar (which at that time was backed by gold), and the stock market index for 1923, the year in which hyperinflation most ravaged the German economy.

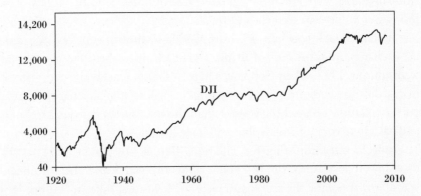

Figure 6.2 Stocks Can Decline or Stagnate for Decades (Dow Jones Industrial Average)

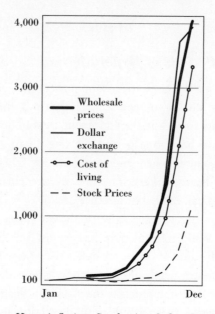

Figure 6.3   German Hyperinflation: Stocks Are Only a Partial Inflation Hedge

As you can see, share prices did rise dramatically during the period—by around 1,200 percent. But over the same period, subsistence costs rose by around 3,300 percent. In other words, when adjusted for inflation, stock investors were among the greatest inflation losers. In real terms, they lost about 80 percent of their wealth.

In Figure 6.3 you can see how German wholesale prices, the dollar exchange rate, the cost of living, and stock prices behaved in nominal terms during 1923, when Germany's hyperinflation reached its nadir. Stock prices did not keep up with rising prices. Hence, stocks acted only as a partial inflation hedge. Much better than the total losses delivered to bond and cash investors, of course, but still huge losses.

Indeed, after adjusting for inflation, German stocks in 1922 fell to their lowest level since the beginning of World War I in 1914. To understand how dramatic the real losses were for investors, take stock price levels in 1913, the last peacetime year of that period, as the baseline. Set that starting value at an index of 100. And then track it through the years of hyperinflation, peaking in October 1922. You will find that, after adjusting for inflation, you wind up with an ending value of just 3.6.

It wasn't until the end of 1923 that inflation-adjusted stock prices rose significantly in Germany—jumping to an index of 21.3. The following Figure 6.4 shows the actual figures for both nominal and real-term trends in German share prices from 1918 to 1923.

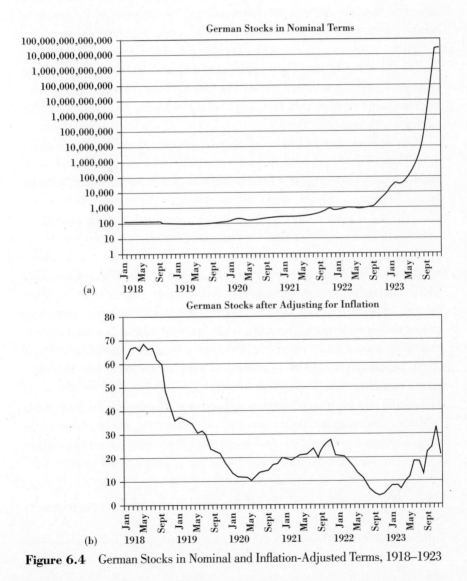

Figure 6.4 German Stocks in Nominal and Inflation-Adjusted Terms, 1918–1923

Bottom line: investors who put, say, 100 marks in German stocks in 1913 and held them through the entire hyperinflationary period would have seen their investment sink to a meager 3.6 marks at the low. And then, even if they could have held on for the subsequent recovery, would have wound up with only 21.3 marks in real terms. They would have managed to salvage 21.3 percent of their purchasing power 10 years later when the hyperinflation came to an end. A loss of nearly 79 percent is, of course, not exactly inspiring. But compared to the total wipeout losses suffered by investors in fixed-income bonds and life insurance policies, stock investors were actually fortunate.

Figure 6.4 shows how stocks were doing during Germany's hyperinflation of the early 1920s. The upper chart uses nominal terms, the second chart real, inflation-adjusted terms. You can easily see that stocks were not a perfect inflation hedge. In fact, stock investors had to endure a real roller coaster and lost considerably.

Our analysis of other hyperinflationary periods produces a similar picture. Thus, if buy and hold is your approach, brace yourself for massive losses on equity holdings in a hyperinflationary environment brought about by our politicians. No, you won't lose everything. Assuming you don't invest in companies that go bankrupt, you will salvage *something*. But wouldn't it be better to preserve everything? Or even make money during the decline?

Remember: the more you preserve, the more ammunition you will have to participate in the next period of growth. A good illustration is Germany's rebirth after what we call "zero hour"—the currency reform of 1948, when the deutschmark was first created. Every German resident was supposedly treated the same. In reality, however, while every German was indeed given a basic allowance of 40 deutschmarks, there was a huge difference. One segment of the population needed every pfennig of their allowance to buy food and keep a roof over their heads. In the meanwhile, other people were able to go to the bank and use their allowances to borrow money against property, gold, or shares. That moment in time was the fork in the road, the road that made all the difference in the world. And we would like to point out unequivocally: it is at times like these that the die is cast for the accumulation of great wealth.

Are We Facing a Shift of Power toward Extremism?

All this assumes that there will still be a stock market and an economic system based on free markets. Unfortunately, however, that cannot be taken for granted, as history shows, particularly in Germany. Fortunately, the United

States has historically proven to be relatively immune to extremist tendencies, and the ideals of freedom are still deeply rooted. Nonetheless, even in the United States there have long been unsettling undercurrents, and there are no guarantees against drastic economic mismanagement by politicians. For freedoms to be preserved, they must be continually fought for.

In the spring of 2009, we saw the first signs of rebellion directed against the government's irresponsible monetary policy, reckless fiscal policy, and cancer-like growth of its powers. And we saw fresh concerns about fiscal irresponsibility from both ends of the political spectrum. Whether a new freedom movement will emerge and change the course of history remains to be seen. But clearly, the resentment of freedom-oriented people is already searching for an outlet.

In previous crises—such as during Latin American debt defaults of the 1970s or the Asian currency crisis of 1997—the United States was at the fringe of the crisis and merely suffered some aftershocks. Now, however, in the global debt trap, the United States is at the center. It is now clear that it has none other to blame than itself. But what will be the social consequences of the next crisis? How will the U.S. population react to the severe reduction in wealth that is now under way? What response will politicians offer?

President Barack Obama put it this way:

> It is true . . . that the crisis began in the United States. I take responsibility, even if I wasn't president at the time.

The United States is the greatest military power the world has ever seen by a wide margin. Will it stand idly by and passively relinquish its status as a world power? Or will it continue to pull out all the stops, mobilize power politics to an extreme, and seek to prevent the decline that is already under way? Some of the best answers can be found in the communiqué from the G-20 summit of April 2009: more control over the financial markets, more bailouts, and even more loans to poor countries. And similar answers can be found in Europe's rescue of Greece and other PIIGS countries. They are out to save the world. But they cannot succeed.

Beware: if the ultimate political response to the global debt trap includes the weakening or abolition of democracy, then we have only one appropriate piece of advice: be sure not only to keep your money safe but also to diversify your investments *geographically*. Transfer part of your wealth abroad. This advice also applies to your gold investments. Which countries will take which paths when the crisis intensifies further, as we expect it to, is very difficult for anyone to predict. And therein lies our greatest concern. So keep track of political developments around the world. Be aware of which countries—especially your own—are shifting toward greater and greater government controls. Only in this way can you avoid the inevitable surprises that come from shifts to more extreme forms of government. Be ready.

You may consider these warnings exaggerated—and we certainly hope they are. But regrettably our knowledge of history makes it impossible for us to downplay them. Again and again, we have seen how economic distress has lead to popular dissatisfaction and dangerous political upheavals. It's precisely with these kinds of pressures that governments seek scapegoats to divert the anger of the people. And it's often ethnic minorities with great wealth or control over assets that are among the first victims. But they're certainly not the only ones. Also targets of scapegoating and witch hunts are prosperous professionals, political opponents, and anyone critical of the government. And if politicians are unable to redirect the wrath of the people to internal scapegoats, they often find another handy diversion—war.

Stocks and Inflation that Is Not Extreme

We've illustrated how stocks can behave in a hyperinflation scenario. Let's hope, however, that the global debt trap never takes us that far. And assuming this hope has a foundation in reality, let's consider what can happen to equity markets in less extreme periods.

In the 1960s and 1970s, for example, we saw a build-up toward low double-digit inflation in the United States, but never reaching hyperinflation. The numbers were not as extreme, but the pattern was similar: like in the more extreme inflation scenario, share prices performed significantly better than fixed-income bonds. And as with extreme inflation, they were *still* not a good investment and again failed to preserve capital.

Figure 6.5 shows the German stock index from 1961 to 1982. As you can see, it went nowhere despite the growth miracle. Inflation rates were relatively high during the 1970s. It follows that stock investors suffered severe real, inflation-adjusted losses during these two decades. Again, stocks were not a good inflation hedge. The same is true for the U.S. stock market during this time.

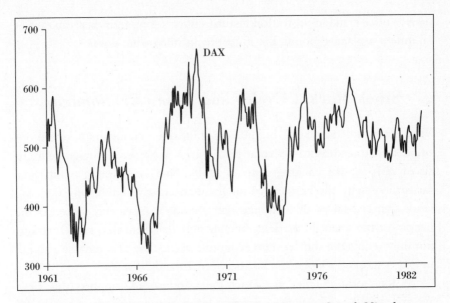

Figure 6.5   German Stock Market Went Nowhere Despite Growth Miracle (German DAX Index, 1961–1982)

We use German stocks as an illustration, but the data for the Dow Jones Industrial Average and the S&P 500 Index lead to similar conclusions. Look at the German DAX index: even in nominal terms, without considering inflation, it was virtually unchanged for 20 long years. Despite the German economic miracle—the so-called *Wirtschaftswunder*—shareholders made nothing. And if you consider the declining purchasing power of their deutschmarks, they lost 58.5 percent. After two decades they not only saw no gains, but their real assets shrunk to just 41.5 percent of their 1962 value.

With these kinds of numbers, how can anyone in her right mind continue to regard equities as a good hedge against inflation? At best, during inflationary times, stocks are like a one-eyed man trying to lead the blind. Are they totally worthless? No. Remember: even in the worst-case scenario for the economy, as long as the companies stay out of bankruptcy courts, it can ultimately be to your advantage to put a small portion of your portfolio in special situation value stocks that pay solid dividends. Just be sure not to forget the lesson recently learned by Warren Buffett—that even value stocks can plunge in value. And never forget that equities do *not* offer genuine protection against either a long-term bear market or an inflation-plagued boom. But if not stocks, then what does?

Stock Market Cycles and *Homo Economicus*

We cannot underscore this big-picture point often enough: stocks did not begin their transition to a secular bear market with the sovereign debt crisis of 2010 or the banking crisis of 2008. That key turning point came far earlier—with the bursting of the great speculative bubble in 2000. We made that critical point then, and we've made it repeatedly since. As the history of the financial markets convincingly demonstrates, stock markets not only reflect the shorter-term economic cycle, they also the rise and fall in longer-term cycles that can last between 10 and 20 years.

A long-term chart of the Dow Jones Industrials supports this view. We are clearly dealing with cycles that bring massive appetite for risk and equally massive aversion to risk. In the upward phases of these cycles, key indicators of fundamental stock valuation climb very steeply, while in the downward phases they fall back to very low levels. The longer the good times persist, it seems, the more adventurous, reckless, and optimistic investors become—a sentiment that is, of course, reflected in share valuations.

How these long-term cycles emerge is hotly contested. But the connection to mass psychology cannot be denied. Ultimately, the cycles can be boiled down to sea changes in human behavior. Experimental psychology and experimental economics, which investigate the behavior of individuals and groups under laboratory conditions, also offer substantial evidence regarding the extent to which human behavior is determined by irrational influences. They convincingly confirm what stock market traders have always known. It is not the rational decision maker—*homo economicus*—that always sets the course of the economy and stock market. It is predominantly the *irrational man,* careering between the extremes of fear and greed—especially when central banks feed the greed with abundant, easy, or even free, money.

Group dynamics—especially the pattern whereby bullish sentiment by some mutually reinforces the sentiment among others—also play a major role. And in the frenzy to join or outdo one's peers, nothing is more bullish for rising prices than rising prices themselves. They attract new investors like moths to a flame. The new investors drive prices even higher, and the higher prices attract still *more* investors. On the way up, it's called a *virtuous cycle*. On the way down, however, it never ceases to amaze us how quickly it can become a vicious cycle.

Indeed, the history of the stock markets has taught us one unmistakable lesson: Unless you have found a trading system with a good track record even in the worst of times, and especially if you follow the crowd, the massive swings from euphoria to panic will quickly empty your pockets.

Whatever the cause of these long-term cycles may be, the most important thing to know is that they *do* exist. And you should also have an idea of where the markets currently are within this big cycle.

Because these cycles can range from 10 to 20 years or even much longer, they consist of several smaller cycles—often (but not always) coinciding with recession cycles. These intermediate cycles, when extreme, can make it difficult to recognize the long-term cycles. So, to clear this fog in the cycle analysis, it can be helpful to look at the stock markets' fundamental valuation parameters, preferably smoothed out over several years.

In the graph shown in Figure 6.6, you will see the trend of the S&P 500, along with its price-to-earnings ratio and dividend yield. Here you can easily see the cycles referred to earlier. In particular, you can see how attractively shares were valued at the start of the 1980s and how the great boom of the 1980s and 1990s led to ever less attractive valuations. Starting around 1995, the boom became a giant speculative bubble as P/E ratios and dividend yields reached absurd, economically unjustifiable levels. In a remarkable exercise of mass self-deception, analysis was replaced with wishful thinking; reason, with euphoria; and the entire market, with a ludicrous episode the outcome of which is now well known. As we mentioned before, the Nasdaq lost nearly three-quarters of its peak value and, even at the peak of the subsequent housing boom, barely recovered to half of its earlier peak. In the German Neuer Markt, which, like the Nasdaq, listed mostly up-and-coming technology companies, the fate was even worse.

Based on this comparison, you can clearly identify the truly best times for buying shares—when the index was near, or even below, the lower thin line. In other words, the best times to buy were when the market's overall P/E ratio was 10 or less. On the other hand, particularly bad times for buying or even holding stocks were when the share prices rose above the upper thin line, that is, when the P/E was 20 or more.

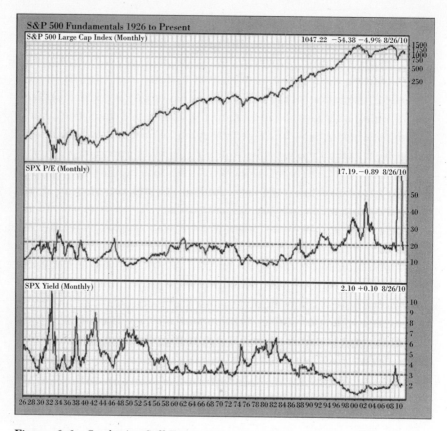

Figure 6.6   Stocks Are Still Expensive

This is not a chart that your broker has probably ever shown you. Nor will you find anything like it in a mutual fund prospectus. Their agenda is to get you to buy stocks whenever you have the money to do so—or even if you don't. Their business would not do very well if you only bought stocks when it's best for you!

The key is that, as of mid-2010, as we finalize the U.S. edition of this book, this chart shows that U.S. stocks are still extremely overvalued. This is clearly *not* the time to buy.

Figure 6.7 shows how German stock investors fared when the stock market bubble burst in the year 2000. They, too, had gone mad as a crowd during the dot-com boom. They exaggerated even more than their American counterparts. When all was said and done, the Neuer Markt

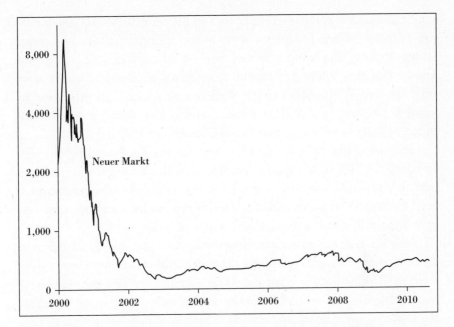

Figure 6.7   Germany's Equivalent to the Nasdaq Imploded by 96 Percent (Neuer Markt Index)

Index, Germany's equivalent to the Nasdaq, imploded by 96 percent. Yes, that's what happened to supposedly "safe" German investments during these remarkable times of mass madness.

Excellent Opportunities for Flexible Investors

Consequently, we are unfortunately unable to recommend the purchase of shares from the perspective of fundamental analysis. However, because both authors are confirmed friends of equity investments and the stock markets, we cannot let this issue rest there.

Remember: within long-term cycles there are often attractive opportunities for making money through equities, but only for the flexible investor. Of course, anyone can buy shares; the great art of equity investing lies in determining when to *sell*.

If your broker or financial planner is typical, he has probably focused mostly on buying but failed miserably in advising when or how to sell. And fund management companies explicitly and deliberately do everything they can to avoid selling. Except for some minor adjustments here and there, selling stocks is simply not a part of their job description. And it is widely known that their entire business model consists in staying fully or nearly fully invested at almost all times. With few exceptions, all they seem to know is buy, buy, buy. And we presume you've had plenty of opportunity in recent years to see where that business model can lead you.

Fortunately, as an individual investor you are not bound by industry standards or inflexible business models. You don't always have to stay invested, and that simple fact gives you an invaluable advantage over a fund manager. This is not rocket science. When the risks are too great, you can simply sell, move to the sidelines, and wait it out.

In other words, you need a compass to show you how great the risks are. In recent years, a handful of independent investment newsletters have effectively found such a compass. Their earnings are derived exclusively from subscription fees—not from the sale of advertising space, let alone the sale of specific financial products. That's how they can afford to provide independent advice—advice that can indeed be used to achieve sustainable returns even in the worst of times. Needless to say, this business model alone is no guarantee of success; investment newsletters are also written by human beings who themselves can sometimes be susceptible to the same kind of mass delusion and folly as their readers. For this reason, those who are in a position to detect negative trends and to warn of recessions and slumps in good times will always remain a small minority. But as we've said, they do exist—not only in the United States, but also in Germany as well.

However, a good advisor and true pathfinder is still not enough. In principle, the old Rothschild adage—"Buy at the sound of cannon; sell at the sound of violins"—applies. As your authors, well known as "crash prophets," we regularly operate according to this maxim.

But no matter whom you follow, there is no way around the fact that you will have to make decisions for yourself. You must be prepared to sell when the majority of your friends and neighbors are doing the opposite; and to invest when others are shaking their heads and declaring you insane. In other words, you need the self-confidence and backbone to avoid crowd behavior and mass psychology, especially at critical turning points.

If you can just master this mental and psychological challenge, then the coming years are set to provide you with many extraordinary opportunities in the equity markets. Ultimately, the instruments you have available to you represent an embarrassment of riches. Not only can you purchase shares and bet on rising prices, you can also profit from falling prices with inverse investments; and with them, the more the markets fall, the more money you stand to make.

The big picture: we anticipate a resumption and continuation of the long-term downward trend. Plus, because we also anticipate rising inflation rates in the near future, we foresee massive price swings in stock averages. The same broad roller coaster of the past 10 years will probably continue for a few years more.

Only when you see P/E ratios under 10 will they be substantially undervalued; only when this undervaluation lasts for several years; only when stocks have largely fallen into disrepute; only when brokers largely give up hyping stocks; and only when the global debt trap has become so severe that a return is finally made to a realistic monetary and fiscal policy—will the equity markets have finally reached rock bottom, the endpoint of their long-term downward trend that began in 2000.

That's when we will be able to advise you to purchase shares for the long term, that is, with a horizon of 10 to 20 years. But until that time, we must advise you to adopt the attitude of a medium-term investor and speculator:

- Either buy special investments like inverse ETFs that are designed to profit directly from the long-term downtrend
- Or, take advantage of the shorter-term intermediate rallies with moderate, in-and-out stock trades
- Or, use a strategy that includes a combination of both. As we can attest from personal experience, both routes are possible and can be very lucrative.

Do You Know How to Play Poker in the Stock Market?

Anyone seeking to profit from stocks in this era must also get used to handling probabilities in the correct manner. This is no simple task, and it requires one ability above all others: discipline. Every good poker player understands the significance of probability calculations to make decisions on when to raise a bet, when to pass, and when to fold. Every good stock market trader does, too.

This is what differentiates a serious player from a careless gambler. The former seeks to calculate the relative probability for each and every bet. His strategy is to maximize the probability of a win, and this entails doing the homework before the game and counting the cards to stay on top of the game. The gambler, on the other hand, is a thrill seeker. Even if he understands probability, it does not interest him. He either enjoys playing and is not troubled by the losses, or he's a masochist, subconsciously seeking his own financial ruin.

Unfortunately, most stock market speculators today behave like the careless gambler. They neither do their homework nor make the necessary effort to ensure they are always up to speed with events to react sensibly to the inevitable twists and turns of the game.

If a player knows the probabilities that result from a given hand, they must continually adapt their game to these probabilities. It makes little sense to play a hand with poor probability. If the chances are slim, you fold early. And you save what's left in your kitty for the next hand.

Beginners do not often understand this process. The timid among them tend to only play hands that are dead certain; the bold, in contrast, seek to bid aggressively no matter what cards they're dealt. Even if they're lucky enough to win, they overlook the primary lesson: it's not just a single round that will make them a winner. Over the long term—over the course of a hundred such games—they are virtually guaranteed to lose in the end.

Exactly the same applies to the stock market. Investors who bet with a poor opportunity-to-risk ratio are making a fatal error: they will lose money in the long term. And even if they get lucky and win on the first few trades, it will make little difference in the long run.

Indeed, beginner's luck can be among the worst of curses—a common psychological trap. The investor feels his hit-or-miss approach is valid. He convinces himself that he understands how to make money. He throws caution to the wind and increases his stake. And he gets caught with the largest positions precisely at the wrong time—often at the end of a long boom. When the inevitable slump occurs, any profits achieved can turn to dust. And unfortunately, this behavior is typical, which helps explain why, during times like these, at the end of each cycle, most individual investors wind up losers.

So, our first important point is to calculate the probability of success for each trade. But that is hardly enough. Our second important point to note, which many investors miss, is this: a high probability of profit does not necessarily mean a good opportunity-to-risk ratio. And conversely, a low probability of profit does not necessarily mean a bad one. You also have to take into account the potential *magnitude* of the profit —the percentage return or gain you can achieve on each dollar you invest. If the potential percentage gain is large enough, it can turn a relatively lower probability trade into a good bet; while a very limited potential gain can transform a high probability trade into a bad bet.

Among the first key factors to consider is the fundamental valuation of the stock market and of the individual company. Think of it as your safety margin. If a company—or an entire market—is undervalued on the basis of classic indicators such as price-and-earnings ratios or dividend yields, then it may be a risk worth considering, even if other technical or macroeconomic indicators are not yet giving you the green light. That's because purchases made at an extremely attractive fundamental level operate as a form of safety net. If the bear market is still not quite over, it should help limit your downside risk. And if a fundamental upturn is beginning, it can help magnify your profit percentage.

Why? Because every stock market boom consists of at least two components: first, rising corporate profits lead to share price gains. And second, as the economic boom progresses, increasing investor interest in equities as an asset class helps ensure that they will pay higher prices.

Let us assume that you purchase a stock valued at the end of a pronounced slump with a P/E ratio of seven. In other words, if the stock is selling for $70 per share, its annual earnings are $10 per share. Now let's say the economy recovers and the company's profits double to $20 per share. If the P/E ratio is unchanged, then the share price will double to $140.

Typically, however, the P/E ratio does not stay the same. It tends to rise significantly over the course of a boom, from, say, 7 to 14. If that occurs in our example, then the share price will double for this reason alone—to $280, a four-fold gain overall.

Now, let's see what happens if you buy a stock with a very high P/E, such as 20 times earnings, or, as we saw in the late 1990s, even as much as 100 or more times earnings. Now, due to the high valuation alone, your profit potential is dramatically reduced. If you're lucky, this high-risk bet may pay off initially or in the short term. But over the long term, it is far more likely to be a loser. The many inexperienced and hopeful stock market newcomers in the dot-com frenzy of the late 1990s learned this simple lesson in fundamental stock valuation the hard way.

What about Bonds?

If you're talking about the majority of fixed-income securities—with a fixed-interest coupon, with a payback strictly at their *nominal* value, and *without* any adjustment for rising inflation—then you're asking for big trouble. In inflationary periods, they are among the very biggest losers, independent of the quality of the issuer. And since the majority of money paid into whole life insurance policies is invested in medium- and long-term bonds, almost all of which are vulnerable to inflation, these policies are also among the biggest inflation losers.

Recall once more the preconditions for all major periods of inflation: discretionary paper money (fiat money) and spiraling national debt, the great majority of which is financed by newly created money. It follows that long-term, fixed-rate borrowers—especially highly indebted governments—are among the biggest winners from monetary devaluation. And it also follows that long-term, fixed-rate lenders—including those who buy the government bonds—are among the biggest inflation losers.

And don't expect the legal system to rescue you from this highway robbery. Certainly not while debts can be met with devalued money and judges are on the government's payroll. It should come as no surprise that they have always decided in favor of the hand that feeds them, opining that it *is* legal to repay fixed-rate debts with inflated, virtually worthless, government-monopolized money. Even in the case of Germany's hyperinflation of the 1920s, when it was obvious that the money was not worth the paper it was printed on, the courts came down on the side of the government. That the government bureaucrats ran the government's finances entirely outside the bounds of any acceptable parameters—and perpetuated outright fraud on the citizenry—was deemed entirely immaterial.

No single historic event can illustrate more clearly the utterly egregious conflict of interest between the citizenry and their highly indebted government. The latter is reduced to nothing other than a band of bandits, leveraging their talents as successful populists entirely for their own gain. They see the public as an anonymous sea of faceless individuals. They exploit this public exclusively to further their own personal interests. And yet, at the end of the day, they are not held personally accountable for the debts they've accumulated, the great damage they've done or the tremendous financial burden that nearly all citizens and their descendants must ultimately bear.

You can safely assume that the global debt trap will lead us to a renewed period of inflation, and that, with the inflation, you will ultimately be treated, to some degree or another, according to the preceding schema. Even during the inflation of the 1970s—relatively moderate in comparison to what the future could bring—government bonds and other fixed instruments acquired the apt nickname "expropriation certificates."

The good news is that, as an investor, you have the *power to decide* whether you will subject yourself to this foul treatment, whether you'll allow your wealth to be expropriated by inflation or not. Fortunately, nobody is forcing you to buy bonds. And if you own them, no one is preventing you from selling them either.

Even better news: today, thanks to handy instruments like inverse bond exchange-traded funds (ETFs), you even have the opportunity to profit directly from falling bond prices. You simply buy the ETF at a low price with the aim of selling it at a higher price. We regard this investment opportunity as extremely promising. Instead of betting on the unlikely scenario that your principal and interest will be worth what's promised—either directly or through whole life insurance policies—we recommend you bet on precisely the opposite. Bet on monetary devaluation and rising inflation by buying inverse bond ETFs, whose prices are designed to rise when government bond prices fall.

One word of warning: Unless you want to keep track of the creditworthiness of the issuer, avoid over-the-counter derivatives and stick with ETFs or other instruments traded on regulated exchanges.

Another key point: Do not confuse medium- and long-term bonds, which are vulnerable to rising inflation, with very short-term instruments that adjust quickly to the rising inflation by giving you a higher rate of return. There will be many viable income opportunities later with:

- Safe short-term instruments that promptly give you better yields as inflation and the government borrowing drives rates higher, or
- Fixed instruments, such as TIPPS, with variable interest rates that are adjusted at regular intervals in line with inflation.

Term and interest, however, are not the only factors you need to take into account as an investor. No less important is the quality of the issuer—the issuer's ability to meet all of its debt payments without missing a beat.

As a vivid illustration of this all-important consideration, never forget the summer and fall of 2008, when so many supposedly strong issuers failed, or came dangerously close to failure. Months earlier, author Claus Vogt warned of these failures in his *Sicheres Geld* (Safe Money) newsletter in Germany. Yes, many banks were bailed out—both in the United States and in Europe. But suppose, in the next round of this great global debt trap, some are not. What might happen then?

We know today that those banks were de facto bankrupt. Moreover, today, despite trillions of capital infusions from the government, and despite so-called stress tests in the United States and Europe, which give the public an entirely false impression of their capital adequacy, they remain, today, extremely vulnerable to the future consequences of the global debt trap.

Our 2004 forecast of impending bank collapses remains intact. Yes, to date, all the major banks that failed have been bailed out with unprecedented goverment generosity using taxpayer funds. And yes, the many bank or thrift failures in the United States have been limited mostly to smaller institutions. But this changes nothing. It is due exclusively to political intervention that cannot be easily sustained.

Our advice: Base your banking decisions exclusively on the merits of each bank—not on the faith that government intervention will continue. That means if a bank is unsafe, you have only one viable choice. Get your money out of there and seek safer banks, or better yet, havens outside of the banking system entirely.

In our writings, we also recommended that investors sell their non-Treasury money market funds—funds that nearly every other adviser on the planet regarded as a crisis-proof resting place for all investor cash. And that recommendation has also proven correct. In the United States, several money market funds "broke the buck," delivering outright losses to their investors. And in Germany, it was worse. Many money market funds sold here had to absorb serious losses, sometimes double-digit losses.

What about government guarantees? In the United States, the government tacitly guaranteed money market funds. But as with the bailout of banks, when the consequences of the global debt trap strike, don't assume that this guarantee will hold. As with banks, make sure you rely exclusively on the merits of the issuer.

With short-term Treasury bills or variable-interest bonds, any inflation-related losses are bound to be very limited. Your interest payments are adjusted to the current interest rate level relatively quickly. But we cannot repeat too often: You must be sure to pay close attention to the quality of the issuer. In a severe stagflation scenario—economic stagnation accompanied by high inflation rates—increasing numbers of companies and municipalities can go under. In such cases, even notes or bonds with relatively short terms could suffer severe losses. Moreover, in a double-dip recession—a scenario that we feel is unavoidable thanks to the global debt trap—we must assume that the banking crisis, with all its dangers, will return. If we're right, you're bound to see further loan writedowns in the trillions of dollars—not only in residential mortgages, but also in commercial real estate loans, consumer credit, and corporate financing.

Plus, in this second, double-dip round of consequences from the global debt trap, we also must also anticipate what we warned about in the German original of this book one year ago:

> [We see] the ever-increasing danger of national bankruptcies. Emerging markets in Eastern Europe, South America, and Asia could in all respects suffer the same fate as Iceland. But a number of developed countries also find themselves in a similarly precarious or weak position. Ireland, Austria, Italy, Spain, even the UK, give us considerable cause for concern, and not merely as investors.

Now, as we go to press with the English edition, much of this forecast has also come to pass—but only partially. The worst is yet to come.

Fortunately, as we mentioned a moment ago, inflation-adjusted bonds such as TIPPS are also a choice for fixed-income investors. These are bonds whose coupons are coupled to a price index.

Warning: These instruments are not entirely inflation-proof—the adjustments can understate and lag the actual inflation. Plus, a related risk in these instruments lies in the calculation of the underlying price index. If actual monetary devaluation is significantly faster than the rise of the price index, you may come to the conclusion that you've been sold a lemon. But they do reduce at least a portion of the inflation-related losses you might suffer compared to fixed-rate bonds.

In sum, our recommendations in the field of fixed-interest securities are threefold:

1. If you're interested in long-term interest rates, don't bet on them staying the same or going lower by locking yourself into a fixed rate. Quite the contrary, bet on rising long-term rates (falling bond prices) with inverse bond ETFs.
2. If it's liquidity and safety that you're looking for with your cash, stick with the very safest, highest quality instruments, including U.S. Treasury bills (or Treasury-only money market funds).
3. If you must have some higher fixed income, invest some money in TIPPS. But given the risks we cited earlier, keep the amounts very modest.

And for the best results, consider a healthy combination of all three.

The reasoning behind our recommendations: the risk that the global debt trap will cause another major crisis is simply too great to justify lower quality issuers, regardless of how much more interest they may pay. Moreover, with government deficits now so large, the crisis could very well reach a level whereby governments will have to give up bailing out every Wall Street firm from a well-deserved collapse.

Real Estate

You've probably heard that real estate is as good hedge against inflation, and traditionally it was. However, in the current context, this assumption is downright wrong. Indeed, the facts and logic we presented earlier— regarding the experience with stocks during the German hyperinflation of the 1920s—applies equally to real estate. In real, inflation-adjusted terms, German real estate also fell dramatically in value during that period.

The only saving grace: As we said before, in the valley of the blind, the one-eyed man is king. It is better to suffer a partial loss than a total one.

Remember: Periods of high inflation throw the entire price structure of an economy out of kilter. As a result, during the German hyperinflationary period of the 1920s, it was possible for a property owner to go bankrupt strictly due to cash flow problems. So if you're thinking of buying real estate with debt in the hope of profiting from a period of anticipated inflation, be sure to learn from this critical lesson of history: It is entirely conceivable that you will run into repayment difficulties because of drastically rising costs and loss of rental income, as tenants become strapped for cash.

This kind of acute cash shortage, despite nonstop government money printing, is why more than 2,000 different kinds of scrip—ad hoc, emergency currencies—were said to be circulating in Germany in 1923. Issuers included not only the federal government, but also local governments; not only institutions, but also industry associations, chambers of commerce, and private traders. Some of these substitute currencies were sanctioned by the government. Most, however, were illegal. And in the final analysis, money that retained any value was still scarce, leading to widespread loan and rent defaults that forced property owners into bankruptcy.

California's debt crisis of 2009—also resulting in the issuance of a substitute currency—is a stark reminder that what happened in Germany in the 1920s is not strictly a bygone early-twentieth-century anomaly. In a future round of the global debt trap, don't be surprised if you see cities, states, and corporations, unable to meet payroll or other short-term obligations, also issuing various kinds of IOUs, which, they hope, can be exchanged at local stores or cashed in at a discount.

At the same time, hyperinflation can also provide exceptional opportunities for flexible and aggressive speculators. Needless to say, each of these opportunities come with corresponding risks. Inflation winners are likely to be in the minority. The majority of the population loses, and many are even reduced to poverty.

Furthermore, experience tells us that the state often seeks to stop its citizens from protecting themselves from its own destructive policies—let alone enriching themselves. Inflation comes with a political and legal aftermath. Legal certainty and the rule of law may wither or even disappear in times of crisis. Remember our detailed discussion earlier of Germany's *Finanzmarktstabilisierungsergänzungsgesetz*, or Supplementary Financial Market Stabilization Act, of 2009. This legal monstrosity is not only unpronounceable by most non-German speakers but its content and intent may ultimately cause many to recoil in horror from the German capital markets. It continues to conjure in our minds flashbacks to Weimar Germany, when credit agreements were declared null and void by political whim.

Neither inflation nor these inflation-related manipulations will be of much help to real estate investors. Instead, as before, the two fundamental drivers of value appreciation in real estate are, and will continue to be, economic growth and population growth. We don't expect much of the former. And the latter will come too slowly and too late to overcome the huge imbalance of supply and demand for real estate in the United States. With all the consequences of the global debt trap—rising mortgage rates, a double-dip recession, high unemployment, more bank failures, and worse— another major decline in U.S. real estate could be very hard to avoid.

The only outstanding difference from the real estate collapse of 2005– 2009 and the next round of the collapse: The former was the primary cause *of* the recession and debt collapse. The latter will be primarily caused *by* the recession and debt collapse.

Commodities—Clever Yet Incorrect Forecasts

In the 1970s, everything seemed to revolve around commodities—not only in the financial markets but also in politics. OPEC held the world in fear of oil embargoes, production cuts, and sudden price hikes. The Club of Rome frightened the world about the limits of growth, warning that we needed to wean ourselves from the idea of a limitless supply of commodities. This latter idea was not entirely new, but the time for its rediscovery, which bordered on hysteria, was ripe. Limits to growth have been discovered again and again throughout human history.

These kinds of pessimistic forecasts have, in retrospect, always proven to be incorrect. Human resourcefulness prevailed. Mankind simply did not observe the postulated limits, always finding a way to dramatically extend them.

Perhaps the most famous example of supposed limits to growth originates with Thomas Robert Malthus, a highly educated British economist and social philosopher, who was a contemporary of Goethe. In his instructive 1798 book, *Essay on the Principle of Population,* he painted a bleak picture of humanity plagued by starvation. The world's population, he argued, was rising exponentially. But food production was growing only linearly. Therefore, he wrote, his conclusion was inescapable.

As we now know, mankind proved itself much more clever and resourceful than Malthus could have imagined. It succeeded in boosting food production and yields to such a degree that, despite some exceptions, it has generally had little difficulty in keeping up with exponentially growing population, right up to the present day.

Malthus provided a prime example of clever misforecasting. His assumptions were thoroughly reasonable, rested on empirical observation, and were validated by some historical experience. What could be more logical than to extrapolate from those assumptions and reach the conclusion of inevitability?

This important example should never be forgotten, especially when reading forecasts about which there appears to be no doubt. Remembering Malthus's work should help you be wary of forecasts that leave no room for doubt or do not envisage the possibility of different scenarios.

Years before the advent of the current climate fears, we saw demands for the government to take strong measures to protect the climate and somehow make the impossible possible. And with that hysteria, came the Club of Rome, largely adopting Malthus's mantle. Their argument was based on the rising raw material consumption levels of the industrialized nations. This, they said, could not and must not be allowed to continue. Growth, they said, must be limited and directed by a strong central government. Otherwise the lights would soon go out, and the end of civilization would be upon us.

The Club of Rome enjoyed the high point of its popularity at the end of the 1970s and the start of the 1980s. At precisely this point in time, commodity prices were experiencing the exaggerated speculation phase of a long-term, secular upward trend that had begun in 1968.

To the surprise of many observers at the time, there then ensued a dramatic, across-the-board fall in commodity prices—starting in the early 1980s and continuing until the turn of the millennium. Yet, at the same time, the global economy experienced a pronounced and broad period of economic growth. Also in these two decades, many developing countries were able to leap into the industrial age, as their populations achieved previously unimaginable levels of prosperity. Not only did the lights not go out, in many parts of the world, they went on for the very first time.

The Club of Rome was wrong, not only in its diagnosis, but especially in its prescriptions. It wasn't central governments but the global market for commodities—largely free to fluctuate despite cartels and government interventions—that naturally cooled the demand for precisely those commodities that were in shortest supply. This, in turn opened the way for entrepreneurs and innovators, also driven by free markets, to develop new technologies to extract the same or alternate resources. Again, the Malthusian approach was wrong.

Are the lights about to go out this time?

The argument about the finite supply of critical resources nonetheless persists. Particularly with crude oil, there are very convincing arguments supporting the thesis that we have already exhausted the most accessible sources and are near or at peak oil supplies and production levels. But the clever-but-wrong prognosis by the likes of Malthus and the Club of Rome should stand as warnings to all those who rush to such conclusions. Even if we do run into supply and demand constraints, the lights will not go out. Instead, the marketplace, if allowed to fluctuate without undue constraints, will again drive prices to levels that force mankind to adjust its behavior. If economic growth comes to a screeching halt, it will be due to equally powerful forces in the financial marketplace—not due to finite supplies of natural resources.

Indeed, the global debt crisis, whether allowed to play out now or later, can itself act as a broad homeostatic mechanism that drives down demand, gives mankind a chance to adjust and react, opening the path for innovative ways to boost food yields, extract resources more efficiently, and build a solid foundation for a new round of future, hopefully balanced, growth.

In this sense, we are incorrigible optimists: we have sufficient confidence in mankind's ability to adapt and innovate to ultimately succeed in mastering the coming decades—and even centuries. But, our optimism stands and falls along with the economic system. Only an open economic system that encourages the human capacity for invention, promotes individual ambition, and continually allows the struggle for a better life can meet these great challenges.

Theory and practice teach us that only a free market economic system is sufficiently flexible to master the challenges of the future. But if the free market is used as a scapegoat in the course of ongoing attempts to overcome the crisis, if the free market is virtually abolished, then the world would, indeed, be well on its way to hitting limits to growth, much as the Soviet Union and the Eastern Bloc hit a stone wall before their collapse.

Up until now, the political responses to the current crisis have, of course, been anything but free market–based, and to this extent we are concerned. It is well known that prosperity does not emerge by decree. Nor does it spring from manipulations by bureaucrats, organizing their grand experiments in interest-rate fixing or wealth redistribution. Prosperity is the result of free enterprise, always exploring new pathways, solving problems through market mechanisms, and generating levels of prosperity undreamed of by previous generations.

The Most Attractive Market in the World?

Real estate, stocks, and bonds are the investment classes that most investors are the most familiar with. Also, life and annuity insurers have supposedly blessed individual investors with their weak but high-margin, tax-protected whole life insurance products. And investment companies have layered on expensive mutual funds, which, despite widespread underperformance, have, nonetheless made the investment companies a great deal of money. In the broad context of the global debt trap, most are booby traps to be avoided, or used only with very strict risk parameters.

The economic significance of stocks and bonds is large and well known. The financial markets ensure a more or less efficient capital allocation, without which a modern economy could not function. That is the true purpose of the financial markets. The fact that, under certain conditions, some investors and speculators can earn money on these markets through shrewd trading is simply a positive side effect. However, this feat is achieved by only a few, as most investors are not sufficiently flexible to embrace both the upside and the downside—or to properly factor them into their investment strategy.

- The number one rule: *Avoid major losses during market downturns.* And if you ever digress from that path, just remember the year 2008, a year that made the importance of this basic rule of successful investing absolutely clear.
- The second rule: *You must also be flexible when selecting investment classes*—not just stocks and bonds, but also precious metals, other commodities, foreign currencies, and inverse investments in each. The history of the financial markets teaches us that all investment classes are subject not only to fluctuations that can be explained by the economic cycle—by shifts from booms to recessions—but are also subject to much longer cycles. Against this backdrop, it is clear that each individual asset class should be considered only at specific times. Or—if possible and within your comfort zone—should also be considered for investments that are designed to profit from falling prices.

Alongside the stocks, bonds, and real estate referred to earlier, do not forget the investment class whose economic significance is equal to that of all the financial markets, and, in some respects, exceeds it: commodities.

Until recently, compared with the real estate and financial markets, the all-important commodities markets were viewed by individuals and institutions as leading a kind of shadowy life. And in the wake of their disastrous price declines of 2008, that notion was again revived in many investment circles.

Jim Rogers is one who has done much to counter this notion. Up until 2008, his well-oiled PR machine had helped commodities achieve an astonishing rise in popularity among investors. As a former partner of George Soros, Rogers enjoyed, rightfully so, a certain degree of star status among speculators. As early as 1998, he began to bet on a renewed and pronounced commodities boom, even creating his own commodities index for this purpose. And indeed, the indices available up to that time had many failings that he wanted to iron out—their lack of internationalization and focus on the United States, plus their poor diversification and energy bias in certain indices.

Rogers wrote a primer on commodities as an investment class that became a bestseller. And he spared none of the many opportunities that came his way to publicly point out the attractiveness of commodity investments. With the German translation of his book *Hot Commodities: How Anyone Can Invest Profitably in the World's Best Market*, he became a household name for commodities investors in Germany as well. He rose to become the leading figure of a very strong commodities boom, which was also forecast by us in *Das Greenspan Dossier*.

Then came 2008 and the harsh setback for global commodities.

Because we predicted the recession that began in the United States in December 2007, we were not surprised by that slump. Historically, virtually all recessions have been accompanied by falling equity and commodities prices. It was consequently easy for us to predict a similar course of events in this instance as well. In contrast to Rogers, we did not advise our readers to ride out the foreseeable cyclical recession, but to drastically reduce their commodities positions.

After the severe commodity price routs of 2008, the next question was this: Was that decline merely a pronounced interruption in a long-term upward trend, or was it the end of the commodities boom? Rogers believes the former to be probable, and we agree. In other words, we believe that the price falls are merely cyclical in nature—an entirely normal trend during a recession.

Important Markets

Despite intermediate sharp declines, never underestimate the importance of the commodities markets. Consider the many critical advantages they offer:

- *Commodities are the basis of all production.* Even in the Stone Age, people worked with different types of stone according to their requirements. Later, they gained collective knowledge in metal extraction and processing. So, the development of mankind without commodities is impossible to imagine. Basic materials such as bronze, silver, gold, copper, tin, iron, and salt have been ubiquitous and indispensable. Nonetheless, in contrast to the financial markets, the commodities market ekes out a veritable wallflower existence. Thanks to Jim Rogers's efforts to popularize commodities as an investment class, this has changed a little in recent years. But most investors continue to focus overwhelmingly on other, traditional investment opportunities. Most institutional and private investors were—and are—largely oblivious to commodities as an investment. For commodity investors, this is a great plus.

- *Commodities markets are characterized by their broad diversity.* There is a wide range of very different commodities, from base metals to energy and agricultural products. Moreover, most of the commodity markets are extremely liquid. They include a broad network of well-organized trading centers spanning the world; and they do not suffer from many of the deficiencies that threaten the stock and bond markets. Indeed, turnover on global commodities markets exceeds that of global equity markets.

- *Commodities have delivered attractive performance in the past.* The price trend of commodities is comparable with the long-term performance of the equity markets. Among others, this is the conclusion of a comprehensive study by the Yale International Center for Finance, which covers the period from 1959 to 2004.

- *Commodities are no more risky than stocks.* The level of risk (measured in terms of volatility or the range of broad market swings) of the two markets was also investigated in the Yale study. The result, which will perhaps surprise many people, was this: overall, equity markets are actually a bit riskier than commodities markets.

- *Commodities help ensure broader diversification.* The correlation (or, to be more precise, the correlation coefficient) is a statistical measure reflecting the degree to which different investment classes move in the same direction. If the prices of two investment classes were to move precisely in unison and the same direction, the correlation would be 100 percent, or plus 1. If the prices of two investment classes were to move in unison but in precisely the opposite direction, the correlation would be –100 percent, or minus 1. The price trends of commodities and stocks show almost no correlation in a monthly and quarterly comparison. However, if one considers a five-year period, then a strongly negative correlation is evident. In relation to bonds, the correlation is strongly negative even when viewed quarterly. Nonetheless, the correlation does not become more negative as the period is expanded. Conclusion: commodities give you a great way to diversify with an investment class that is not correlated to stocks in short or medium term, and is inversely correlated in the long term.

- *Commodities provide the best protection against inflation.* The correlation between commodity prices and the inflation rate is already positive when viewed over a quarterly period, and becomes extremely positive when viewed over five years. High inflation rates are strongly correlated with rising commodity prices, but also with falling prices for stocks and bonds. Thus, in contrast to bonds and even stocks, commodities do offer genuine protection against inflation. The fact that equity investments have historically offered poor protection against inflation may come as a surprise to many readers. But the unambiguous result of the study is confirmed by other research. And you saw earlier, it also applies, for example, to the period of German hyperinflation in the early 1920s. Never forget: in that episode of extreme inflation, stocks lost between 80 and 90 percent of their value, when adjusted for inflation. In that scenario, commodities, especially precious metals, are among the *only* investment solutions.

- *Generally speaking, commodities have a place in every portfolio.* The results of the Yale study are very important from an investor's point of view. Because of the negative correlation to other investments—coupled with attractive performance—commodities are an essential asset class for every portfolio. They can significantly reduce a portfolio's overall volatility, and do so without diminishing overall returns.

Figure 6.8 shows the trends in real, inflation-adjusted terms, for bonds, stocks, and commodities over the period in question. As you can clearly see, up until the 1990s, commodities were slightly ahead. It was not until the great stock market bubble of 1995 to 2000 that the performance of the equity markets succeeded in overtaking that of commodities. However, with the bursting of that speculative bubble, the situation reversed once again.

Figure 6.9 shows the correlation between return and risk (standard deviation) of four investment classes—short-term government securities, long-term government bonds, stocks, and commodities. It is well known that higher returns must typically be paid for with higher levels of risk. Yet this chart proves that the risk over the period was somewhat greater for the equity markets than for the commodities markets—*with nearly identical returns.*

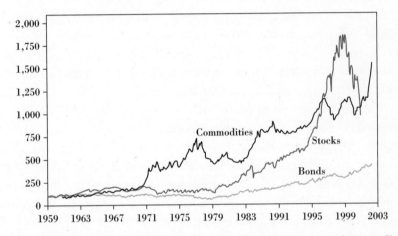

Figure 6.8 Commodities and Stocks Are Equally Attractive over the Long Term

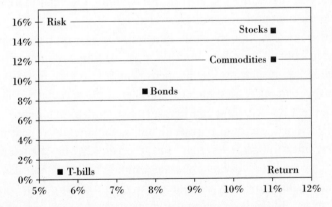

Figure 6.9 Commodities Have a Better Risk/Return Profile than Stocks (Average Return and Standard Deviation)

Commodities Are a Must for Every Investor, Just as Equities Are

As you've seen, the 2004 Yale study highlights several advantages of commodities that you, as an investor, should be aware of and incorporate in your investment strategy. The performance of commodities are every bit as attractive over the long term as stocks. The risk level of the two investment classes is also nearly identical. For these two reasons alone, you should be familiar with both investment classes to the same extent, and include them in your portfolio as a matter of principle.

A further advantage: as we mentioned earlier, because of the negative correlation between commodities on the one hand and stocks and bonds on the other, you can reduce the overall risk of your portfolio by adding commodities to the mix. And in contrast to stocks and bonds, you can also effectively protect yourself against inflation.

Why then is this investment class still relatively unpopular despite its very attractive characteristics? Here's one explanation: around 1980, a long-term slump began in the commodities and precious metals markets, leading to considerable price declines after adjusting for inflation. At the same time, traditional financial investments began one of the greatest booms of all time, with share prices rising by more than 15-fold during that 20-year period through the end of 1999.

It is well known that, in markets, no argument is more convincing than rising prices. Consequently, the attention of investors, banks, and the media was increasingly drawn to the booming financial markets while interest in the commodities markets waned.

Another key reason: investors generally believe that the logistics of investing in commodities are more difficult. Although commodities trading is highly liquid, that trading happens primarily on the futures markets, which have a bad reputation and are considered too speculative. Thanks to robust clearing houses, these markets give investors a high degree of security in the event of trading partner defaults. But they also give investors the opportunity for great leverage—in other words, the chance to invest in large amounts with relatively little capital. This leverage can be an advantage if you know how to control the risk. And of course, nobody is required to use all the leverage available. But it is the examples of investor losses multiplied by the large leverage that make the headlines. And it is those headlines that have given futures markets a bad reputation that has endured up to the present day.

Only recently have easy-to-use commodity vehicles been created beyond the futures markets—through the introduction of commodity-based exchange-traded funds (ETFs) in the United States and exchange-traded certificates (ETCs) in Europe.

They are practical and easy to buy and sell in a regular stock broker-age account. However, some these certificates—particularly the certificates in Europe—also have a disadvantage: they can be subject to issuer risk. If the issuer of a certificate goes bankrupt, the certificate can also suffer substantial losses. Particularly since 2007, when the prospect of bank fail-ures began to loom ever larger, we pointed out this risk to our readers in increasingly pointed terms. Nonetheless, the banking crisis that began in 2007 is an extreme case. And if it returns, we should also be in a position to detect the burgeoning risk early so we can warn our readers accordingly.

To illustrate a key point, let's go back to the extreme and rare stock market boom of the late 1990s—when the long-term stock market boom, which had begun in 1982, morphed into a giant speculative bubble, draw-ing large numbers of new investors like groupies to a rock star.

In its final stages, the attention, imagination, and most important, the greed of almost all individual and institutional investors was turned almost exclusively toward the equity markets. Above all, the Nasdaq in the United States and the Neuer Markt in Germany, almost forgotten today, experi-enced a veritable stampede driven by a rare bedazzlement of the masses going berserk over technology.

In contrast, while the technology sector was in the spotlight, commodi-ties were considered almost exclusively a boring and grimy sector that one could happily ignore. This belief was so widespread and deeply ingrained that even college programs related to commodities, such as geology and certain engineering courses, were largely abandoned in favor of programs related to high tech. Most young people wanted to seek their fortunes either in the increasingly glamorous technology or in the extremely lucra-tive investment banking sectors. It did not occur to them to explore the archaic world of the commodities. As frequently happens, this extreme cyclical behavior—often known as the *pork cycle*—was to have its sweet revenge. Just a few years later, experts in the commodities sector were in desperately short supply, while computer scientists fell on hard times.

And in the most recent cycle, it was investment bankers who suffered their own Armageddon, facing a tough job market that persists to this day.

Not surprisingly, it was during this phase of its widespread, deeply ingrained bad reputation that most commodities markets made a broad, long-term bottom. Investors, obsessed with the Nasdaq and Neuer Markt and ignoring financial market history, repeatedly passed over highly attractive entry opportunities in the commodity markets. Only a small minority recognized the long-term trend reversal—and the birth of a new commodities boom—that was in the making.

This helps explain why so few investors bought commodities in this initial phase of the new bull market. To do so, they had to be among the contrarians, such as Jim Rogers. By contrarians, we mean the small band of independent-thinking investors who refuse to heed the siren songs of Wall Street or be lulled by the pressures from mass psychology—who are able to swim against the tides and are in a position to form their own opinion. We, the authors of this book, live, breathe, and write within this tradition.

Arguments for a Continuation of the Commodities Boom

Even a cursory glance at any long-term price charts of free markets can lead to only one conclusion: prices change in accordance with clearly visible trends. If you cannot recognize this, you're probably an economics professor subscribing to an extreme version of the random-walk school of thinking. This worldview maintains that prices move entirely by chance and therefore cannot be forecast. Perhaps some folks can build their university careers on this theory. But as pragmatic investors, it makes us chuckle.

Starting way back in 1968, inflationary monetary and fiscal policies, among other factors, lead to a dramatic rise in commodity prices. This boom lasted until 1982. And it did not end until President Jimmy Carter allowed Fed Chairman Paul Volcker to combat inflation with drastic interest rate hikes.

This kill-or-cure remedy was successful. Inflation rates fell dramatically. And a new age of declining inflation, falling interest rates, and rising share prices—the great financial market boom of the 1980s and 1990s—got under way. At the same time, commodities experienced a deeply entrenched, long-term bear market, which also lasted approximately 20 years. It was only at the turn of the millennium—at the peak of the greatest stock market bubble of all time—that chart analysis of the commodities markets began to reveal a very promising bottoming pattern.

Sure enough, starting in 2001, in a knee-jerk response to the bursting of the stock market bubble, a highly inflationary monetary and fiscal policy was introduced around the world. Official policy was dominated by substantial interest rate reductions and dramatic rises in national debt levels. And with this massive policy shift, the foundation was laid for a new commodities boom.

Now the question: did that commodities boom come to an abrupt end in 2008? Will commodity prices now once again go into a Rip Van Winkle–like slumber that endures for nearly a generation? Or should we expect a continuation of the boom that began in 2001?

A key to the answer lies in the emerging markets. In recent years, many have enjoyed a veritable economic miracle, a process that hardly seems reversible to us. To be sure, disaster scenarios are not inconceivable in the emerging markets as well. Nor do we subscribe fully to the decoupling theory. So you cannot expect emerging markets to escape cyclical disruptions, or even crises on a scale similar to those seen recently—or historically—in the industrialized countries. But the rapid industrialization and urbanization underway in China, India, and elsewhere are bound to have an enduring impact on the world economy and on commodity consumption.

As you can see in Figure 6.10 commodity prices rose to new all-time highs in 2007 and 2008. Because of the economic and financial crisis, they, too, slumped precipitously thereafter. We think this decline will prove temporary, because there are very strong arguments for a long-term bull market in commodities.

Strongly growing economies, which not long ago started out from a very low base, are exhibiting rapidly increasing demand for raw materials. Consequently, the growth in demand from the emerging market nations is many times faster than that of industrialized nations. At the same time, in the emerging markets, per capita consumption of nearly all key commodities is still substantially below that of the industrialized nations. This is true not only for industrial raw materials, but also for agricultural commodities. And as people's eating and consumption habits change when they achieve prosperity, per capita consumption is bound to rise dramatically over time. This game of catch-up—with many emerging markets leapfrogging

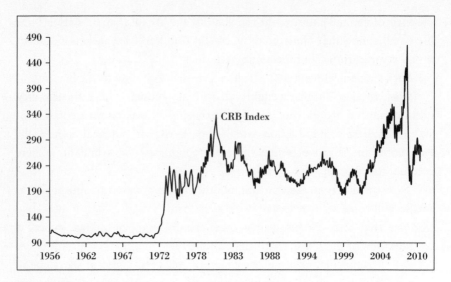

Figure 6.10 Commodities Are Temporarily Back Down to Near Pre-Boom Levels (Thomson Reuters/Jeffries CRB Index)

from the nineteenth to the twenty-first century—is an ongoing, long-term megatrend that, in all probability, is bound to continue.

We base this forecast primarily on the history of industrialized economies—countries that followed a similar trajectory in the past. Their consumption of raw materials followed the same growth path we now see in China, Brazil, and India today. And despite temporary interruptions, we have no reason to believe that this long-term trend will be permanently altered by the current economic crisis. The economic cycle, with its upturns and recessions, does indeed determine the short- and mid-term behavior of global markets, including commodities. But the long-term cycles are driven by broader, more enduring changes in supply and demand—not to mention inflation.

The Chinese government clearly sees the world in very large-scale strategic terms and has absolutely massive currency reserves in U.S. dollars. This combination is giving China the opportunity to use any sluggishness or corrections in global commodity markets to make equally massive strategic purchases. In the future, this, in turn, could of course lead to some degree of decoupling of commodity prices from the impact of the economic cycle and trigger surprises in commodity price trends. We can see this already in some select commodities, particularly gold. But it is not yet clearly visible in most other commodities, notably energy. So don't count on decoupling to prevent cyclical downturns in commodities. Quite the contrary, use them as buying opportunities.

The strongest argument supporting our forecast of a long-term commodities boom lies in the big-picture trends of real, inflation-adjusted commodity prices: in 2001, they reached their lowest level since the 1930s. And thanks to the dramatic price drop in the second half of 2008, even in nominal terms, many commodity prices fell nearly to their lows of 2001. As long as these two massive declines remain mostly intact, commodity prices will continue to be extremely attractive.

For a long-term perspective, consider the three big commodity booms of the twentieth century: the first lasted from 1906 to 1923; the second, from 1933 to 1953; and the third, from 1968 to 1982—17 years on average. So based on this alone, the current commodity boom, which began in 2001, is still only from half to two-thirds through its likely life span.

If it ended in 2008, as some seem to argue, it would have lived a half-life of only seven years. A more likely scenario is that it merely experienced an extreme setback due to the global economic crisis and is likely to resume after that crisis plays itself out. This scenario is further supported not only by the highly inflationary monetary and fiscal policies we see today but also by the trends in real commodity prices. Even during the boom of recent years, they remained far below the high water marks of previous boom periods.

In fact, many commodity prices have recently been so low they were close to their average cost of production. This means that cost-intensive extraction operations were costing their owners money. If this situation were to continue, we'd see another, new wave of mine closures. The exploration and mining of new deposits would be choked off.

During the last economic upturn, this typical production cycle led to considerable supply bottlenecks, which, in turn, drove prices skyward. The tight credit conditions that persist today—despite government efforts to encourage bank lending—seem to ensure that we'll see similar supply bottlenecks in the future.

Remember: with mining and other key resources, there is a particularly long time lag between the discovery of new deposits and actual extraction. Before an ounce of ore or barrel of oil is extracted, producers must wade through feasibility studies, approval procedures, mine construction, and expansion of the necessary infrastructure. If, because of low inflation-adjusted prices or tight credit conditions, exploration activities are cut back today, then it won't be long before you again hear complaints about supply bottlenecks and large price increases.

Also remember: in a dramatic move, between mid-2008 and early 2009, commodity prices fell to levels that marked the lower limit of a pronounced, long-term sideways move that prevailed in the 1980s and 1990s. Thus, from a technical point of view, that level is a massive *support zone*—a floor below which prices are unlikely to fall.

With all of these factors converging, it therefore makes sense to consider strategic purchases. Yes, the *upper* boundary of the 1980s-to-1990s sideways movement was also viewed as an important *resistance zone*—a ceiling beyond which traders thought commodities were unlikely to rise. But if the recent past proved anything, it proved that the so-called resistance zone was entirely meaningless—in many commodities, it was breached to the upside without hesitation.

Because of our forecast of a recession and temporarily low inflation, we were prepared for falling commodity prices from 2007 onward. But the extent of this decline—in combination with the speed at which the prices collapsed—still surprised us. This crash exceeded what might be expected in a normal, cyclical, recession-induced slump. Instead, the crash in commodity prices was more in keeping with a true global economic crisis.

In our economic analyses, we continue to come to the conclusion that the current crisis is far from over: Don't be surprised to see a further intensification of the crisis. Don't be shocked if it's very dramatic in scope. Don't be surprised by intermediate commodities price declines.

But by the same token, don't be deceived by interim economic recoveries that may occur at any time, always remembering that, even in the 1930s, key economic measures did not fall in a straight line. They exhibited relatively small intermediate rallies. And like today, those rallies tempted many investors to hail "the end of the crisis." On that long downward path—as on this one—there was no scarcity of opportunities for stock investors to lose money.

Just remember: the stock rallies are bought and paid for by massive government interventions. But as we have explained thoroughly in this book, it is precisely because of those interventions that we anticipate a substantial continuation of the crisis. In the interim, however, false starts—both in the stock market and the economy—are also highly likely.

Against this background, we're currently in no rush to jump into the commodity markets in a big way, despite the unambiguous course toward inflation that has been set. Instead, we can afford to be patient, waiting for clear signals from our macroeconomic leading indicators that the economic cycle is at the end of its downward phase and has begun a renewed upturn. At mid-year 2010, there is very little to suggest that this is the case. Quite the contrary, all the early evidence is in place for a new recession in the United States. This gives you the best of three conditions:

1. You have the clear knowledge that commodities are very attractively valued.
2. You can see how they are bound to begin a steep climb as the inflationary course set by governments takes hold.
3. And, thanks to a new recession in the United States, you should have abundant opportunities to buy at better prices.

In the long term, we anticipate a renewed commodities boom that could put previous commodity booms to shame. However, over the course of the coming two years (2011 to 2012) we anticipate an intensification of the global economic crisis, which will likely *delay* the start of this boom.

Those Who Buy and Possess Gold Have Many Enemies—A Tough Recommendation

As we did in our 2004 book, *Das Greenspan Dossier,* we recommend that investors who want to protect their wealth invest at least 25 percent of their portfolio in gold. From that time until mid-2010, the price of gold in dollars has risen sharply, both in dollars and in euros. Nonetheless, we continue to recommend investing a high proportion of one's assets in gold and precious metals.

This is a tough recommendation to make, because the proportion of gold in a model portfolio, which we recommended at 25 percent in 2004, has, in the interim, risen to more than 50 percent, thanks to highly encouraging price gains. And this overweighting of gold would be even more extreme for any investors who failed to heed our advice to get out of stocks, which are down substantially since late 2007.

Our recommendation: If you read and followed our earlier advice, hold. If you are new to gold investing, use setbacks to build your positions, step by step, up to the 25 percent recommended allocation.

But the path to these impressive price gains was not always easy. As in all boom periods, gold did not rise continually, suffering relatively pronounced setbacks and corrections along the way. The same is likely to be true going forward; so be prepared for a bumpy road in the coming years as well.

Why? First, because the history of the financial markets teaches us that 50 percent retracements—giving back half of the prior upswing—are both possible and normal within the context of a long-term uptrend. Second, there are simply too many institutions in our society that will do everything they can, including attempts to manipulate prices, to prevent the price of gold from rising too sharply.

Rising gold prices can, or actually *must,* be viewed as a vote of no confidence in a currency and in the policies behind it. Since citizens have no choice but to live within the confines of the state's money monopoly, and since they have no vehicle for influencing the machinations of politicians or their central banks, virtually the *only* outlet for expressing their mistrust of their rulers, now both evident and largely justified, is by joining a mass movement toward gold. And given the extremes politicians are going to with their policies, such a movement may become a veritable panic, threatening the financial system and the political structures. Even revolutions are possible—and have often occurred historically—in response to the destruction of the currency, which, in turn, is almost invariably triggered by an entirely deliberate inflationary policy on the part of the government itself.

An early indication of these reactions can be seen in a minor episode that took place at the pro-regulation Attac conference in Berlin. In his opening speech, Germany's former secretary of state for finance, Heiner Flassbeck, compared the financial markets to a gambling casino. He suggested that this casino is broken and should be repaired. In response, the audience, including more than 1,000 in the great hall, began to boo and protest, to which the speaker corrected himself, saying: "Not repaired, closed! It must be closed!" Then the audience, evidently not well educated in finance, cheered its approval.

It was a classic illustration of the misguided perspective of the wise careerists. They blame the market for the very excesses they themselves create with their interventions. Then, when those markets, such as derivatives trading, overheat and explode, their emotional, knee-jerk reaction is to shut the markets down.

Plus it also stands as an illustration to the lengths politicians could go toward trying to manipulate and control markets, especially if they are viewed as a threat.

Friend *and* Foe

The government is both the mightiest friend *and* the greatest foe of gold investors—friend, because the inflation that drives gold prices higher is almost invariably created by government; and foe, because gold is in direct competition with the state's monopoly over money.

Even to most politicians, it must be clear that gold is the antithesis to the state's power over fiat money. If the state's fiat money were to collapse, then, in the absence of government interference, gold—along with silver and other alternative currencies—would replace it as the most generally acceptable form of money.

Right now, we have unequal competition between ever-deteriorating government-backed money (fiat currencies) on the one side and free-market money (gold) on the other. And right now, the outcome is decided by the central banks responsible for administering the state's monopoly over money.

Their purpose? To ensure order in the financial system. According to the letter of the law, they are supposed to be independent—not bound by the directives from the government or its finance ministers. However in practice, central bankers, who are appointed and largely financed by federal governments, know all too well that they must not bite the hands that feed them.

Result: In the real world, there's no such thing as an independent central bank. They are a fiction, and central bankers either already know it, or they're quickly reminded of this fact of life as soon as they seek to strike a more independent path.

In the 1960s, Federal Reserve Chairman William McChesney Martin Jr. was harshly scolded by President Johnson whenever he raised the discount rate. His 1970s successors, Arthur Burns and G. William Miller, learned the lesson and largely did the bidding of the presidents they served. Alan Greenspan took the helm at the Fed 69 days before the worst stock market crash in America's history and, despite lip service to independence, almost invariably supported White House inflationists. And Ben Bernanke will go down in Fed history as the chairman who printed more money more quickly than any other—precisely what Washington's inflation witch doctors ordered. Only Paul Volcker struck a truly different course, but even he rarely did so without a tacit green light from the Oval Office.

In Germany, the prime example of central bank subservience that comes to mind is when Bundesbank president Karl Otto Pöhl spoke out against the early introduction of the deutschmark in East Germany in 1990—and against an economically absurd, politically determined exchange rate. His reward for being independent (and right): public humiliation by German Chancellor Helmut Kohl, a man who knew virtually nothing about monetary policy. Lacking the authority and stature to defy the country's political leaders, Pöhl resigned in 1991, partly in protest. We think he did the people a disservice. Instead of deploying his knowledge in their interest, he folded his tent.

Three Hundred Percent Profit Given Away, but Nevertheless the Right Decision?

When Gordon Brown was still Britain's Chancellor of the Exchequer he told the Bank of England to throw half of Britain's gold reserves (400 metric tons) onto the market, heralding the sale in a public forum and *in advance*.

Generally speaking, if you want to achieve the best possible prices in a sale, especially one of that magnitude, you do so with the appropriate degree of discretion and caution, in a manner that will not disrupt the market. The approach Brown took—and which was later followed by other politicians and central bankers—deviated radically from normal procedure, and had precisely the opposite goal: They actually wanted to sell their gold for the *worst* possible price. But why?

The answer: By shocking the gold market, Chancellor Brown wanted to prove to the British people and the entire world that his so-called anti-inflation policy was successful. This is why he repeatedly and publicly announced the planned gold sales. Sure enough, gold prices, which were already down dramatically in prior years, fell even further—to $252.80 per ounce, an historic low. Brown then proceeded to sell 395 tons of gold over

17 auctions from July 1999 to March 2002, at an average price of about US$275 per ounce. Yes, it may have achieved a short-term political purpose. But it was one of the costliest ones on record—a great financial blunder.

Consequently, Brown could boast the thoroughly questionable success of being the largest seller at the worst levels of gold's longest bear market. The ones who could truly celebrate their success, however, were anonymous buyers. They did not trumpet their intentions far and wide. They did not have an agenda other than to make money. And they succeeded in acquiring a large portion of Britain's gold reserves at fire sale prices, gold that had been plundered—sorry, "obtained"—from the four corners of the world.

Way to Go, Mr. Brown!

In trading circles, he has the honor of having given his name to the low point in gold prices reached at that time—the "Brown bottom." Credit where credit is due. . . .

As you can see in Figure 6.11, Gordon Brown, the then–U.K. Chancellor of the Exchequer, sold half of the country's reserves at the bottom of a secular bear market. Obviously, the British were not resentful. They later made him their Prime Minister.

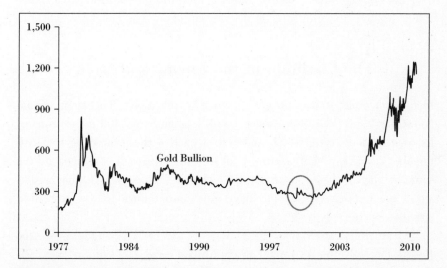

Figure 6.11 The Brown Bottom: Gordon Brown Sold Out the United Kingdom's Gold at Precisely the Wrong Time—Near a Major Historic Low (Gold Price per Ounce in U.S. Dollars)

The Gordon Brown Gold Indicator

Analysts at financialsense.com have even derived a gold indicator from Gordon Brown's actions. With a nod and a wink, its creators tell us that this contrarian indicator is one of the more reliable of an imminent rise in the gold price, as the results in Figure 6.12 seem to confirm.

Figure 6.12 illustrates the poor performance of the wannabe gold expert Gordon Brown. With tongue in cheek, a clever analyst used Mr. Brown as a contrary indicator.

Not surprisingly, on February 3, 2009, the British Parliament conducted an inquiry into Gordon Brown's gold sales. Conservative Party MP Peter Tapsell had questioned Brown's decision to sell large parts of the gold reserve from the start. Now he pressed his point home. Brown's noteworthy response: it had been the correct decision to diversify Britain's reserves. That response comes as no surprise to us. And had they diversified the reserves into Zimbabwean dollars, it would not have shocked us either.

The reality: Had Gordon Brown waited a few years to sell Britain's gold reserves, the United Kingdom could have been 5 billion to 7 billion pounds richer. But alas, this reckless transaction apparently did little political damage to Brown, who went on to become prime minister, presided over sales of still more reserves, and left Britain to his successor in a sorrier state than any citizen or foreign observer could have dreamed possible.

The Coalition of the Enemies of Gold

In the concerted attacks on gold, Brown wasn't alone. The International Monetary Fund (IMF) followed Brown's lead and sold 408 metric tons of its own gold reserves, which make up a part of the reserves of the IMF member countries. Many central banks on the European continent did the same, selling off their countries' gold reserves. The people, had they understood the implications, would have gone into mourning. Investors and speculators cheered.

Meanwhile, rather than go it alone as the United Kingdom did, the European central banks sought to coordinate their gold bullion sales, celebrating this coordination as a "great achievement": In 1999, they signed the Washington Agreement, agreeing to sell "no more than" 400 metric

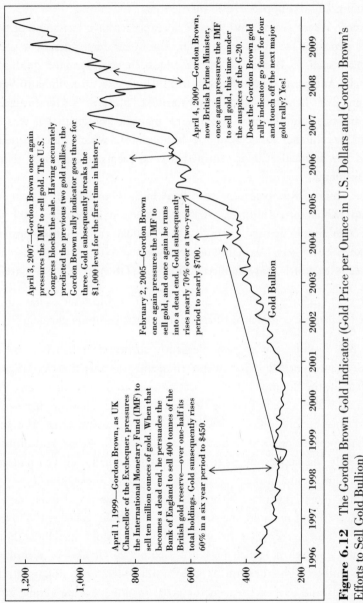

Figure 6.12 The Gordon Brown Gold Indicator (Gold Price per Ounce in U.S. Dollars and Gordon Brown's Efforts to Sell Gold Bullion)

SOURCE: www.usagold.com.

tons of gold per year over the subsequent five years. And in 2004, when the five years were up, a new agreement was promptly signed, with the cap on annual gold sales upped to 500 metric tons.

In more recent years, central bank bureaucrats have lost some of their previous penchant for large, spectacular, loudly heralded sales. A few central banks, such as Portugal's and Belgium's, have suspended gold sales completely. And some central banks—from China to Russia, India to South Africa, and even Argentina—have even started to buy gold for their reserves.

Meanwhile, the Swiss National Bank made it known that it was not planning any further sales. And the Bundesbank, which had frequently opposed the political zeal of central bankers, seems to subscribe to this new movement.

Yes, Steffen Kampeter, a so-called budget expert in Germany's Christian Democratic Union (CDU) recommended in March 2009 that gold reserves should be used to combat the financial crisis. But Bundesbank chief Axel Weber—yes, the man who once wanted to emulate Greenspan—countered with words that sounded nothing like Greenspan. He declared:

> The German gold reserves are not for sale. The gold reserves have a role in ensuring confidence and stability for the common currency.[2]

We heard, and we were very pleasantly surprised. It had been a very long time indeed since anyone had spoken of the monetary function of gold.

Officially, the Bundesbank's reserves amount to 3,412 metric tons. And it is to Axel Weber's credit that the German Bundesbank has not disposed of any gold since he took office in 2004. Weber's predecessor, Ernst Welteke, a thoroughly pitiful Bundesbank head for a number of reasons, had different ideas entirely: his suggestion at the time was to actually sell German gold reserves and put some of the proceeds into European stocks. Ouch!

In this context, one more surprising fact is very worthy of note: the U.S. Federal Reserve has not sold one single gram of gold in recent years. In fact, the United States recorded its last outflows of gold in 1968. That's around the time when French president Charles de Gaulle—in accordance with the rules of the Bretton Woods system—tendered dollars to the United States and cashed them in for gold. In doing so, de Gaulle effectively unmasked the great currency deception of Bretton Woods, and, sure enough, it was only three years later that President Richard Nixon declared the end of that monetary system.

However, we should introduce one more caveat at this juncture: it is entirely possible that some central banks cannot sell gold because they have effectively already loaned that gold to investment banks. This factor is difficult to prove and impossible to measure; on central bank balance sheets, the items *gold* and *gold receivables* are combined into a single entry. In other words, some unknown portion of the gold reserves are actually not reserves at all—but merely gold receivables, held by the banks, which, as we have seen, do not exactly adhere to sound business models.

Nor must we ignore the investors who buy gold and keep it in a precious metals account with their bank and are also in the dark—*they have no way of knowing where the physical gold actually is.*

For some proof, consider this example from Switzerland. Kaspar Villiger, the board chairman of UBS, Switzerland's biggest bank, at the time this chapter was written, once commented on gold in a manner that vividly illustrates this dilemma. At the time, he was still Switzerland's finance minister. He even was the man who wrote legislation and constitutional amendments that later allowed the Swiss National Bank to reduce its gold reserves from 2,600 metric tons to 1,000 tons. Surprisingly, however, in 2003, when this same Kaspar Villiger was questioned by parliamentarian Paul Günter—who wanted to know exactly *where* Switzerland's gold was located—he responded:

> Where these gold bars actually are, I'm afraid I cannot tell you, as I do not know myself. I do not need to know, nor do I want to know.[3]

We hear, and we are amazed. If the man who wrote Swiss laws governing Swiss gold sales has no clue where the Swiss gold is, how can the average investor in the United States, the United Kingdom, or anywhere else on the planet?

Alas, foes of gold are not new entrants on the world scene; they've been around for a long time. Consider, for example, the Exchange Stabilization Fund (ESF), formed on April 27, 1934. Its explicit agenda: to protect the international value of the U.S. dollar and to depress the price of gold. At that time, its nominal capital was two billion U.S. dollars. With the aid of the Gold Reserve Act (signed in 1934), the ESF was released from its accountability to the U.S. Congress and is subject to no public, judicial, or parliamentary control. The fund has over $100 billion at its disposal, including about half of that in the form of Special Drawing Rights (SDR) from the IMF, which can be used by the U.S. Treasury Department as it sees fit, subject to the approval of the president. Since 1962, the U.S. Federal Reserve has acted as designated agent (under the direction of the Federal Reserve Bank of New York), which executes the ESF's orders on foreign currency markets.

Overall, we now have the distinct impression that central banks' enthusiasm for selling gold has been reduced sharply since the price of gold has surged in recent years.

Why? Perhaps it's because the central bankers actually fear their day of reckoning, when they will be called to account for their actions. For example, what will be their fate when citizens one day realize precisely how many pounds or euros per capita have gone down the tubes thanks to their wanton squandering of national treasures?

Perhaps the central bankers are also worried that, with every ton of gold they sell, the remaining gold reserves available for sale are greatly diminished, and that one day they will be exhausted.

However, there is a further, much more important argument: Even the worst and most nefarious central bankers in the world are presumably familiar with the history of money and gold that we have outlined in this book. In that case, they must undoubtedly know that every fiat money system always ended in failure, and sometimes can do so in a relatively short amount of time. It cannot have escaped even the most naïve of central bankers that this fate may be lying in wait for our present system as well. To regain the trust they have gambled away, they know they will probably need to start again with a halfway serious, credible currency. And what better instrument for this purpose than tried and tested precious metals?

Anyone involved in power politics who thinks beyond the here and now must surely come to the conclusion that she must keep at least some of her powder dry. If, someday, the prevailing global monetary order ends in chaos and a new one needs to be negotiated on an international scale, gold will probably play an important role. And in that scenario, any nation left with no gold reserves whatsoever will be very poorly equipped for this new beginning, relegated to the sidelines of any international negotiations.

One indication validating this view can be seen in the actions of the central banks in January 2009. Overall, the central banks were active on the markets as net purchasers, acquiring 1.1 billion ounces of gold in net terms. Ecuador, Venezuela, and Russia were among the largest buyers. Meanwhile, China had risen to become the world's largest gold producer, while production fell in South Africa. The Chinese government does not publish data on its gold reserves, so we cannot form an accurate picture of precisely what kind of leverage China might have in the kind of worst-case scenario we have sketched out here. But it could be very substantial.

The world's largest manager of private wealth assets is presumably still the Swiss bank, UBS; and in March 2009, it published an extensive study on the subject of gold. In it, the analysts speak of an ideal environment for gold investors, as the central banks have been forced into a corner. Their conclusion: the price of gold could rise to $2,500 per ounce, as an inflationary trend was highly probable in the near future.

In general, we agree. But, at the same time, the very existence of this study also triggers warning signs for us. Our experience teaches us that the big banks are not among the first to detect a boom, but tend to jump on the bandwagon in the later phase of a trend. We are reassured, however, when we consider that this late phase in a long-term boom can last many years, much as the late phase of the 18-year stock market boom of the late twentieth century—a spectacular surge that began in 1995 and did not end until 2000.

The key question to be asked about the bullish UBS gold study is this: How much gold will this market leader purchase for its customers? And the answer depends on the degree to which studies like these will send a signal to institutional investors—such as insurance companies, pension funds, and sovereign wealth funds—to start buying gold. Yes, some are prevented by their statutes from buying gold at all. So, until now, they have remained almost entirely absent from the initial phase of the gold boom. But we presume that this will not last. If the gold boom reaches the scale that we anticipate, those statutes will be amended.

Indeed, we have seen similar statutes, laws, and guidelines fall by the wayside throughout the history of the financial booms. In this context, UBS could be a trendsetter among otherwise slow-moving banks and institutional market participants.

A Q&A between UBS CEO Grübel and Swiss newspaper *Neue Zürcher Zeitung* throws some light on this issue:

Neue Zürcher Zeitung: "How much gold is UBS buying? How much gold do JP Morgan and HSBC have in short positions?"

Grübel: "The law of the jungle rules."

In other words, it's time for banks to sink their teeth into gold, and those who are caught on the wrong side of the market could become dead meat.

The Bernanke Top

How will we know when the gold boom is near an end? We believe we have a contrarian indicator that will give us some valuable clues: it will be when the world's leading central banks begin to publicly consider *increasing* their gold reserves. That's a signal to watch out for that the final, highly speculative phase of the gold boom is under way. And when those same central banks actually jump in to the market as big buyers—that's when you should offer to sell them your personal gold investments. In other words, the Brown Bottom will be followed, years later, by a Bernanke or Weber or Whomever Top, as blundering central bankers and the gold market come full circle.

The next question: When will this occur? The first signs of a change in thinking within the central banks are already here. Indeed, as we mentioned earlier, some less influential central banks were already adding to their gold reserves in the period from the fall of 2008 to the spring of 2009. Ecuador added 28 metric tons, doubling its reserves in one fell swoop. Venezuela added 7.5 metric tons.

Russia increased its gold stocks by 90 metric tons to 495.9 metric tons. Although relatively modest at first, President Putin publicly declared his aim of adding even more. And experts have calculated that Russia will purchase at least 360 metric tons of gold per year and will not export its own gold production. These annual purchases alone would largely offset any potential sales by European central banks, estimated at 500 metric tons per year.

In the opinion of the World Gold Council, gold will also play a role in the planned currency union among the Gulf states—the gold dinars. If, in the future, crude oil is traded and priced in Dubai in gold dinar, then the role of the U.S. dollar as the world's leading reserve currency—the anchor of the global monetary order—would be placed in question.

In March 2009, the head of the Chinese central bank struck a similar tone, publicly demanding a new global reserve currency to be administered by the International Monetary Fund. His exact words: "The present crisis once again cries out for creative reform of the international monetary system."[4]

We give little credence to the concept of making the IMF the world's central bank. But the proposal by the Chinese, who become stronger and more influential by the day, is another symptom of a global monetary system on a collision course for a major turning point. Meanwhile, in the words of the World Gold Council, "Gulf central banks, along with the central banks of Brazil, Russia, India, and China are expected to increase their gold reserves."

Moreover, the developments described here could of course influence the behavior of other market participants, and ultimately, the herd instinct is likely to prevail. Thus, institutional investors could also follow the example of the central bank bureaucrats and begin to diversify their very substantial assets in favor of gold.

If this process progresses as we expect it could, then we are talking about massive sums that would drive the relatively small gold market to previously unimagined highs. As of March 31, 2010, for example, U.S. pension funds alone managed $12.3 trillion. If just 10 percent were allocated toward the future purchase of gold-related assets, it could drive $1.2 trillion into the gold market, or the equivalent of 21 years of global gold production. We don't anticipate that U.S. pension funds will buy that much. But we also don't anticipate they will be alone in the buying frenzy. Institutional and individual investors all over the world will likely seek to jump on the same bandwagon.

Hide Your Gold

In the short term, the investor should act cautiously, as sales of gold by the European central banks are still to be expected. And those sales could temporarily mask the highly inflationary monetary policies pursued by the U.S. Federal Reserve and other central bankers in response to the global debt trap.

In March of 2009, the Federal Reserve, in particular, held out the clear prospect of a turning point in monetary policy. To any who cared to listen, they declared that they would be running the printing presses at full throttle with the blatantly deliberate and immediate intent of monetizing U.S. government debt, as Helicopter Ben actually realized the dream he had verbalized a few years before.

The danger: as a gold investor, you must be prepared for the possibility that, in the not-too-distant future, governments may try to follow in the footsteps of Franklin Roosevelt, the U.S. president who confiscated the gold of private investors. We expect to see telltale warning signs, however, before such a radical step is taken. For example, you could see jawboning and tongue-lashings for gold speculators coming from the White House, the SEC, or Congressional leaders. You could even see a hike in capital gains taxes restricted to gains on gold investments. Their battle cry: "Irresponsible gold speculators are profiting from the suffering of the American people."

Under such circumstances, people who hide gold bars and gold coins in their homes may one day hear an unwelcome knock at the door. And it's with this in mind that we issue the following entirely serious warning: Tell no one about your gold. Word could get around and reach the ears of the wrong people. Here in Germany, we can already see some signs or movement down the road of recreating conditions reminiscent of the former East Germany. And simultaneously, we also see a real danger that a grand coalition of tax raisers, debt creators, and nationalizers could take us even further down that path in fairly short order.

We already have hard data that show that the sale of small and medium-sized safes has risen on an unprecedented scale; and the mistrust their owners have for the state's monetary monopoly is justified. But safes alone do little to protect you from the state. So, as we have urged earlier, also consider diversifying your assets across different countries.

A Curious Test Result

We were delighted to see the German *Warentest* (Product Testing) Foundation publish a test result in January 2004 under the heading *Gold—A Risky Road to Eldorado*. It contained the following observation:

> In the recent past the value of gold has been anything other than stable. It is therefore of interest primarily to speculators.[5]

We are intrigued to see whether or not the foundation will also put gold's competitor—fiat money—to a similar test someday. Of course, such a test would be totally unnecessary; the result has long been well known: nearly all fiat currencies in history have ultimately become worthless. Fiat money is the goal and tool of economically irresponsible governments, institutions that have always managed to trash the currencies they've been entrusted to protect.

CHAPTER 7

A Future Retrospective

Coming generations will probably share the opinion we published some years ago—that the bursting of the great stock market bubble in the year 2000 marked the beginning of the end of the great twentieth-century booms. At that time, we were already talking about a grand turning point. And perhaps, even at that late date, a somewhat *less* painful reversal of direction by our leaders may have been possible. But it was not to be. The monetary and fiscal road to catastrophe that they had embarked upon has been pursued relentlessly ever since.

With a degree of probability verging on certainty, future generations will at least see the year 2007, when the great real estate bubble burst, as the end. They will recognize it as the end of an era characterized by excessive debt accumulation by both private and public institutions. They will see it as the key turning point when the entire financial system nearly collapsed. And hopefully, they also will recognize it as evidence of the great dangers implicit in a monetary system based on fiat paper currencies.

Hopefully, they also will look back on a catastrophe that was used to lay the foundations for a new and better system—the return to the proven principles of responsible and sustainable economics, principles that form the essential precondition for promoting prosperity and the long-term welfare of mankind. Harvard economic historian Niall Ferguson put it this way:

> Future historians will look back on the crisis as an event comparable
> in its significance to the Depression of the early thirties.[1]

Then, too, the crisis created the preconditions for the creation of a new system. Unfortunately, that opportunity was not only passed up in large parts of the world, but betrayed in the most horrific manner: Germany, decimated by a world war and hyperinflation, by a heinous band of criminals that exploited the destruction as an opportunity to seize power, and by murderous fascism that plunged the world into a second catastrophic war, again reducing half the world to rubble.

Regrettably, an objective reading of the past admits only one conclusion: Despite some notable exceptions and variations, by and large, history does repeat itself. Human nature rarely changes. Both politicians and their supporters, when confronted with similar external conditions, react in a comparable manner. All are an integral part of the same basic, subconscious or conscious, mass-psychological processes.

No, they are not making *precisely* the same mistakes they made during the Great Depression of the 1930s. But they are certainly making very *similar* ones. The monetary and fiscal policy currently being pursued is not all that different from the one pursued then. To the contrary, within the context of what was possible in the 1930s, the government at that time also attempted to pull out all the inflationary stops, to rescue failing banks, and to prevent the worst-case scenario from unfolding. True, it was all in vain, the problems could not be solved politically, and the Great Depression did occur. But that does not change the fact that, like our leaders of today, they did try to do everything within their power to avert that outcome.

Thus, the Bernankes of this world have, in our opinion, drawn entirely wrong conclusions from the experiences of the 1930s, believing that, at critical junctures of the 1930s crisis, governments and politicians of that era did too little, too late to change the course of history. And, based on that erroneous conclusion, this time around they think they are learning the lesson of that era, acting more aggressively, more quickly—first in response to the stock market bust of 2000–2001, second in response to housing bust of 2006–2009, and third, in reaction to the sovereign debt crisis of 2010.

This is why the U.S. Federal Reserve more than doubled its balance sheet from $1 trillion to more than $2 trillion within just a few short months following the collapse of Lehman Brothers in September of 2008. And this is why the quality of the Fed's balance sheet has declined dramatically, stuffed with all kinds of toxic assets acquired as collateral—both from member banks and a host of institutions that traditionally had no right to those facilities.

The Fed has left no doubt that it would do whatever it takes to perpetuate this policy and would not let anything or anyone divert it from this path. Nor did U.S. and European governments leave any doubt that they would do everything to provide private banks and failing countries with gigantic cash injections—tax dollars that future generations are supposed to pay off.

However, the bottom of this pit is still not in sight. In the meantime, the people responsible—or rather, the people *ir*responsible—are going to be forced by events to admit that the banks' losses far exceed their equity capital, that the entire fractional reserve banking system was insolvent and that the end of the flagpole had been reached.

Sure, governments were able to temporarily stabilize the banking system with their massive bailouts. And yes, they were able to bring about dead cat bounces in their economies through gigantic Keynesian stimulus packages.

But what has all this bought them?

- It has bought high, quasi-permanent unemployment. In the United States, the unemployment rate, even when measured by distorted official yardsticks, is holding at peak levels; and when measured on an all-inclusive basis, is close to *double* those levels. Worse, the percentage of long-term unemployed—out of work for six months or more—has reached a level that is *double* the worst level ever recorded in U.S. history.

  In Europe, thanks to widespread laws and massive programs that guarantee job security for incompetent jobholders—while encouraging would-be job seekers to stay out of work—we have been caught in a similar long-term unemployment syndrome for many years. Now, the United States, thanks to its new, ever-more generous bailouts, handouts, and rescue packages, is falling into a similar trap. Instead of finding ways to dig themselves out of the global debt trap, they sink their fists and their feet deeper and deeper into the tar baby.

- Both in the United States and in Europe, it has bought them federal budget deficits on a scale never before seen in peacetime.

- The unthinkable but inevitable happened: global investors began to rebel against sovereign debt bonds. Like great predators stalking their prey, they began by singling out the weakest of the herd and then attacking with a vengeance. First Greece, then Portugal, then Spain.

Slowly at first, but with growing momentum as the sovereign debt crises hit the headlines, a growing group of investors became aware of the risks of the absurd monetary and fiscal policies. More and more, they recognized the giant speculative bubble that had formed in the government bond market itself.

Again, despite some initial hesitation, the authorities came to the rescue, and a new grand coalition—this time between the European Union and the IMF—emerged to put down the global rebellion.

But despite any temporary respite they can achieve, once shattered, the thin glass of trust that shielded sovereign government from these attacks will be difficult to restore. There is no turning back the clock. The first steps toward the first global hyperinflation in the world history have already been taken. Undoing broken promises and restoring public trust will take political courage that is currently lacking. And it will take tolerance for economic pain that few currently have.

A Final Word of Hope

The situation is indeed dramatic. But the global debt trap need not be permanent. And, as we've stressed repeatedly, inflation does not fall from the skies—it is created by politicians and their central bankers. Thus, in principle, a policy reversal, no matter how painful in the short term, *is possible* at any time.

With this book, the greatest success we can hope for is to be able to say, with hindsight, that we made a constructive contribution to such a policy reversal. We have no illusion, however, that this outcome—avoiding a global inflationary crisis of historic dimensions—is a probable one.

In 1931, Italian economist Costantino Bresciani-Turroni published a comprehensive analysis of the hyperinflationary period in the Weimar Republic. He spent time in Berlin as an eyewitness to this important period in history, committing his observations to a book that is, more so than ever before, worth reading. We conclude our book with a quote from his own conclusion:

> The inflation retarded the crisis for some time, but this broke out later, throwing millions out of work. At first, inflation stimulated production because of the divergence between the internal and external values of the mark, but later it exercised an increasingly negative influence, disorganizing and limiting production. It annihilated thrift; it made reform of the national budget impossible for years; it obstructed the solution of the Reparations question; it destroyed incalculable moral and intellectual values. It provoked a serious revolution in social classes, a few people accumulating wealth and forming a class of usurpers of national property, whilst millions of individuals were thrown into poverty. It was a distressing preoccupation and constant torment of innumerable families; it poisoned the German people by spreading among all classes the spirit of speculation and by diverting them from proper and regular work, and it was the cause of incessant political and moral disturbance. It is indeed easy enough to understand why the record of the sad years 1919–23 always weighs like a nightmare on the German people.[2]

Memories fade, and the global interconnectedness of a flawed monetary system based on fiat currencies no longer allows a focus on a single country. Inflation has gone from being a national problem to a global one. Let us hope that the coming years will not one day weigh like a nightmare on the people of the world.

Notes

Chapter 1: Why the Debt Crisis *Was* Predictable

1. Friedrich August von Hayek, *The Denationalisation of Money*, 3rd ed. (London: The Institute of Economic Affairs, 1990), 102.

2. Friedrich August von Hayek, *The Road to Serfdom* (Chicago: University of Chicago Press, 2007).

3. Friedrich August von Hayek, *The Denationalisation of Money*, 3rd ed. (London: The Institute of Economic Affairs, 1990), 133.

4. Roland Leuschel and Claus Vogt, *Das Greenspan Dossier*, 3rd ed. (Munich: Finanzbuch Verlag, 2006), 30.

5. Reuters News, "The Financial Crisis Continues—ECB Chief Warns Against Complacency," September 10, 2008.

6. Jean-Claude Trichet, quoted in Reuters News, May 12, 2009.

7. Henry Kaufman, *On Money and Markets* (New York: McGraw-Hill, 2000), 292.

8. Milton Friedman, "We Are All Keynesians Now," *Time* magazine, December 31, 1965.

9. Hermann Hesse, *The Glass Bead Game* (New York: Picador USA, 2002).

Chapter 2: Real Estate, Banks, Bubbles, and Debts

1. Barney Frank, cited in "How Housing Masked a Weak Economy," by Bill Fleckenstein, *MSN Money,* February 5, 2007.

2. "Poor through Work," *Der Spiegel,* October 2007.

3. An article did appear in early 2009 in which a couple of voices demanded the introduction of a proper and reliable monetary system—albeit in a somewhat different context.

4. Jeremy Grantham, GMO *Quarterly Letter,* January 2009.

5. Milton Friedman, *There's No Such Thing as a Free Lunch* (Chicago: Open Court Publishing, 1977).

6. Niall Ferguson, "We Experience the Financial Symptoms of a World War," *Frankfurter Allgemeine Zeitung,* February 24, 2009.

7. Incidentally, when he was awarded the prize, Wuffli stressed that it was, above all, the consistent, long-term strategy pursued by UBS since the mid-1990s that had been decisive for its success, while the laudatory speech was delivered by none other than fellow bad banker, Herr Klaus-Peter Müller, of Commerzbank. If those are not credentials for the new bad-bank CEO job, we do not know what is.

Chapter 3: The Great Money Game

1. Otmar Issing, *Einführung in die Geldtheorie,* 12th ed. (Munich: Verlag Vahlen, 2001).

2. Murray N. Rothbard, *What Has Government Done to Our Money?* 4th ed. (Auburn, AL: Ludwig von Mises Institute, 1990), 15.

3. Ibid.

4. Ibid.

5. Karl Marx and Friedrich Engels, *The Communist Manifesto* (London: The Communist League, 1848), 26.

6. Peter Bernholz, *Monetary Regimes and Inflation* (Cheltenham, UK: Edward Elgar, 2003), 18, 110.

7. Alan Greenspan, "Gold and Economic Freedom," in Ayn Rand, *Capitalism: The Unknown Ideal* (New York: Signet, 1967), 101.

8. Ludwig von Mises, *Human Action* (Auburn, AL: Ludwig von Mises Institute, 1998), 424.

Chapter 4: The Road to (Hyper)Inflation

1. Ben S. Bernanke, "Deflation: Making Sure 'It' Doesn't Happen Here," speech delivered at the National Economists Club, Washington, DC, November 21, 2002.

2. *Jahresgutachten 2007–2008 des Sachverständigenrats,* November 7, 2007, 77, 79.

3. Claus Vogt, "Our Indicators Increasingly Point toward Recession," *Performance,* December 2007, 3.

4. *Jahresgutachten 2007–2008 des Sachverständigenrats,* November 7, 2007, 98.

5. Ibid., 76.

6. Axel Weber, in: "The Case IKB Exacerbates the Crisis," *Frankfurter Allgemeine Zeitung,* August 3, 2007.

7. Roland Leuschel and Claus Vogt: "Does the Bursting of the American Housing Bubble Threaten the Global Economy?" *Smart Investor,* March 2007.

8. Mortgage Bankers Association Press Release, August 26, 2010, http://www .mbaa.org/NewsandMedia/PressCenter/73799.htm

9. Ibid.

10. Federal Reserve, *Flow of Funds Accounts of the United States,* 96.

11. Mike Larson, "Double-Dip Disaster Directly Ahead," *Safe Money Report* special edition, September 2010, 7.

12. Paul Krugman, "Where Are the Bond Vigilantes?" *New York Times,* August 25, 2009.

13. "Anleger blicken sorglos auf Inflation," *Frankfurter Allgemeine Zeitung,* April 6, 2009.

14. Ben S. Bernanke, "Deflation: Making Sure 'It' Doesn't Happen Here," speech delivered at the National Economists Club, Washington, DC, November 21, 2002.

15. Roland Leuschel and Claus Vogt, *Das Greenspan Dossier* (Munich: Finanzbuch Verlag, 2004), 249.

16. Gideon Gono, "It Can't Be Any Worse," interview, *Newsweek,* January 24, 2009.

17. "The Curse of Cheap Money," *Der Spiegel,* January 19, 2009.

Chapter 5: How Could It Have Come to This?

1. William Poole, "Inflation Dynamics," speech delivered at Truman State University, Kirksville, MO, February 20, 2008.

2. Frederic S. Mishkin, "Outlook and Risks for the U.S. Economy," speech delivered at the National Association for Business Economics Washington Policy Conference, Washington, DC, March 4, 2008.

3. Claus Vogt, *Performance,* October 2001, 5.

4. Mervyn King, speech delivered at the Northern Ireland Chamber of Commerce and Industry, October 9, 2007.

5. One-liner, accredited to Eugen Roth.

6. Ben S. Bernanke, "Deflation: Making Sure 'It' Doesn't Happen Here," speech delivered at the National Economists Club, Washington, DC, November 21, 2002.

7. Alan Ahearne et al., "Preventing Deflation: Lessons from Japan's Experience in the 1990s," *International Finance Discussion Papers* 729 (June 2002).

8. Ben S. Bernanke, "Deflation: Making Sure 'It' Doesn't Happen Here," speech delivered at the National Economists Club, Washington, DC, November 21, 2002.

9. Ben S. Bernanke, "On Milton Friedman's Ninetieth Birthday," speech delivered at the University of Chicago, November 8, 2002.

10. Bill Gross, "Beep Beep, " *Investment Outlook,* February 2009.

11. Horst Köhler, *Die Welt,* May 14, 2008.

12. Michiyo Nakamoto and David Wighton, "Citigroup Chief Stays Bullish on Buy-Outs," *Financial Times,* July 9, 2007.

13. Paul O'Neill, quoted in *Reuters,* September 17, 2001.

14. Joseph E. Stiglitz, "America's Day of Reckoning," *Project Syndicate,* August 6, 2007.

Chapter 6: What Can You Do Now?

1. Warren Buffett, letter to the shareholders of Berkshire Hathaway, March 2009.

2. Axel Weber, quoted in "German Gold Reserves Not for Sale," *Wirtschaftswoche,* March 9, 2009.

3. Kaspar Villiger, quoted in *Zeit-Fragen,* March 10, 2009.

4. Bloomberg News, March 17, 2009.

5. *Stiftung Warentest,* January 2004.

Chapter 7: A Future Retrospective

1. Niall Feguson, "We Experience the Financial Symptoms of a World War," *Frankfurter Allgemeine Zeitung,* February 24, 2009.

2. Costantino Bresciani-Turroni, *The Economics of Inflation* (Surrey, UK: Unwin Brothers Ltd., 1937), 404.

About The Authors

Claus Vogt is known in Germany as one of the few analysts who clearly predicted, well in advance, the global market declines of both 2000–2002 and 2008–2009.

In his 2005 German bestseller, *Das Greenspan Dossier*, also co-authored with Mr. Leuschel, Mr. Vogt wrote: "When the U.S. real estate bubble bursts, it will not only trigger a recession and a stock market crash, but it will endanger the entire financial system, especially Fannie Mae and Freddie Mac." With that sentence alone—plus their constant reminders throughout the 2005 book—the authors gave readers an unambiguous forewarning of the housing bust, the worst recession and stock market crash since the Great Depression, the near meltdown of the entire financial system, and the virtual demise of America's two mortgage giants.

Mr. Vogt's financial market career spans two decades—first as a financial consultant with the London division of Merrill Lynch, and more recently as the Research Director and strategist for an independent German bank, which, thanks largely to Mr. Vogt, was one of the few to make money for its clients during the financial crisis. He is currently Managing Director of Aequitas Capital Partners, an asset management firm serving institutional and individual investors.

Mr. Vogt is editor of *Sicheres Geld*, one of Germany's largest circulation investment newsletters, and also writes a regular weekly column in *Money and Markets*, reaching over a half million U.S. and international readers. He graduated with a degree in business and economics from the University of Frankfurt am Main.

Roland Leuschel, who began his career over a half century ago, has been one of the most highly respected stock market analysts in Europe for over thirty years, known both for his strongly bullish arguments prior to major rising markets and his equally strong crash warnings before nearly all major bear markets since the early 1980s, earning him the title of "Crash Prophet."

Mr. Leuschel is a regular columnist for several international finance publications, including *Börse Online*, Germany's leading stock market publication. His prior books include not only *Das Greenspan Dossier*, which warned readers about the U.S. housing bust and financial crisis, but also the 1984 European edition of *The American Idea—Growth is Our Future,* co-authored with former congressman and Housing Secretary Jack Kemp. He has degrees in engineering and economics from Karlsruhe University and in economics from the Free University of Berlin.

Index